FICTIONS, LIES, AND
THE AUTHORITY OF LAW

CATHOLIC IDEAS FOR A SECULAR WORLD

O. Carter Snead, series editor

Under the sponsorship of the de Nicola Center for Ethics and Culture at the University of Notre Dame, the purpose of this interdisciplinary series is to feature authors from around the world who will expand the influence of Catholic thought on the most important conversations in academia and the public square. The series is "Catholic" in the sense that the books will emphasize and engage the enduring themes of human dignity and flourishing, the common good, truth, beauty, justice, and freedom in ways that reflect and deepen principles affirmed by the Catholic Church for millennia. It is not limited to Catholic authors or even works that explicitly take Catholic principles as a point of departure. Its books are intended to demonstrate the diversity and enhance the relevance of these enduring themes and principles in numerous subjects, ranging from the arts and humanities to the sciences.

FICTIONS, LIES, AND THE AUTHORITY OF LAW

STEVEN D. SMITH

University of Notre Dame Press
Notre Dame, Indiana

Copyright © 2021 by the University of Notre Dame
Notre Dame, Indiana 46556
undpress.nd.edu

All Rights Reserved

Published in the United States of America

Library of Congress Control Number: 2021942320

ISBN: 978-0-268-20120-3 (Hardback)
ISBN: 978-0-268-20126-5 (WebPDF)
ISBN: 978-0-268-20119-7 (Epub)

CONTENTS

	Acknowledgments	vii
	Prologue: The Puzzling (Alleged) Disappearance of Authority	ix
ONE	The Fictional Foundations of (Modern) Political Authority	1
TWO	Fictional Authority and the Problem of Constitutional Interpretation	29
THREE	Our Quasi-Fictional Government	75
FOUR	From Political Fictions to "Living with Lies"	123
FIVE	Authority and Faux Authority	157
SIX	Is Genuine Authority Possible?	189
	Epilogue: Authority outside the Cave?	219
	Notes	225
	Index	269

ACKNOWLEDGMENTS

The chapters in this book, although intended to constitute a unified argument, were written (or were derived from things written) over a period of years, and I have received helpful suggestions and criticisms from more people than I can possibly remember at this point. I thank all who have assisted and guided me; naming some would be an injustice to the others. But I do need to thank more specifically the wonderful colleagues and friends who not only read and commented on all or parts of this book but who have influenced me more generally over the years through ongoing conversation, criticism, and encouragement: my San Diego colleagues Larry Alexander and Maimon Schwarzschild, my Notre Dame friends Rick Garnett and Jeff Pojanowski, my international consultants Jim Allan and Luis Pereira Coutinho, my electronic correspondents Michael Perry and George Wright, and my familial advisers Merina Smith and Nathan Smith. I also benefitted from comments and criticisms at workshops on various chapters of the book with the law faculties at Arizona State, George Mason, and the University of San Diego. Juan Villalvazo and Kendall McKee provided valuable help with the footnotes. And Liz Parker and Sasha Nunez were a tremendous help with the index.

PROLOGUE

The Puzzling (Alleged) Disappearance of Authority

In the middle of the twentieth century, the political theorist Hannah Arendt made a disconcerting announcement. "[A]uthority has vanished from the modern world," Arendt declared. "Practically as well as theoretically, we are no longer in a position to know what authority really *is*."[1] And she added that "[t]he moment we begin to talk and think about authority, it is as though we were caught in a maze of abstractions, metaphors, and figures of speech in which everything can be taken and mistaken for something else, because we have no reality, either in history or in everyday experience, to which we can unanimously appeal."[2]

Suppose for a moment that Arendt was correct: Would her surprising news be cause for lamentation, or rather for jubilation? Typically, the invocation of "authority" does not prompt spontaneous rejoicing; it may instead evoke images of arrogant, pretentious people who think they have the right to boss us around. So, if authority has indeed "vanished," perhaps we should celebrate? "Free at last! Thank God, we are free at last!"

Arendt thought otherwise, though. She suggested, ominously if obscurely, that the disappearance of authority amounted to some kind of catastrophe for humanity. The "loss [of authority]," Arendt observed gravely, "is tantamount to the loss of the groundwork of the world."[3]

It is an intriguing metaphor—and a disturbing one. "*The loss of the groundwork of the world.*" What *is* "the groundwork of the world"? What would it mean to lose that groundwork? The image elicits an unsettling vision of people with nothing firm to stand on—people lurching and staggering and reeling as they vainly try to plant themselves on some liquid or lava-like surface that shifts and disintegrates beneath their steps. Like children in one of those amusement park exhibits—or maybe "The Flopper" in a famous Cardozo decision[4]— in which the floor is constantly moving, everything is off-kilter, and everyone keeps tumbling down. Except that this time the victims would be not children but all of us, and the spectacle would be grim, not amusing. Modern civilization—lost in the funhouse?

Coming from one of the most respected political thinkers of the last century, these are sobering if cryptic words—words deserving of examination and reflection. Because if Arendt was right, understanding how authority somehow "vanished" from the modern world and how that disappearance amounts to the "loss of the groundwork of the world" might offer us a valuable insight into our times, with their distinctive frustrations and dysfunctions.

But *was* Arendt right?

Surely there is cause for skepticism. After all, isn't "authority"— as a word, as a concept, and as an operative reality—a perfectly familiar feature of modern life? Don't we have authority, or authorities (plural), all around us? Primarily, perhaps, we attribute "authority" to governments and to government officials—and to the laws that such governments and their officials promulgate. And government officials with their teeming hosts of laws and regulations and requirements have hardly vanished; on the contrary, they swarm about us on every side. It might be a huge relief if they *would* vanish, or at least back off a bit: No such luck! In addition, there are plenty of other nongovernmental figures to whom we ascribe "authority." Bosses, school principals, parents. Teachers. Coaches.

In short, far from having disappeared, authority seems virtually ubiquitous.

Beyond its prima facie implausibility, Arendt's claim also seems paradoxical—because if the claim were correct, we might think, it would be one that she could hardly make, and that we could hardly respond to. If it were actually true that "we no longer have any idea what 'authority' is," as Arendt contended, then saying as much would be like saying "We have no idea what 'glumph' is." To which we might respond, "That's correct. What on earth *is* 'glumph'? What are you even talking about?" But Arendt's declaration doesn't seem like that; it seems like a statement that we *can* understand, discuss, agree or disagree with. How is this possible unless we do have some conception of what authority is?

Still, it would be rash to dismiss the considered statements of a respected political theorist too quickly (or after just two or three paragraphs of skeptical reflection). Moreover, Arendt was not alone; other thinkers have sometimes made similar observations. R. B. Friedman reported that the claim "that the very concept of authority has been corrupted or even lost in the modern world" is "an opinion frequently expressed in some of the most well-known discussions of authority in recent years."[5] In our own century, the philosopher Michael White has remarked that "[a]n enduring problem concerning authority for us post-Enlightenment moderns, it seems to me, is that natural authority has largely disappeared from our most common worldviews."[6] Going back in time, the Christian existentialist Soren Kierkegaard lamented that "the concept of authority has been entirely forgotten in our confused age."[7]

So the claim that authority has disappeared, with confounding or even catastrophic consequences for us, deserves our attention and our investigation. And in preparing for that investigation, we might break down Arendt's indictment into three separate claims:

First, authority has disappeared from the modern world. Vanished. This claim is counterintuitive because, as we have already noted, it *seems* that authority is all around us. But of course Arendt was perfectly aware of this fact; she did after all write a much-admired study of totalitarianism (which we will consult in a later chapter).[8] So if she and Professor White and Mr. Kierkegaard and others say that "authority has disappeared from the modern world," it seems they must be asserting that what we typically call "authority" is not really authority. Instead, they imply, what we call "authority" is some kind of imitation or impostor or counterfeit. Faux authority. That is one claim that calls for investigation.

Another claim is that the disappearance of authority is a loss for us — even a catastrophic loss. That conclusion is hardly self-evident. There are astute and respectable theorists who agree with Arendt in saying that authority is absent from our world but who contend that we can get along just fine without it, thank you.[9] So we will need to consider whether the loss of authority, if that is indeed our situation, is actually a lamentable development, and if so, in what way.

A third claim calling for our investigation asserts that we no longer understand what authority even is. This third claim goes beyond the first one: not only is authority missing from the modern world, but the very term or concept has become unintelligible to us.

The claim that we no longer understand the meaning of authority is the most elusive of the three. It stands in a complicated, puzzling relation to the other two. In one sense, it seems to reinforce the first claim: the disappearance of authority from the modern world is so complete (or so critics like Arendt assert) that we no longer even understand what the term refers to. That, presumably, is why we might routinely mistake the counterfeits or substitutes that we call "authority" for the genuine article.

But the third claim also subtly subverts the first one, and also the second one. If we do not understand what authority is, how can we be sure that the thing has disappeared? And how can we say whether the loss of authority is a misfortune or rather a blessing if we do not even know what it is that we have lost? Its puzzling quality will make investigation of this third claim a tricky but potentially revealing endeavor.

So there are three related but separate claims, and we will engage them in the following order. Chapter 1 will be devoted to supporting Arendt's first claim, at least obliquely. My contention in this chapter will be that political authority in the American legal and political system, and probably in other liberal democracies as well, has a fictional quality. Authority itself *is* a fiction, perhaps, or at least it is grounded in fictional foundations.

While resonating with Arendt's claim, this contention is more modest, in two ways. First, my contention addresses only the matter of authority as it is conceived in the American political tradition (and like-minded liberal democracies); it does not deny the possibility that authority might be alive and well in other contexts or in other conceptions. Second, there is—or at least there can be—an important difference between saying that something has "vanished" and saying that it is "fictional" in character. Santa Claus may be a fictional character, but he has hardly vanished. On the contrary, he is very much with us, wielding considerable cultural power. Authority might be like Santa Claus—fictional, yes, but present and powerful (for good or ill) nonetheless.

So the contention of chapter 1, even if persuasive, will fall short of corroborating Arendt's more radical claim that "authority has vanished from the modern world." We will defer consideration of that more radical claim until later in the book.

Before reaching that issue, though, we will first consider whether the disappearance of authority—or, at least, its fictional character—is worrisome or even catastrophic (perhaps even amounting, as Arendt claimed, to the loss of "the groundwork of the world"). Chapters 2 through 4 will address aspects of that question, in different ways. In chapters 2 and 3, I will argue that the fictional character of authority lies at the bottom of many long-standing legal or jurisprudential disputes in the American legal system—disputes about the nature of the union, for example, and about constitutional and statutory interpretation—and it is what makes those disputes so intractable. Shifting the focus from America to Eastern Europe, chapter 4 will suggest that the fictional character of authority has the potential to lead to the nightmarish condition that Vaclav Havel and others discerned in later Communist countries and that Havel described as "living with lies" (and that some perceive as being replicated in Western societies).

We will save the last and most elusive claim—that we no longer understand what "authority" even means—for the last two chapters. I will suggest in chapter 5 that we can appreciate the sense and plausibility of Arendt's claim by reflecting on and extending a famous argument made by a thinker whom many regard as the greatest English-speaking legal philosopher of the twentieth century—the Oxford scholar H. L. A. Hart. Most of what we call "authority," Hart's analysis as extended will entail, is not really authority (and not even a fictional version of *actual* authority). It is something else—the counterfeit of authority, perhaps. Faux authority, if you like. This conclusion, if persuasive, would reenforce Arendt's contention that "authority has disappeared from the modern world."

Nonetheless, I will suggest in chapter 6 and also in the epilogue that, with effort, we *can* get a sense of what genuine authority is or would be. That we find the concept so elusive today is, as Arendt suggested, an indication that although the "groundwork of the world" may not have been altogether lost, we have great difficulty in getting our footing on that groundwork. And there is at least one tradition—the Christian tradition—that has for centuries maintained the hope that although the governments and law we live under today may be mere simulations of authority, the day will come in which real authority will present itself.

One preliminary clarification may be helpful. We have taken as a starting point and provocation for our inquiry Hannah Arendt's contention that "authority has vanished from the modern world," and we will refer to that contention at times as we proceed. But our inquiry will not be primarily exegetical. Given Arendt's stature and given the intriguing quality of her claim, we would expect that scholars might devote considerable attention to figuring out what Arendt meant; and they have.[10] Our inquiry will not attempt to cover that ground again. As we have already noted, Arendt was merely one among a number of thinkers who have perceived that in our time the idea of authority seems problematic or profoundly puzzling. Our concern will not be to engage in exposition of the particular diagnosis offered by Hannah Arendt—or Professor White or Soren Kierkegaard or anyone else—but rather to do our own investigation of the puzzling condition they perceived.

Why is authority such a difficult matter in our day? Has it disappeared? How could that have happened? And if so, is this cause for lament, even alarm, or rather for rejoicing? These will be our guiding questions.

POSTSCRIPT. Readers who have themselves published books will understand that the publication date listed at the front of a book may bear only a tenuous relationship to the time when the book was actually written. In the present case, this book was largely completed by the fall of 2019. Seven months later, as I begin revisions in the summer of 2020, the world has already changed in ways that could not be anticipated then. Most obviously, who could have imagined the massive alterations in the way life is lived that have been prompted by the COVID-19 pandemic? Millions of people quarantined in their homes, thousands of businesses shut down, professional sports put on hold for who knows (as of when I write) how long? Some of the hypothetical scenarios presented in chapter 3, intended at the time I devised them to be quite fantastic, now seem not at all far-fetched—for example, the possibility that Congress might meet and vote remotely in response to an epidemic.

A different unanticipated development has been the massive political reaction to the killing by a Minneapolis police officer of an African American man, George Floyd. The ensuing protests have underscored the fragile nature of political authority. Perhaps the most conspicuous instance to date has been the decision in Seattle to declare a section of the city an autonomous zone in which the police will not enter. As of this writing it is impossible to know how long such protests may last or how deeply they will affect our institutions of authority and law enforcement.

Another relevant development is the Supreme Court's decision in *Bostock v. Clayton County*; in an almost made-to-order illustration of the implications of the textualist approach to legal interpretation criticized in chapters 2 and 3, the court construed the 1964 Civil Rights Act to prohibit discrimination based on sexual orientation even though the court acknowledged that no one in the enacting Congress intended such a prohibition and that Congress had repeatedly declined to adopt any such prohibition in the years since. And yet another relevant development is the escalation of the "cancel culture" described at the end of chapter 4. In the aggregate, these various unanticipated and disruptive (for good or ill) developments make Hannah Arendt's description of "the loss of the groundwork of the world" seem a little less hyperbolic. The developments make some of the questions raised in this book seem more urgent and less academic.

In a world in which crisis seems to follow on unexpected crisis, there is no way to know what may happen between this stage of revision and the actual publication of the book. One can only hope. The satisfaction of having one's argument confirmed by events would hardly compensate for further collapse of "the groundwork of the world."

CHAPTER ONE

The Fictional Foundations of (Modern) Political Authority

We saw in the prologue that according to respected political thinkers like Hannah Arendt, "authority has vanished from the modern world." This claim seems puzzling, though, and prima facie implausible, because it seems obvious that *claims* of authority confront us on every side. You cannot cross the street or drive to work without encountering a host of regulations and prohibitions promulgated by governments asserting the authority to enact and enforce such laws. You cannot buy a cheeseburger or a tube of toothpaste without paying an increasingly hefty tax imposed by some self-declared governmental authority. You cannot collect a paycheck without having a substantial portion of your hard-earned salary withdrawn in advance, again at the behest of an institution—several of them, actually—claiming the authority to make these extractions.

If you are a minor, you are likely confronted with assertions of authority by your parents. If you are a student, you are subject to the authority of your teachers, who (like you) are themselves subject to the higher authority of the principal or the dean. If you are an employee, you deal daily with claims of authority from your boss. If you belong to a baseball team or an orchestra or a platoon of soldiers, you are constantly under the authority—or what surely appears to be authority—of your coach, your director, or your sergeant.

In short, every facet of your life and of mine is hemmed and hedged by assertions of authority.[1] But what is the nature of this authority? Is it "real" authority or rather, as Arendt implied, some sort of simulation or counterfeit? Where does it come from? What is it based on?

The Consent Account

In the American political system, and in like-minded liberal democracies, there is a standard and official perspective on these questions, at least with respect to political or governmental authority. That answer was put forward in the American Declaration of Independence as a "self-evident truth"—namely, that "Governments . . . deriv[e] their just powers from the consent of the governed."[2]

Let us call this "the consent proposition." The consent proposition has been recited ad infinitum, and it has become part of the bedrock of the American political tradition. Don Herzog observes that "[c]onsent theory has an extraordinarily firm hold on our imagination. It provides perhaps the single most prevalent paradigm structuring our thinking about law, society, morality, and politics."[3] An occasional theorist will soften the requirement slightly, saying that what is needed is not "*con*sent," exactly, but rather "*as*sent";[4] but the basic idea is the same.[5]

To be sure, in describing the consent proposition as "self-evident," the Declaration exaggerated a little, or maybe a lot. In other regimes—communist regimes, for example, or theocratic regimes—very different accounts of authority (or "legitimacy"[6]) have prevailed. We will encounter some of those accounts later in the book. And even in Western democracies, both theorists and ordinary citizens often find the consent account of authority to be, as John Marshall might have put it, "too extravagant to be maintained."[7] (Our discussion will suggest that these skeptics are right—and also wrong.) Theorists of this more skeptical bent often propose alternative, nonconsensual explanations of how governments may come to have authority over us or of why we ought to acknowledge at least a prima facie obligation to conform to the rules and commands issued by government. We will consider some of these alternative accounts in due course as well.

In the American political tradition, however, and in liberal democratic regimes generally, the consent proposition has dominated. Alexander Meiklejohn asserted that "[g]overnments . . . derive their just powers from the consent of the governed. If that consent be lacking, governments have no just powers."[8] Rogers Smith explained that a feature of "the course of America's constitutional development" has been an "expanding legal emphasis on consent as the *sole* source of political legitimacy."[9]

Nor is this domination merely an accident. On the contrary, there are understandable reasons why in *our* tradition, the consent account not only has been but needs to be the official account. Whether it is plausible or not.

THE NECESSITY OF CONSENT

More specifically, in the liberal West a commitment to freedom—and, more specifically, to freedom understood in terms of individual autonomy—has been pervasive. "[W]herever we look," John Crosby remarks, "we find some variation on the theme of independence, autonomy, belonging to oneself, existing for one's own sake, living out of one's interiority, acting through oneself, determining oneself."[10] Gerald Dworkin explains that the "view of the moral agent as necessarily autonomous" is "a philosophical view that is shared by moral philosophers as divergent as Kant, Kierkegaard, Nietzsche, Royce, Hare, Popper, Sartre, and Wolff."[11] Indeed, the commitment to autonomy is sometimes thought to be the defining feature of modernity,[12] as well as being a foundational element of liberal democracies. Ekow Yankah observes that "[f]rom the point of view of liberalism, human beings are defined first and foremost by their autonomy or freedom-preserving nature."[13]

But this commitment to autonomy is in tension with the very idea of authority.[14] And the consent account may seem to offer the only way of reconciling autonomy with authority.

The opposition between autonomy and authority has been a common subject of reflection; one such forceful reflection was put forward by the philosopher Robert Paul Wolff.[15] Wolff's core point can be simply stated. We are, or at least we aspire to be, autonomous beings. Nor is this merely a contingent wish; on the contrary, our moral worth and dignity inhere in that autonomy.[16] And "[t]he autonomous man, insofar as he is autonomous, is not subject to the will of another. He may do what another tells him, but not because he has been told to do it."[17] Government and its laws, by contrast, are heteronomous relative to us: they are outside forces ordering us to obey their commands because we have been commanded. And that is a demand that we can never acknowledge without compromising our autonomy.

Wolff stated the basic point succinctly:

> The defining mark of the state is authority, the right to rule. The primary obligation of man is autonomy, the refusal to be ruled. It would seem, then, that there can be no resolution of the conflict between the autonomy of the individual and the putative authority of the state. Insofar as a man fulfills his obligation to make himself the author of his decisions, he will resist the state's claim to have authority over him. That is to say, he will deny that he has a duty to obey the laws of the state *simply because they are the laws*.[18]

On this reasoning, "[a]ll authority is equally illegitimate."[19] To be sure, some laws and legal regimes will be more admirable than others. If we have the good fortune to live under a just and benign government, then we may have excellent reasons for complying with many or most of the laws that such a government enacts or for being what Heidi Hurd approvingly describes as "law-abiding anarchists."[20] What we cannot do, without compromising our autonomy and hence our dignity, is acknowledge that government has *authority* over us, or a "right to rule" us.

There is a powerful and almost axiomatic force to this challenge, and, as Joseph Raz has observed, much modern theorizing about authority can be understood as an attempt to respond to it or deflect it.[21] Can "autonomy" and "authority" coexist, or are the two simply antithetical and mutually exclusive, as Wolff argued? It is a difficult question, but one that can help to underscore the distinctive attractiveness of the consent proposition. That is because, far from transgressing the commitment to autonomy, the consent proposition may seem to embrace and build on that commitment. So you are an autonomous agent, yes; but if you yourself voluntarily consent to be governed by, say, Parliament, or by the czar, then the authority of Parliament or the czar does not *violate* your autonomy, but rather is *derived* precisely from the exercise of that autonomy.

So goes the argument, in any case; we will see later, in chapter 5, that things are more complicated. For now it is enough to say this much—that given the pervasive commitment to autonomy, if there is to be authority at all it seemingly will have to be based on consent. If we are committed to being autonomous agents, how is it possible that we could acknowledge the authority over us of anything or anyone unless we had consented?

Consent as a Fiction

So the consent proposition is attractive, even mandatory, under modern conditions and given the commitment to autonomy. But the proposition also has its notorious difficulties. Amanda Greene remarks that the consent-grounded criteria of voluntarism and contractualism "advance a standard of legitimacy that no society has ever met or could ever hope to meet."[22]

The most conspicuous difficulty with the consent proposition, probably, is that if the proposition is correct, then we are seemingly forced to conclude that all or virtually all contemporary governments lack authority. Theorists have discussed this difficulty at length. But we need not become mired in the intricacies here: it will be enough for us to notice the essential difficulty and the inadequacy of the most common and direct ways of deflecting that difficulty. This is well-trodden ground, and we will try to traverse it quickly. We can then consider a more promising and commonsensical way of overcoming that difficulty—albeit one that raises a different set of intriguing and portentous challenges.

The consent proposition tells us, once again, that governments must get their authority from "the consent of the governed." But as it happens, *I* am one of "the governed," and I do not recall ever giving *my* consent. As far as I'm concerned, me personally, it never happened. Same for you, most likely. Maybe a few of us did give our consent—immigrants who achieved citizenship through an official ceremony of naturalization, for example. But it seems almost certain that the vast majority of people who are citizens or residents of the United States (or Britain, or France, or . . .) never actually consented to the authority of the governments that rule us—not, at least, in the ways or forms that we typically count as manifesting "consent."

Indeed, we were never even afforded an opportunity to give or refuse our consent. Nobody ever sat us down and asked, "Do you consent to be ruled by this government? If so, initial right here, by the X." What actually happened was quite different: we were born—not through any choice of our own—and almost before we could utter our first wails of protest or squeals of approval, the government (along with our parents, of course, and later our teachers, and others) just started bossing us around, whether we liked it or not.[23]

And so if governments can gain authority only through the consent of the governed, the stark conclusion promptly follows (or so it seems): none of these governments actually possess authority. Leslie Green remarks that "consent theory may offer a correct conception of what it would be for the authority of states to be justified while at the same time offering an explanation of why it is not. Just as the best conception of free will may support the conclusion that we do not have it, the best conception of authority may show that it does not exist."[24]

The consent proposition is closely tied in modern political thought to the idea of a "social contract." We—or was it our ancestors? or has the distinction somehow been effaced?—once lived in a "state of nature" without government or law. But whether life in this condition was relatively idyllic (as Locke portrayed it) or "nasty, brutish, and short" (as in Hobbes's depiction),[25] it had its inconveniences.

And so we contracted with each other to relinquish some of our natural freedom in order to form a government. This contract conveyed and embodied our consent; and it is the basis of the government's authority over us.

In one version or another, these notions—of the state of nature, or the prepolitical state, and the social contract—pervade modern political thought, showing up in different versions in the thinking of luminaries like Locke, Hobbes, Rousseau, and (more recently) Rawls.[26] Kent Greenawalt thus explains that "[f]or most of the history of liberal democracies, the dominant theory about why citizens are obligated to obey the law has been social contract."[27]

The problems with the idea of a social contract, however, are once again notorious. There are two main difficulties. First, the contract is a blatant fiction or, as Ronald Dworkin put it, a "fantasy."[28] As a matter of actual history, there never was a social contract. It is imaginable, just barely, that such a contract *could have been* formed. But it wasn't. Thus, during the English civil wars of the mid-seventeenth century, when modern ideas of popular sovereignty were in their nascent stage, one group—the so-called Levelers—took the notion of consent and contract seriously enough to write up an actual "Agreement of the People" and present it to Parliament. The agreement, as Edmund Morgan explains, was supposed to receive "the signature of every man, woman, and child to be governed and protected under it."[29]

Parliament, which purported to exercise authority based on its supposed representation of the people, could hardly object to this proposal, could it? Well, actually, yes, it could. "The response of the sitting Parliament to the proposal," Morgan relates, "was as might have been expected: the Agreement of the People, the House of Commons proclaimed, was seditious, 'destructive to the Being of Parliaments, and Fundamental Government of the kingdom.'"[30] And so, alas, the contract was never signed.

The Levelers' futile campaign is useful in showing what genuine consent to authority might look like—and in showing that our actual governments are not based on any such thing. But suppose the Agreement of the People *had* been implemented. Or, more generally, suppose our distant ancestors *had* entered into an actual social contract of some kind. Even so, it is not at all clear how and why their agreement would be binding on you and me. Maybe they—our ancestors—consented to authority, but they are long since dead. *They* are not "the governed"; *we* are. And the fact would remain that we never did consent.

This is not to say that hypothetical thought experiments about what people would be willing to contract for in some imaginary state of nature or "original position" might not be illuminating, as in John Rawls's extensive and influential theorizing. But as a basis for actual governmental authority, the idea just doesn't work; it doesn't work because it isn't true.

These conclusions are quite obvious, but they are also inconvenient. (And perhaps also, in a certain sense, sophomoric: we will see later that in one perspective, arguments such as "I never consented" or "There never actually was any social contract" may be both plainly correct on the level of mundane fact and also, in a loftier sense, misguided and obtuse.) The conclusions are sufficiently inconvenient that both ordinary citizens and political theorists often look for ways to avoid them.

One common expedient suggests that we did consent to our respective governments after all—not in so many words, perhaps, but by implication. And how did we give this implicit consent? Well, by not choosing to leave the country, maybe, when at least in theory we *could* do that. Or by accepting benefits from the government (such as police protection). Or by voting, paying taxes,[31] or otherwise participating in public life.[32]

For some situations, implied consent accounts can be quite persuasive. You decide to join the football team, maybe, or the orchestra: you will be taken to have impliedly consented to the authority of the coach or of the director, even if you never explicitly said so. This conclusion will seem quite plausible, for a couple of reasons. First, you actually did choose to join the team or the orchestra. There was a time when you did not belong to these groups, and then, as of some identifiable date and as a result of your uncoerced decision, you became a member. Second, a commitment to follow the coach or the director is a well-understood feature of being a football player or an orchestra musician. That's just part of what it means to be on a team or in an orchestra: everyone knows this.³³

Conversely, it is hard to say that you ever freely chose to join the society ruled by the particular government that purports to exercise authority over you.³⁴ Most likely, you just somehow found yourself there, not through any choice of yours.³⁵ So the contention that you gave "implied consent" seems to rest on a fiction just as much as the "social contract" does.

Indeed, in other contexts where we care about consent, these sorts of claims about "implied consent" would seem laughably inadequate, or even offensive. It is a common assumption today, for example, that sexual relations among adults are presumptively permissible, at least so far as the state is concerned, so long as they are consensual. Conversely, sexual relations inflicted on someone without their consent constitute a serious wrong and injustice. So suppose some frat boys are accused of sexual aggression against a young woman who became inebriated during a fraternity party. They defend by saying that the sex was consensual. And *how* did the woman consent? Well, . . . by voluntarily coming to a party where she knew such conduct was likely to occur, . . . or maybe by choosing to dress in an alluring way with the knowledge that this attire would be enticing to frat boys, . . . or by not leaving the party when things began to get rowdy, . . . or by drinking to the point of vulnerability with the knowledge of what might follow. It may well be true that the woman did these things, and also that such conduct involved both more genuine choice on her part and more awareness of predictable consequences than is present in a citizen's "decision" to live in the country where he or she was born or to accept police protection. And yet far from exonerating the frat boys, these claims about implied consent will be viewed as additional outrages—as insults both to the victim's dignity and to our intelligence. However knowing and deliberate, this sort of conduct just does not qualify as "consent" to be sexually assaulted.

So if we reach a contrary conclusion in the context of political authority, it seems that we are being driven by necessity to indulge what is at bottom a fiction. Rights to emigrate, to vote, and to participate in the political process may be valuable endowments, and they will also turn out to be relevant, in a more roundabout way, to the question of authority. But they do not make for genuine "consent."

A DIFFERENT EXPEDIENT resorts not to "implied consent" but to something like "constructive consent" or "imputed consent"—notions much exploited in some contemporary moral and political theorizing. Whereas "implied consent" suggests that someone actually did consent to something (albeit not explicitly), "constructive consent" treats "what a reasonable person *would* consent to" as the equivalent of consent. But then the very notion of constructive consent (like other constructive entities in law—constructive notice, or constructive possession) quietly acknowledges that the "consent" that is being invoked to justify something is not real: it is something that is imagined and ascribed, not something that actually happened.[36]

So suppose I have the *power* to force you to do something that I believe (perhaps correctly) will be for your benefit. You have fallen into a decadent, drunken lethargy, maybe, and I have the power to force you to lay off the liquor or get up off the sofa and take a job or go to school. Let's say I exercise this power, and you indignantly protest that I'm not the boss of you. And suppose I respond that, yes, I *am* the boss of you—on the basis of your consent; and when you insist that you never did consent, I explain, "Well, a reasonable person in your pathetic condition *would* consent; and so if you were reasonable *you* would consent; and that's basically the same as consenting." The claim that a reasonable person would consent to my authority is surely contestable. But even if we stipulate to the correctness of that claim, it simply doesn't follow that *you* consented. The whole point of insisting on consent is to ensure that *you* and *I*, not somebody else, and certainly not some fictional "reasonable person," are the ones who get to do the consenting.

"Constructive consent" thus amounts to a false facade of consent invoked in support of an exercise of power that is justified, if at all, on some other ground.[37] That theorists would resort to dressing up their fundamentally nonconsensual ethical claims in the costume of constructive consent is testimony to the enormous power that the ideas of autonomy and consent wield in our modern political culture.

Even so, constructive consent, to put the point bluntly, is simply not consent.[38] (If this dismissal seems peremptory, let me say that the considerations supporting "constructive consent," like those supporting "implied consent," will turn out to be relevant in a more indirect way to the question of authority. But not because they actually supply the consent demanded by the consent proposition.)

Other theorists propose different accounts of authority. They may argue, for example, that a person who resides under the jurisdiction of a governmental regime and receives benefits from it—police protection, for example—has an obligation to respect the laws of that regime. Or they propose that we have "associative obligations" to our fellow participants in a common venture. Theorists have examined these theories in great detail.[39] Although we will in due course look at several of these theories a bit more closely, for present purposes we need not descend into the details. Instead, it will be enough for now to take note of a dilemma faced by such theories.

Theories based on conferred benefits or gratitude or associative obligations may be taken either as accepting and attempting to satisfy the consent proposition or, instead, as offering nonconsensual alternatives to that proposition. But if they are offered as rationalizations for concluding that we have implicitly consented to the government's authority, such theories are compellingly unpersuasive. Once again, we are not given any realistic choice to refuse government's authority, along with the putative benefits it provides, or to opt out of the common venture. Just try moving to the desert or the forest: the long arm of the government will still reach you. Or imagine that someone kidnaps you, confines you in a locked cell, but also offers you food—or maybe even a choice between a grim gruel and nourishing and delicious food. If you eat the food, or if you choose the nourishing and tasty food, could you plausibly be said to have consented to your confinement?

So it seems these theories are better understood as alternatives to the consent proposition. Thus construed, the theories may or may not be persuasive: we need not reach any verdict here. If we think the theories are persuasive, then they may succeed in giving us *reasons to obey* laws and commands issued by governments. We might even conclude that they succeed in demonstrating the existence of something that we might choose to call "authority." (Whether that would be the apt conclusion, or the apt terminology, is a question we will look at more closely later, in chapter 5.) But they still do not serve to confirm the consent proposition or to extricate the dominant account of authority from the category of "fiction."

Consider a more extreme example. Suppose someone says, "Although it is true that few of us ever consented to this government, the government has authority nonetheless—and we have an obligation to respect and obey it—because God has so ordained. Check out St. Paul's Epistle to the Romans, chapter 13." Just as a historical matter, this sort of theological rationale has often been invoked to support governmental authority, and even today there are surely devout citizens who accept the rationale: I myself know any number of them. But even if we stipulate for purposes of discussion that the theological rationale is correct, and thus that it gives us a reason to respect the authority of government, it still would not confirm the received, official account—which, once again, is based on . . . consent. Governmental authority as claimed by the government and as commonly understood in the American political tradition would still be based on a fiction.

Alright, but then how unsettling is this conclusion? Is there anything disturbing in the conclusion?

Up to this point, we have been saying two things as if they were synonymous. We have said that if the consent proposition is correct, then government *lacks authority*. We have also said that if the consent proposition is correct, government's authority *is based on a fiction*. But are these claims actually synonymous? Does saying that authority is based on a fiction entail that the authority itself is . . . what? Nonexistent? Illusory? Fraudulent? Can authority be grounded in a fiction and nonetheless be real authority?

Maybe it can. To see how, consider a different account of authority—one that purports to dispense with the need for "the consent of the governed" but that may have the inadvertent effect of revising and rehabilitating the consent proposition or of making "fictional consent" a sufficient basis for actual authority.

Authority and Coordination

This alternative account can be called "the coordination account" of authority. A version of this account is well articulated by the Oxford philosopher John Finnis. Finnis's account occurs as part of his "natural law" account of law, which might lead one to expect something starry-eyed and medieval. But in fact the theory is closer to being brutally realistic and is not dependent on any sort of medieval or theistic premises.

Finnis observes that in a complex and pluralistic society in which a variety of agents pursue a vast array of different goals and agendas, it is to everyone's benefit to have someone or some institution that can issue directives and rules by which people can coordinate their projects and activities with those of other people. In part the need is for someone or some institution that can maintain order and punish the violent and the antisocial. But the requirement is hardly limited to that basic law-and-order function: on the contrary, even if the people in a society were all as amiable as angels, the need for coordination would persist, and indeed would likely increase. People would still want to work together to organize business enterprises, charitable foundations, birdwatching societies, athletic associations, opera companies; and they would need coordinating rules in order to pursue these common projects. "[T]he greater the intelligence and skill of a group's members," Finnis observes, "and the greater their commitment and dedication to common purposes and common good . . . , the *more* authority and regulation may be required, to enable that group to achieve its common purpose, common good."[40]

But the necessary coordinating rules and directives do not just appear out of nowhere; they must come from someplace—or, usually, from *someone*. So if there is a person or persons with the power and propensity to issue such coordinating rules and have them obeyed, their very ability to provide such coordination gives this person or persons authority. Their authority derives from "the sheer fact of [their] effectiveness" in satisfying the need for coordination—from "[t]he *fact* that the say-so of [these people] will in fact be, by and large, complied with and acted upon."[41]

Authority is thus not dependent, Finnis argues, on "[c]onsent, transmission, contract, custom."[42] Neither does it depend on virtue in the rulers: authority can exist in "the very frequent case where bad men establish their rulership over a realm."[43] All that is needed, once again, is "effectiveness"—sheer power—accompanied by the willingness to use that power to promote order and social coordination.

Finnis criticizes "[t]he tendency of political thinkers to utter legalistic fictions about the original location of authority."[44] And it is true that by contrast to other accounts that exude a sort of fictional quality (with exotic and imaginary "states of nature," "original position[s]," "veil[s] of ignorance," and "social contracts"), the coordination account seems grittily realistic. Thus, if we look at our actual real-world situations and ask how it is (not in theory but in actual practice) that governments manage to claim and exercise authority over us, isn't something like the coordination account the most eligible explanation? As citizens, we may not recall ever actually consenting to be ruled by our governments—or even being given a genuine opportunity to do so. And we may not regard the rulers as possessed of extraordinary (or even ordinary) virtue or wisdom. Even so, we *do* need someone or some institution to enforce and maintain order and to provide and enforce the rules by which we can live and interact with each other. That need is a fact, not a fiction. And the government provides these essential goods: that is why we accept that we should support the government and its laws. Isn't it? Something along these lines?

Coordination and (Fictional) Consent

The coordination account thus seems both prima facie plausible and refreshingly realistic. Pretty much fiction-free. On first inspection anyway. But then a question arises. Granted that the government has authority if it has effective power to provide social coordination, how does the government acquire that effective power?

The answer may be complicated and may vary from one government to another. One source of governmental power—perhaps the most obvious one—consists of control over the means of force and violence: the army, the police, the courts.[45] Law operates, in Robert Cover's memorable description, upon "a field of pain and death."[46]

Some regimes depend heavily on such violence. And yet this is surely not the full story. For one thing, it seems unlikely that raw force unaccompanied by anything more will be sufficient over an extended period to maintain power over the subjects, or even over the various people and officials who constitute the government itself. "The government," after all, is not some unitary and self-sustaining organism, but rather a vast and complex network of diversely motivated and differently minded people. The means of violence—the actual guns, tanks, bombs, jails—are widely distributed among these people. So if there were nothing to the government other than sheer force, it would have difficulty even holding itself together, much less governing its subjects.

The fact is, usually, that to a large extent and to varying degrees, people obey the government and its laws—and the government therefore has power—because people believe that they are supposed to obey the laws.[47] That is just what decent people do—or what decent people think decent people do. And why are people supposed to obey the laws? They are supposed to do this, or so they believe, because they believe that the government has . . . authority.[48]

And thus a circularity appears. A government has authority, Finnis tells us, if it has effective power. And a government has effective power, we now see, if it has authority—or at least if it is *perceived as* having authority. Conversely, if a putative government came to be widely perceived as *lacking* authority (or as "illegitimate," as we say), compliance would likely decline, resistance would increase, and the government would soon encounter serious difficulties in exercising power over its subjects, and indeed over its own agents and institutions. Losing its "effective power," government would thereby lose its authority.

To put the point bluntly, if a bit oversimply: if the people generally accept that the government has authority, it does. And vice versa. This perception doesn't need to be universal, to be sure, but it needs to be widely enough shared so that together with the government's other resources (guns, jails, and so forth), "the say-so of [the government] will in fact be, by and large, complied with and acted upon."

But then the initial question is just pushed back a step, and slightly reformulated. We began by asking how government comes to have authority. Now we have to ask how government comes *to be perceived* as having authority.

Again, the answer to that question is surely complex, varying from one government and one context to another. If we step outside the seminar room and pay attention to the ways governments in fact operate, it becomes overwhelmingly obvious that they maintain their effective power—and hence, in the coordination account, their authority—in part by cultivating what we might describe as the "aura of authority." In this vein, under the heading of "political aesthetics" (and echoing an observation of Pascal[49]), Michael Huemer explains that "[m]odern governments rely on a rich collection of nonrational tools, including symbols, rituals, stories, and rhetoric, to induce in citizens a *sense* of the government's power and authority."[50] Huemer itemizes some of these tools, including flags, anthems, uniforms (including police uniforms with badges and judges' robes), stately or majestic architecture, rituals and ceremonies (such as presidential inaugurations and solemn swearing-in ceremonies), and ponderous official language.[51] Such impressive or gauzy manifestations and performances have constituted a central part of how governments have maintained their authority in the eyes of their subjects.

Exactly how such political aesthetics work to enlist allegiance presents an interesting psychological question. In premodern times, it seems plain enough that such pageantry and ritual functioned to endow rulers with some association with the divine: hence the pervasive involvement of priests and religious rituals in the performances.[52] Arguably a similar function is still in force today: Bibles, prayers, oaths (ending, often, with "So help me God"), and incantations of "God Bless America" remain standard ingredients in the public performance by which American governments present and sustain themselves. However much American courts may insist that government be "secular," they intuitively understand that these religious trappings cannot be dispensed with.[53] A similar sacralizing function is apparent in the English coronation ceremony.[54]

But another more rational or intellectual means by which governments maintain the perception of authority is through the cultivation of legitimating rationales.[55] Such rationales vary from one regime to another. In premodern times, rulers often succeeded in being perceived as having authority in part by invoking the ostensible favor of heaven—by convincing subjects, for instance, that the rulers enjoyed some sort of "divine right":[56] in this respect the nonrational and more rational means of maintaining authority ran together. But in liberal democracies such as America, the primary legitimating rationale, as we have already seen, is that government's legitimacy is based on "the consent of the governed." That, once again, is *our* "self-evident truth."

And thus it seems we are back to "consent" after all. Finnis argued that his coordination account of authority did not depend upon "[c]onsent, transmission, contract, custom." In one sense that is true: effective power to provide coordination is sufficient. But at least in modern democratic states, effective power is to a significant extent dependent, not on actual consent, perhaps, but upon maintaining the legitimating fiction of consent.

Notice, though, that the authority itself is not thereby rendered unreal or fictional. So long as the fiction of consent is widely enough embraced, the government *does* have coordinating power—and hence it does have authority.

In this respect, the coordination variation on the consent proposition seems a significant advance beyond the straightforward consent account. Under the unrefined consent proposition, authority depends on "the consent of the governed"—upon their *actual* consent. So, no real consent, no real authority. In the coordination account variation, by contrast, the "consent of the governed" might be wholly fictional and yet the authority might still be real—if, that is, the fiction is widely enough accepted that the government retains effective power.

We can now refine our initial contention that governmental authority in the political tradition of America and other liberal democracies has a fictional quality. Under a straightforward application of the consent proposition, it seems that governmental authority itself is fictional. Authority depends on the consent of the governed; but that consent is a fiction, and so the authority derived from the fictional consent would likewise be fictional authority. (In the same way that if I dress up like a police officer I do not thereby acquire any actual authority to arrest you or to search your house. A fictional officer has only fictional authority.) Under the coordination account, by contrast, the authority is real, derived not directly from consent but from effective coordinating power. Even so, insofar as that coordinating power depends on the perception of authority, which in turn is based in large part on the fiction of consent, authority still rests upon a fiction.

In his audacious history of humanity, Yuval Noah Harari contends that what initially separated humans from other animals was our ability to invent and deploy fictions.[57] "Any large-scale human cooperation," Harari argues, "—whether a modern state, a medieval church, an ancient city or an archaic tribe—is rooted in common myths that exist only in people's collective imagination."[58] "People easily understand that 'primitives' cement their social order by believing in ghosts and spirits, and gathering each full moon to dance together around the campfire. What we fail to appreciate is that our modern institutions function on exactly the same basis."[59]

Harari is, to be sure, somewhat peremptory in his pronouncements about what is and is not a fiction. Our foregoing discussion would suggest, however, that Harari is fundamentally correct with respect to the American and similar modern legal orders. The founding myths or fictions for these orders are, it seems, "the consent of the governed" and "the social contract."

TRUTHS, FALSEHOODS, AND FICTIONS

Once again, though, we can ask: Is there anything especially troubling or even surprising about this conclusion—namely, that political authority in the American constitutional tradition (and, most likely, in other democratic traditions as well) rests upon a fictional foundation? Is this tantamount to saying that government is based on lies? Wouldn't it be at least paradoxical, and probably perverse and even preposterous, to say that real authority can be derived from falsehoods?

The question requires us to think a bit more deliberately about what fictions are and how they work. A binary-minded rigorist might argue that all propositions—or at least all propositions that appear to make representations about features or states of affairs in the world—must be either true or false. And since a proposition that is fictional is by definition not true, it must therefore be . . . false.

Sometimes our usage follows this binary conception. "Fictions" can sometimes be a polite term for "lies." And yet in other contexts we understand fictions to be their own special genre situated somewhere in between straightforward truth (in a factual sense) and outright falsehood. Suppose that after listening to a reading of *Moby Dick* or *The Brothers Karamazov* someone asks, "Did all of that *really* happen?," and, upon being told that it didn't, exclaims, "So then it was all just a pack of lies?" This rigorist response fails to grasp the nature of a fiction. The fiction is perhaps not "the truth" (in a factual sense), but neither is it merely a "lie."[60] It is its own special genre.[61]

But then how do fictions, in this less censorious usage, differ from mere falsehoods? An initial response might suggest that a fiction—think of a novel or a film—does not hold itself out as true in a factual sense. It comes with a disclaimer, so to speak, which saves it from being a mere falsehood or a lie. But this response is not entirely satisfactory, because a disclaimer of factual truth seems neither sufficient nor necessary to qualify as a "fiction."

Suppose I utter this statement: "The following propositions are false: Benjamin Franklin was the first president of the United States. Two plus two equals five. The moon is made of green cheese." My introductory disclaimer should insulate me against any accusation that I have been telling lies, but does it convert my unfactual statements into "fictions"? This would seem an odd characterization. Conversely, many works of fiction do not make any explicit disclaimer of facticity; they may, on the contrary, adopt elaborate measures to make their narratives appear to be factual reports. Naive readers might even be taken in by such measures. Think of the classic radio broadcast of a reading of H. G. Wells's *War of the Worlds* and the public response to it.[62] And yet the overall character of such works is still evidently "fictional"; the narratives are neither "factual" nor simply "false."

The special character of a "fiction," it seems, is that while containing implicit or sometimes explicit indications that it is not factual in a conventional sense, the fiction does offer something that listeners or readers are invited to treat *as if* it were factual, at least within a limited context or for particular purposes. The attentive audience may be assumed to understand that the fictional statement or narrative is not "the truth" in a standard factual sense; even so, that audience is called upon to suspend this understanding, at least while appreciating or participating in the fiction, and to enter into a sort of imaginative, alternative world in which the statement or narrative *is* the truth. As Jerome Frank explained with respect to legal fictions, "[i]n the case of a fiction the mind is obliged to regard a subjective idea 'as if' it were objective but, at the same time, to remain aware that the idea is really subjective."[63]

Hence the novelistic devices calculated to impart an air of facticity: these are designed not so much to induce actual or literal belief as to facilitate the bracketing of disbelief that is necessary for the fiction to perform its function. So we will understand that space aliens are not *really* invading the earth or that there is not *really* a man named Ishmael floating on a coffin left from the wreckage of a whaling ship destroyed by a massive and malevolent milk-white whale. And yet while listening to the broadcast or reading the novel, we enter into a world in which we bracket this understanding, and so we treat the story *as if* it were true.

Fiction as Cooperative Conspiracy

Fictions thus depend on a delicate mental operation that can easily go wrong—an operation that presupposes a kind of cooperation or conspiracy between author and audience. For this operation to succeed, the author must provide the audience with something that elicits and supports the suspension of disbelief, and the audience must cooperate in that suspension. Even a brilliantly executed fiction will fail if viewers or hearers refuse such cooperation.

Thus, perverse or immature audiences may ruin a fine theatrical performance or film by constantly pointing out every tiny departure from factuality. ("Look, you can tell that isn't a real gun!" "That isn't blood; it's ketchup." "Those mountains in the background aren't real; if you look closely you can see they're painted.") We understand that such behavior is boorish. The person who insists on pointing out such discrepancies, thereby spoiling the performance, is like a disloyal conspirator who exposes the plot (and both fictions and conspiracies can involve plots) to the public or the police.

Still, what is it that would induce an audience to cooperate in this conspiracy? Part of the answer is that the fiction promises a payoff to those who make the effort to engage with it. The payoff might be merely entertainment, or a delicious feeling of fright: that, presumably, was the intended result of the "War of the Worlds" broadcast. Or it might be something like insight or wisdom. Surely great novels—*Moby Dick*, *War and Peace*, *Crime and Punishment*—serve to provide this kind of benefit.

Or the payoff might be authority, and the benefits of order and coordination that are associated with authority. Our foregoing argument suggests that in the political context, legitimating fictions (like consent or social contract or, in an older view, "divine right") may help to secure the benefits of a coordinating authority that makes collective life possible.

And yet a promised payoff is not enough to sustain the operation essential to a successful fiction; it is also necessary that the fiction itself possess sufficient plausibility to sustain the suspension of belief called for by the fiction—so that readers and viewers can engage with the story *as if* it were relating something that happened. A successful fiction must be, not true, but believable. It must be sufficiently believable so that at least within the frame of the fiction readers or viewers can set aside their awareness that this "didn't really happen" and instead suppose that it did happen.[64] We might say that a fiction, while not purporting to be "true," exactly, nonetheless attempts to be "truish."

A novelist, to be sure, may not pretend that her story is the same kind of thing that the historian or the chronicler purports to give us. If asked, the novelist might quickly acknowledge: "Of course, none of this *really happened*." Indeed, movies or television shows sometimes begin with an explicit (and sometimes false!) declaration that none of the events or characters in the show are meant to resemble actual events or people. And yet almost all fictions nonetheless attempt to instill in readers or viewers a suspension of disbelief. Thus, with reference to a novel in which the Roman Empire is imagined as having modern technology (something no reader could mistake for a historical claim), novelist Helen Dale nonetheless observes that "[t]he best speculative fiction persuades you that its alternative world is real."[65]

So suppose that after watching a movie with a friend, you explain that you didn't enjoy the film because you "just couldn't believe it," or because you found it too "implausible." And suppose your friend responds: "You're just being obtuse. Don't you know that it was *fiction*? A story? It wasn't a documentary; it never pretended to be factual in the first place. You weren't *supposed to* believe it." In this case, it is your friend—not you—who is being obtuse. True, the movie didn't exactly hold itself out as factual. But it did attempt to elicit a suspension of disbelief so that within the frame of the film it could be taken as true—or treated *as if* it were true. And if the film lacked this kind of plausibility or believability, so that viewers could not take it as true, then it failed as a fiction. "Implausibility" is thus a common and recognized flaw in fictions.

In the same way, studying the transition from "divine right" theories of government to popular sovereignty, Edmund Morgan explains that "the success of government . . . requires the acceptance of fiction, requires the willing suspension of disbelief, requires us to believe that the emperor is clothed even though we can see that he is not." For this to happen, though, the political fictions need to believable. Not true, but believable. As Morgan puts it, they need to maintain "a viable relation with fact."[66]

These two features of fictions—that they seek to provide benefits such as entertainment or insight or wisdom, or legitimacy; and that they attempt to be "truish" and hence to sustain a suspension of disbelief—are related. If the payoff offered by a fiction is meager or nonexistent—the movie wants to entertain but in fact it is just boring or offensive—viewers will have little motivation to muster up the necessary suspension of disbelief. Conversely, even if the fiction does offer benefits of entertainment or insight—or order and coordination—it still needs to be sufficiently believable, or "truish," that it can sustain the suspension of disbelief that is a requisite of its success.

The (Potential) Efficacy—and the Limitations—of (Fictional) Consent

We can now appreciate how the fiction of consent functions in a liberal democracy. Consent is mostly a fiction, as we have seen, and to succeed as a fiction it needs to satisfy the requirements of payoff and plausibility.

The coordination account explains how the fiction of consent can meet the first requirement. We need the benefits of authority—its benefits in satisfying our need for order and social coordination. And if we believe, as in the modern Western political tradition, that authority must be based on "the consent of the governed," then the fiction of consent will be vital in maintaining the authority from which those benefits flow.

But of course, to say that "authority provides the benefit of social coordination" is an abstract proposition. In reality, the benefits of authority will vary dramatically, depending on how well a government functions and how respectful it is of its citizens and their interests. Thus, under a benign and well-functioning government, the motivation to indulge the fiction of consent and suspend the skepticism that would remind that the consent is fictional rather than real will presumably be strong. Under such a regime, critics who observe (as we did earlier in this chapter) that "we never really consented" will likely be dismissed as obtuse and subversive—like the adolescent who throughout a well-made and suspenseful movie keeps exclaiming that "That isn't actually blood!" or "That isn't a real gun!" If a story is going well—if it is providing us with entertainment or wisdom, ... or with well-functioning and beneficial authority—then it is merely boorish to disturb the story with such subversive observations (true though they may be).

Conversely, as a government becomes more dysfunctional or unjust, the motivation to believe the fiction will weaken. A group that sees itself as systematically oppressed or discriminated against will have little incentive to overlook the fictional quality of the "consent" on which the government's assertion of authority depends. "*We* never consented!" will seem not only a true but also a perfectly appropriate and cogent thing to say—to the oppressed group, that is.

Even a generally well-functioning government, however, still needs to satisfy some requirement of plausibility. And thus the features pointed to by theorists of implied and constructive consent—police protection, for example, or the right to vote—become relevant after all, because they affect both the benefits of the fiction of consent and the "truishness" of that fiction.

Take the right to vote. We have already noted that a citizen who exercises the right to vote for legislators or executive officials (like the president) does not necessarily thereby give genuine consent to the authority of the government. Even so, the right to vote is powerfully relevant to the maintenance of authority, for two reasons. First, most citizens will likely view the right to participate in governance as an important privilege or benefit: hence, a government that affords them this right will be to that extent more attractive, and their motivation to accept the government's authority will be greater. Second, and even more importantly, although the right to vote may not amount to genuine consent, still the fiction of consent will be far more believable or "truish" in a government that permits people to vote and participate. The point is probably even clearer if made in the negative: the proposition that the government is based on "the consent of the governed" will be starkly implausible if the government does not even allow the governed to vote or otherwise participate in governance.

So it seems that it is possible to derive actual authority from a fiction—from the fiction of consent. (Or at least to derive what we typically *describe* as "authority": we are deferring until a later chapter Hannah Arendt's suggestion that even what today is called "authority" is not the genuine article, but rather some sort of counterfeit.) Not only is this feat possible in the abstract: as with the old joke about baptism by immersion, we've seen it done. The last two centuries or so of American history, along with the history of other liberal democracies, corroborate the possibility.

And yet authority grounded in a fiction has its limitations. One limitation we have already noticed: such authority is potentially vulnerable to criticism calling attention to its fictional foundation. So long as government is functioning well to provide the benefits that government is supposed to provide, citizens will presumably be disinclined to make—or to listen to—such criticisms. But if the government comes to be perceived as unjust or oppressive or even merely ineffectual, such criticisms are likely to gain greater purchase, thereby eroding the authority of the government.

Embarrassing Questions

This sort of limitation will likely become apparent in times of political strife and stress. But there is a different sort of limitation that will quietly impose itself even in normal, healthy periods. This limitation follows from the fact that a fiction is, after all, . . . fictional. Because it is fictional, it will be unable to yield answers to particular kinds of questions that overlook its fictional quality. And if such questions arise, the result will be a kind of embarrassment and futility and, at least potentially, an erosion of the fictional framework.

To illustrate: Imagine an audience in a literature class that has listened for the first time to a reading of Charles Dickens's *A Christmas Carol*. After the reading, the instructor tests the students' comprehension with a series of questions. Who was Jacob Marley? What was the name of Scrooge's former employer? How many spirits did Scrooge see? These questions can all be answered from within the framework of the fiction. Marley was Scrooge's now deceased business partner. Scrooge's former employer was "Old Fezziwig." Scrooge was visited by three spirits. So far, so good. And anyone who objected that the questions are nonsensical because the story is merely fictional would be demonstrating his obtuseness: it is true that the story is fictional, but within the framework of this fiction there are correct (and also incorrect) answers to these questions.

But now suppose that the students respond with some questions of their own. Which political party did Scrooge support—the Whigs or the Tories? Did he ever consider running for Parliament? Did his net wealth increase or diminish after he began to be more philanthropic with his money? Was Scrooge a member—or did he become a member—of a Christian church? Which denomination? In what month was he born? What were his height and weight? Was he right-handed or left-handed?

These questions *are* nonsensical; they mistake the character of the story, treating it as factual rather than fictional. If the story were about some actual historical person—some real-life English commodities trader, for example—the questions would be cognizable, and we could say that at least in principle there are correct (and incorrect) answers to the questions, even if we have no way of ascertaining what the correct answers are. (The commodities trader died decades ago, perhaps, and there is no record of whether he was right-handed or left-handed.) But with a fiction, there simply is no "fact of the matter" that could supply the answers.

To be sure, it might be possible to extrapolate from the story and hazard tentative guesses about the best answers to *some* of the questions. Literary critics sometimes engage in such an exercise; so do the rest of us. So we might argue that a person with the personality and character ascribed by the story to Scrooge would more likely vote Whig, or Tory, or that he would (or wouldn't) be likely to belong to a Christian church. These would not be correct or incorrect answers, exactly, but rather conjectural and interpretive attempts to fill out the character of Scrooge beyond what the story itself gives us. And for other questions—about Scrooge's birthday or handedness, for example—it would be simply pointless even to engage in this kind of conjecture.

This sort of misunderstanding in which someone treats a fiction as factual, and as a result makes demands that a fiction cannot answer, is not unfamiliar. Children ask factual questions about Santa Claus. How does he manage to get around to every household in the world in just one night? Is his house at the North Pole made of ice, and if so, how do Santa and Mrs. Claus manage to keep from freezing during the perpetual Arctic winter? Biblical literalist students may ask a more modernist Sunday school teacher what kind of fruit it was that Adam and Eve ate—an apple? a pomegranate?—or how their sons Cain and Seth managed to find spouses.

These are examples arising from specialized contexts. But are there examples that are more widely applicable—that occur in the experience of most of us? And if there are, would we even recognize them? Because after all, we would ourselves be under the misapprehension of treating as a fact something that is actually a fiction. And yet, as we have seen, it is the character of a fiction that even as we treat it as if it were true, we are also aware at some level that it is not "really true." So perhaps we would or could notice, at least with effort, that we are participating in a fiction.

So, does this limitation on the efficacy of a fiction have any relevance to the legitimating fictions on which the authority of law is based? I will argue in the next two chapters that it does. More specifically, I will argue that many of the most persistent controversies in law and jurisprudence are intractable precisely because they overlook the fictional quality of authority and thereby ask factual-type questions and make factual-type claims about matters that are merely fictional. When we ask what the Constitution means or what some statute means with respect to some contentious question, experience shows that notwithstanding all of our debate and research, we are unlikely to agree. An important reason for this impasse, I will suggest, is that we are trying to squeeze factual-type answers out of things that are, at their core, fictions.

CHAPTER TWO

Fictional Authority and the Problem of Constitutional Interpretation

So it turns out that legal authority in modern democratic regimes is grounded in a fiction, or in a family of fictions whose leading characters include "the consent of the governed" and "the social contract." *So what?*

As the previous chapter argued, a fiction that is widely enough accepted can support actual practical authority. To be sure, it would be imprudent to go around constantly proclaiming that our law is based on a fiction, because that would undermine the fiction and hence its ability to sustain the authority of law.[1] (Just as it would spoil a movie if your friend kept leaning over and whispering, "None of this *really* happened, you know.") There may also be something faintly embarrassing in the admission that the majestic empire of our law—the columned courthouses, the austerely robed judges, the badges and uniforms, and of course the high razor wire fences and guard towers and prison bars—that all of this is ultimately traceable back to a sort of carefully maintained collective self-deception. Still, does that embarrassment have any inconvenient practical implications—any adverse consequences for the ways in which lawyers, judges, sheriffs, magistrates, and other officials actually carry on the business of law? Or for the ways in which the rest of us experience that law?

Maybe not. It might be that the edifice of law is like a vast family dynasty in which the estate can all be traced back to some dubious ancient grant or bequest. The investigations of a meddlesome historian reveal, perhaps, that the family's founding patriarch actually stole the original property or swindled someone out it or took it by violence, and only pretended to have acquired it legitimately. The ostensible title deed is a forgery, maybe—like the Donation of Constantine. Even so, at this late date, decades or centuries later, any imaginable statute of limitations has long since run; there is no chance that the originary fraud or violence will somehow be reversed. So although the fictional nature of the founding event might be a minor source of mortification to the family, it has no practical implications for the persistence of the family dynasty—any more than the exposure of Romulus and Remus as mythical characters will undermine the de facto dominion of the Caesars.

Maybe law with its fictional fundaments is like that? Legal authority has a fictional element, maybe, but this element has no consequences for the practical business of lawyers, judges, and subjects generally?

This would perhaps be the most comforting answer to the "so what?" question. It is also the most common answer. Common not in the sense that it is frequently asserted—this again would be a subversive or self-defeating practice—but in the even stronger sense that it is universally, silently assumed. Thus, the question of legal authority—of whether law has authority and, if so, how—is typically treated as a discrete philosophical question for specialized jurisprudential seminars and scholarship.[2] In less rarefied contexts, the authority of law is taken as a given, and officials just get on with the business of law. So if you were to explain to a lawyer or judge, over dinner maybe, that the "consent of the governed" on which law's authority is based is actually fictional, he or she might politely respond, "That's an interesting theoretical perspective." Or maybe, a little less politely: "Well, yes, obviously. Tell me something everyone with any intelligence doesn't already know." And the next day it would be back to business as usual, with nary a qualm lingering over from the previous evening's discussion.

Against this virtually universal if unspoken (or rather *because* unspoken) consensus, I will argue in this chapter and the next that the problem of law's authority cannot be so neatly sealed off. The fictional elixir seeps out; it permeates law throughout its reaches, coating even the mundane workings of law with a fictional aspect.

As we have already noted, this fictional dimension need not deprive law of its practical authority. And yet it is legal authority's partly fictional quality, I will argue, that is a principal reason for the irresolvable character of many of the familiar and perennial debates that engage and engulf down-to-earth lawyers, scholars, and judges who would have not the slightest interest in theoretical questions of law's authority. Debates about mundane issues of statutory interpretation or exercises of presidential power. Constitutional debates about the nature of the union. Debates between "originalists" and "nonoriginalists." These debates are unsettlable, I will suggest, because the contestants suppose they are contending over some contested fact when in reality they are arguing about a fiction.

It is as if readers got into a dispute about whether Captain Ahab had been abused as a boy, or about whether Hamlet was suffering from some sort of Oedipal complex or gender dysphoria, or about whether Frodo and Sam's relationship went beyond mere friendship. Such questions might be asked; in the right kind of crowd they might even elicit animated, learned, impressively sophisticated discussions. In the end, though, there is simply no "fact of the matter" that could establish what the correct or true answer is. The same holds, I will argue, for many of the most common questions and debates in law.

In this chapter, we will consider debates in the area of constitutional law. In the following chapter we will consider statutes, judicial decisions, and presidential decrees.

Interpretation and Authority

Start with a mundane observation: the everyday business of lawyers and judges involves interpretation. Interpretation of law—or, more precisely, of laws. Of statutes, regulations, executive orders, judicial precedents, sometimes constitutional provisions. Interpreting laws is central to what lawyers and judges do.[3] Consequently, the texts that embody our law—constitutional texts (like the Fourteenth Amendment), statutory texts (like the Fair Housing Act or the Civil Rights Act of 1964), regulatory texts like the sprawling conglomeration compiled in the Code of Federal Regulations—come in for intense, ongoing scrutiny.[4]

What is it about these legal texts that elicits such massive and perpetual attention—attention vastly exceeding the wildest hopes of the writers of, say, poems (or, a fortiori, law review articles)? It is surely not their prose style or their poetic quality. There is nothing eloquent or witty or insightful about these official legal texts: they are, rather, a kind of dense semantic sludge. No one would ever put a statute book on her bedside stand, except perhaps as a desperate remedy for insomnia.

So then why *do* multitudes of people devote their professional lives to studying these tedious texts? But then the answer to that question is obvious, isn't it? We read and study the legal texts because they are the expressions of legal authorities—of persons or institutions to whom we believe that governing authority has been assigned. These persons or institutions have been entrusted with the authority to make and implement the rules and norms that regulate our collective life, and they exercise that authority by enacting or adopting laws, which are communicated through the legal texts that lawyers and judges (and, more intermittently, the rest of us) interpret. That is why—for the most part, that is the *only* reason why[5]—we make the painful effort to read and interpret these turgid texts.

It is an elementary and obvious point, but it needs to be plainly stated because its significance is often overlooked. If the reason for studying and interpreting a text is that the text is the communication of a legal authority, that reason will dictate what sort of interpretation we perform or what sort of meaning we seek. More specifically, if we are reading the texts *because* they are expressions of legal authorities, then we will read them *as* expressions of legal authorities, and we will try to ascertain what rules or norms or commands the authorities were attempting to communicate and impose through those texts.

Oliver Wendell Holmes Jr. put it this way: "[I]n the case of a statute . . . , as we are dealing with the command of the sovereign the only thing to do is to find out what the sovereign wants.'"[6]

To be sure, this is not the only thing we can do with texts—as modern scholarship on the subject of hermeneutics has amply shown. We might instead study a text to discern whether the author was sexist or racist or religious, or to chart the author's grammatical proclivities, or to ascertain the historical or philosophical or literary influences that shaped the text. Or, bracketing questions of authorship and historical context, we might take the *words* and playfully ask how many different senses can be assigned to those words—a bit like a game of Boggle but with words and phrases instead of letters. A junior high friend of mine, Brad, was a lackluster student but a literary genius, in a somewhat specialized and perverse sense: to his own endless amusement, Brad (like some Freudian literary critics) could find a salacious or erotic meaning in just about anything anyone said. A cigar was never just a cigar.

So we can do any of these things, and others, with texts, including legal texts; nor is there anything to prevent us, if we are so inclined, from describing any of these activities as "interpretation."[7] Who can stop us? And yet if we are reading a text because it is an expression of a legal authority, and thus *as* an expression of legal authority, then we will practice a different kind of interpretation. We will interpret the text to ascertain what the legal authority was trying to convey though the text.

Thus, if you are reading the king's decree because it came from the king and because the king is, . . . well, the king, then you will want to figure out what the king meant by the decree. Same for a statute enacted by Congress. (Although "Congress," as we will see in the following chapter, is a more ethereal entity than we might initially suppose.) Same, for that matter, with a scriptural text, if you believe the text is a communication from God. True, it might be possible to treat any of these texts as a source or locus of some other kind of what you are free to call "meaning"—something other than what the king or Congress or God was trying to do or convey with the text. But in that case you would be detaching the text from the authority that made it and gave it the character of law (or scripture), and so you would be separating the text from your reason for consulting or caring about it in the first place.

THE SEPARATION ERROR

This particular misstep is one we will encounter frequently in this chapter and in the next one, so it will be helpful to give the misstep a name. Let us call it "the separation error." This is the error, once again, that would occur if you are reading or interpreting a text because you think it is an expression of a particular legal authority, and yet you employ a hermeneutical technique that has the effect of separating the text from that authority. In calling this sort of interpretive move an "error," I am not denying that there might be good reasons in some contexts and for some purposes to engage in such "interpretation." It is an error only in the sense that it will defeat your purpose for caring about the text in the first place—if, that is (and this is a crucial qualification), you actually care about the text as an expression of a legal authority.[8]

If you are reading a friend's note or email telling you where to meet her for dinner, then you will try to interpret the words to figure out what your friend was communicating—even if the terms are ambiguous and *could be* read to indicate a different restaurant that serves tastier food. Sure, you could go to the better restaurant and later excuse yourself to your friend by explaining how her note could be read to indicate the restaurant you prefer. And if you care more about the quality of the food than about spending time with your friend (but don't want to offend her), that might even be a sensible thing to do. But if your goal is actually to meet up with your friend, what would be the point of this excuse? Likewise, if you are interpreting a legal text because it is an expression of a legal authority, you will try to interpret the text to ascertain what the authority was trying to communicate by it.

In this vein, Larry Alexander explains that "[a]ny meaning [a law] is given other than its authorially intended meaning renders nonsensical the idea of designating its authors as having the authority to determine the norms to govern us."[9] "[T]he reason we should seek the actual authors' intended meaning," Alexander elaborates, is that the actual authors possessed the legal authority to promulgate norms, and their texts just are their communications of the norms they intended to promulgate. If we ignore their intended meanings in favor of any of the infinite possible meanings someone else might have intended through this set of symbols, then we are ignoring the legal norms promulgated by those with legal authority in favor of norms promulgated by persons who lack that authority. If, for example, Congress has the legal authority to make federal statutory law, then to ignore the congressionally-intended meaning of a federal statute in favor of a meaning that was not congressionally intended is to construct a federal law that lacks constitutional authorization. So, too, if the ratifiers of the Constitution and its amendments are the persons with authority to make and change constitutional norms, then to "interpret" the Constitution as if it had been authored by someone other than its ratifiers is to make constitutional "law" without authority to do so.[10]

Alexander suggests that the practice of reading legal texts as expressions of legal authority entails that we ascertain their meanings by looking to the actual subjective intentions of the lawmakers. That is a natural and commonsensical conclusion; but it is also controversial, and we need not prejudge the question at this point. Perhaps there is some other way of linking a text and its "meaning" to the legal authorities that made and promulgated the text. It is enough for now to say that a mode of interpretation that severs the connection between the text and the legal authority that enacted or promulgated that text will in effect deprive that designated legal authority of actual lawmaking authority. It will take away with the left hand what the right hand purported to give.[11]

What Do Fictional Authorities Mean?

But now we come to an unsettling, perhaps impertinent "what if" question. *What if . . . the legal authorities from which the texts are thought to emanate are not "real," but rather fictional?* Now, what sort of meaning are lawyers and judges looking for? And when they disagree about what the text means, what exactly are they disagreeing about? What sort of fact or evidence could resolve this sort of disagreement?

The answer to that impertinent question seems clear enough: *if* the legal authorities were fictional in character, then in the case of ambiguous texts there would be no fact of the matter regarding what the authorities have commanded or forbidden (any more than there is a fact of the matter about whether Captain Ahab was abused as a boy); and there would thus be no fact or evidence that could determine which among rival interpretations of the contested texts is the correct one. Suppose we have been scrutinizing a particular enigmatic command and treating it as authoritative because we have believed it to be an utterance of the Delphic Apollo (a deity who by all accounts had the annoying habit of speaking in ambiguities and riddles). If it then turns out that Apollo is nothing more than a mythical or fictional character, it will now seem quite pointless to waste time arguing about what the command "really" means. We can construct a fictional Apollo in any way we like; we can thus construct the meaning of Apollo's command to be what we want or need it to be. Except that it would no longer be Apollo's command, so why would we bother?[12]

To be sure, some interpretations might still be *better* or more attractive than others—better with respect to either of the factors considered in the previous chapter as essential to a successful fiction. They might be better in the sense of being more desirable, or more admirable or just. Or they might be better in the sense of being more "truish"—not *true* in a factual sense, but more plausible so as to support the suspension of disbelief on which a successful fiction depends. So we could still argue about rival interpretations with respect to those sorts of criteria. As with other fictions, though, we could tell or spin out authority fictions in various ways, and there would be no "fact of the matter" that could ultimately determine (not even "in principle") which of these tellings is the *true* or *correct* one.

This point may seem plausible in the conditional abstract but inapplicable to our actual situation. Unlike Apollo, after all, the authorities that make *our* law—the legislators, judges, administrative agencies, convention delegates, executive officials—are not mythical or fictional, but rather actual flesh-and-blood human beings. So even if the legal authority they exercise is ultimately traceable back to a fiction (such as the "social contract" embodying "the consent of the governed"), the functioning legal authorities that are the immediate sources of our laws are utterly and often inconveniently real. They are emphatically not fictions.

Or are they?

"We the People": (Fictional?) Author of the Constitution

A good starting point for pursuing the question is the fundamental legal document to which the rest of American law is subordinate: the Constitution. Although the document is sometimes described as if it were some compendium of lofty political principles,[13] in fact even a moderately careful as opposed to ardently wishful reading will discover in it very little of an inspirational character: once you get past its brief aspirational preamble and at least until you get to later amendments, the Constitution reads more like a workmanlike, nuts-and-boltsy blueprint of the basic structure of government. It may be a noble document, but it is hardly something that anyone would read for inspiration. A prominent and imaginative constitutional scholar once suggested that we should read the Constitution for wisdom or insight in the way we study Aristotle or John Stuart Mill,[14] but one could only wonder: Had she ever actually looked at the thing? Americans nonetheless treat the document as sacrosanct because it is deemed to carry ultimate authority; it is the highest or supreme manifestation of authority in our legal and political system (as the document itself somewhat immodestly declares[15]). Presidents, senators, and justices—well, presidents and senators anyway—all must bow before the commands and prohibitions of the Constitution. Or at least they must pretend to bow to those commands and prohibitions.

And how or from whom did the Constitution acquire this extraordinary authority? The document itself gives us the answer in its very first words: the Constitution is the expression of, and it acquires its authority from, "We the People of the United States." Other answers are possible, of course: an unimaginative entry on the Amazon website for a paperback of the Constitution lists the author as "Delegates of the Constitutional Convention."[16] But that is not what the Constitution itself says: it presents itself as the expression of "We the People of the United States."

Nor does the Constitution just *happen to be* an expression of "We the People"; it *needs to be*, or at least it needs to be received as, an expression of "We the People." That is the condition, under the "self-evident truth" that authority must be derived from "the consent of the governed," for the Constitution's claim to ultimate legal authority. Not surprisingly, therefore, the Constitution's populist provenance has been recited and invoked reverently and endlessly throughout American history.[17]

And yet we can still ask: Who exactly (or what, and where?) is this "We the People"? Who or what is this almost mystic author not only of the original Constitution but also, it seems, of the Bill of Rights, and of the transformative Fourteenth Amendment, adopted four score years later? And also of the Twenty-Seventh Amendment? You remember: the one that "We the People" took under advisement in 1789 and then mulled over for more than two centuries before finally making up its (their?) mind in favor of ratification. Who or what is this always-present, ever-changing, sometimes precipitous and sometimes glacially dilatory, seemingly deathless prodigy—"We the People of the United States"?

Scholars sometimes have the candor, or the impertinence, to pronounce "We the People" a fiction. Randy Barnett says it bluntly: "'We the People' is a fiction."[18] James Boyd White explained that "the People" functions as "a kind of fictive entity constituted over time, in the life of the nation as a whole and in our institutions."[19] The eminent historian Edmund Morgan wrote a learned and engaging book explaining how, as his title suggested, "the People" was "invented."[20]

We might say that the story of "We the People" creating and sustaining the Constitution is America's distinctive version of the "social contract" story. It is the American story of how people in a state of nature or prepolitical state (or at least preconstitutional state) got together and agreed to relinquish some of their freedom in order to gain the benefits of government and law.[21]

That comparison will provoke objections, though. After all, by contrast to the social contract, the Constitution itself is not a fiction, but rather a real document. Or so it seems. You can check the thing out in a book or online; if you are still suspicious you can go and inspect the original document in the National Archives. Moreover, that real document was written and ratified by real people at a real point in our history. Fair enough. And yet there is at least one component of the story—one very essential component—that is nonetheless fictional. That fictional component is, once again, the document's ostensible author or enacting authority—namely, "We the People of the United States."

We can even say with some precision when the fiction of "We the People" came into being, and how, and by whom. (Or at least we can say when *the Constitution's* "We the People" came into existence: as Morgan explains, politicians and theorists had been working on fashioning "the people" as a usable political entity for at least a century-and-a-half.[22]) As of September 10, 1787, with just a week remaining in the deliberations of the Philadelphia Convention, the prospective constitution still described itself as the work of "We the people of the States of New Hampshire, Massachusetts, Rhode Island and Providence Plantations, Connecticut, New York, New Jersey, Pennsylvania, Delaware, Maryland, Virginia, North Carolina, South Carolina, and Georgia."[23] At that point the document was sent to a Committee on Style: Alexander Hamilton (later to regain fame as the protagonist of a popular Broadway musical) and James Madison were on the committee, but Pennsylvania delegate Gouverneur Morris served as the principal draftsman.[24] The committee returned two days later with an improved version. Among other refinements, the committee had dropped the reference to the various states and had attributed the document instead to a newly concocted entity: "We the People of the United States."

This attribution was not only rhetorically exhilarating; it was also necessary, in a very practical and also technical sense.[25] Under existing law (the Articles of Confederation), no constitutional change could be effected without the approval of the national legislature and the unanimous consent of the states. The Philadelphia delegates understood that the national legislature, and even more so the state legislatures, would be disinclined to ratify a new frame of government that would reduce their own power (or eliminate them altogether).[26] And so the delegates circumvented legal requirements by inventing and then appealing to a more primal authority: "We the People of the United States."[27]

Patrick Henry objected indignantly to the delegates' presumption: who had licensed them to speak for "We the People of the United States"?[28] It was a cogent enough question. Authorized or not, though, the delegates took that license upon themselves—and they got away with it.

Fact and/or Fiction?

And yet . . . is it really fair to say that "We the People" is a fiction? Perhaps we—or the scholars who offer this peremptory judgment—have been too hasty? Because much hinges on the point, and because in some contexts some of us may be resistant to the claim that "We the People" is a mere fiction, the question deserves a closer look.

Start with some obvious, undisputed facts. In 1787, there *were* a few million flesh-and-blood human beings living in the geographical spaces that comprised the thirteen "United States of America." Surely these human beings—these *people*, or at least these *persons*—were real, not fictional. If you had lived back then, you could shake their hand, take their pulse, punch them in the jaw. And these people—or at least some of them—did actually select delegates and send them to conventions in the various states, where the delegates did actually meet and deliberate and eventually vote to ratify the new Constitution.

Similar things might be said with respect to later amendments to the Constitution: these were all written and debated and ratified by real human beings. So isn't it mere effrontery for scholars like Professors Barnett, White, and Morgan to declare that "We the People" is a "fictive entity"?

Well, yes . . . and (more importantly) no.

Consider a perhaps irreverent analogy. Imagine an accomplished ventriloquist—call him Lester—who speaks through a dummy whom he introduces to audiences as "Frank the Magnificent." In shows, Frank the Magnificent purports to talk to audiences, to listen to and then answer questions, to give sage advice, even to deliver messages from heaven and hell.[29] The performances are so convincing that audience members in some cases are not merely entertained but are inspired to follow Frank's advice.

All seems to be going well—for Lester, for Frank, and for Lester's and Frank's enthralled audiences. And then an insolent skeptic steps forward and objects that Frank the Magnificent isn't real. Frank, the skeptic says, is "a fraud"—but we will soften the skeptic's objection into the claim that Frank is "a fiction."

Is the objection correct? Well, Frank is surely not *merely* a fictional character in the way that, say, Rumpelstiltskin is a fictional character. After all, there is obviously something real—the dummy—that performs in the shows. The dummy is there for anyone to see, touch, and hear—because audible sounds do appear to be emanating from Frank, or at least from Frank's vicinity, simultaneously with the movements of Frank's painted wooden mouth (and indeed even when Lester's mouth appears *not* to be moving!). So there is *something* real; nor is there anything to prevent us from giving that something any name or label we like. Such as . . . "Frank the Magnificent." Why not?

And yet, sadly, it seems that in a more important sense the skeptic is correct. Because although there is something real in the shows (namely, the dummy), and although nothing prevents us from calling that something by whatever name we choose, the fact is that this something cannot actually hear and understand questions, cannot actually give intelligent responses, cannot actually deliver messages from heaven or hell. *The dummy* is real, we might say, but "Frank the Magnificent" *as he is presented* is a fiction in the important sense that he is presented as possessing qualities and powers that the real entity—the dummy—does not actually possess.

In a similar way, there have in fact at all relevant times been real, flesh-and-blood human beings, or "people," living in the geographical territory called "the United States." Nor is there anything to prevent us from mentally grouping those human beings together as a class and calling that class by whatever name we like—such as, maybe... "We the People of the United States." Nothing fictional thus far. And yet an equivocation seems to be at work here, because the "We the People" that ostensibly created and spoke through the Constitution is presented as possessing—and *needs* to possess, in order to perform its political and legitimating functions—qualities and powers that the mere persons, or the aggregation of individuals living within the United States, never have possessed.

For one thing, in order to satisfy the "consent of the governed" condition for authority, the Constitution's "We the People" needs to be able to represent and reflect the will of *all* of the human beings living in the region.[30] All of those human beings, after all, will be treated as subject to—and thus, inferentially, as having consented to—the Constitution. For another, "We the People" needs to be capable of speaking in a unitary voice. And it is arguable (although the point is complicated and debatable) that "We the People" needs to be capable of persisting over decades and centuries—if, that is, the document is going to be deemed binding on later generations and if the original document is going to be treated as of a piece with provisions written and enacted decades and centuries later (or as in the case of the Twenty-Seventh Amendment, written and approved by Congress in 1789 but *enacted* more than two centuries later).

But of course there is no entity possessing all of these features. Even in 1787, when Gouverneur Morris and the Committee on Style concocted the idea, and the phrase, there were numerous humans living in America who were excluded from the processes of governance—slaves, women, Native Americans. These individuals were part of "the people"—the empirical class of human beings living within the geographical territory—but they were not realistically part of "We the People." Not of *the Constitution's* "We the People." *They* had no say in what "We the People" ordained and established.[31]

We might pause at this point to clarify why the fact of unenfranchised persons is being mentioned here. Critics of the American constitutional tradition—and the critics have always existed, and seem to be proliferating of late—often point to this fact as a way of casting blame on the founding generation and perhaps of arguing that the framers acted unjustly in creating the Constitution. The so-called three-fifths clause is often invoked in such castigations.[32] Defenders of the framers may in turn respond that these indictments are themselves unfair and that we need to judge historical persons and events in the context and against the possibilities of their own times.[33] But we need not enter into this quarrel here. The question we are considering is not whether the founders were wise and righteous or, conversely, wicked and oppressive. Nor is it whether in creating the Constitution those men accomplished a grand achievement or instead committed some kind of grave injustice. The point for our purposes is more elementary: insofar as millions of Americans were not permitted to participate in the creation and approval of the Constitution, the claim that the document and the new government were the creation of "We the People of the United States" traded on a fiction. A noble and beneficent fiction, if you like, but a fiction nonetheless.

And indeed, beyond those who were formally unenfranchised, there were surely numerous other Americans who might in principle have participated in governance but did not do so—because they were ignorant of what was happening, or were busy tilling their fields or selling their wares, or were simply not interested. And even those who did participate did not agree or speak with one voice. Moreover, both they and their nonparticipating neighbors were mortals who died—alas, every last one of them—within a relatively short time: many generations separate them from us. None of those "people" were around when the Fourteenth Amendment—or the Twenty-Seventh—was ratified.[34] In sum, as Gary Lawson and Guy Seidman observe, "[t]he document was written, read, debated, and eventually ratified by a very small subset of any plausible grouping of 'We the People.'"[35]

So, yes, there have at all times been human persons within the land. You can if you like refer to those human persons as "We the People." But the "We the People" that established the Constitution and conferred authority on the new government, and then persisted to maintain the continuity of that document and that frame of governance, ... *that* "We the People" was and remains a majestic fiction.

Consider a humble analogy. Suppose that some of the residents of Capitoline Subdivision believe that in order to achieve an immaculately upscale tone for the neighborhood, it would be a good idea for everyone to mow his or her lawn every other day. Mow on Monday, Wednesday, Friday, and so forth. Some of the residents—Julius, Portia, Brutus, and Festus—accordingly invite all of the important people in the neighborhood to a meeting to consider the matter. Some of these invitees show up at the meeting, some for various reasons fail to attend, and some come but then become bored or irritated and leave. At the end of the meeting, the remaining attendees draft and sign a document in the name of "We the Residents of Capitoline Subdivision," covenanting that everyone in the neighborhood will mow every other day and that any violators of this covenant will be subject to a five-hundred-dollar fine.

A month later, Portia and Festus notice a perky yellow dandelion growing in the lawn of Julia (who was not invited to the meeting or who, if you like, *was* invited but was out of town or out shopping on the day of the meeting or who moved in just last week). And so Portia and Festus serve a demand on Julia requiring that she conform to the mowing requirement or else pay the fine. "And why should I? Five hundred dollars for a *dandelion*?" Julia asks indignantly, and Portia and Festus explain that she is a resident of Capitoline and this is what "We the Residents of Capitoline Subdivision" have agreed to. They even show her the document that explicitly declares as much, hold it in front of her face as she reads the words.

Are Portia and Festus right? Well, in a word, no. It seems obvious, rather, that they are indulging in an equivocation. The ostensibly authoritative "We the Residents of Capitoline Subdivision" is plainly not the same thing as the empirical class of residents of Capitoline Subdivision, of which Julia *is* a member. Thus, Julia can rightly respond to their claims by explaining that while there are indeed residents of Capitoline, and while *some* actual residents of Capitoline may have agreed on the mowing requirement, the "We the Residents of Capitoline Subdivision" that is being presented as an authority for the mowing requirement is nothing more than a fiction. It is a fiction in much the same way that "We the People of the United States" is a fiction.

This is not of course to deny that "We the People of the United States" may have been (and may be) a glorious fiction—one that arguably has done magnificent work for which we should be grateful. It is also true that were it not for the fact of "the people"—the actual, empirical human beings—and also for the fact of elections and conventions and similar governmental processes, the fiction of "We the People" would be far less plausible than it is. It is these facts that have served to make the fiction believable—to render it "truish," as discussed in the previous chapter. Without "the people," and without the processes of democratic governance, the fiction of "We the People" might well become so transparently implausible that it would be unable to perform its function in creating and maintaining authority. So we might say, if we like, that the fiction of "We the People" is *grounded in* facts (as successful fictions usually are). Or we might say that "We the People" is only *partly* fictional, or perhaps "quasi-fictional."

Fine. Even so, "We the People" remains in an important sense fictional (even though real people exist) in the same way that "We the Residents of Capitoline Subdivision" was fictional (even though there were residents of Capitoline Subdivision), and in the same way that "Frank the Magnificent" was fictional (even though there really was a dummy called by that name).

Moreover, this fictional dimension helps to explain some ongoing, seemingly irresolvable arguments that have run through the American constitutional tradition. Let us consider two of these arguments—two especially important ones. The first raged in the republic's early decades. The second flourishes today.

Nation or Confederation?

Probably the most recurring and incendiary constitutional issue during the first seven decades of the country's existence—and an issue that still resurfaces in subdued form from time to time—has concerned the nature of the union. Is it a unitary political community, with ultimate sovereign authority lodged in the *nation*? Or is it something closer to a confederation of *states* which retain their separate sovereignties?

The framers at the Philadelphia convention struggled with the question but did not succeed in resolving it. They were accordingly forced to send on to the state ratifying conventions a somewhat awkward concoction[36] that they described as "in strictness, neither a national nor a federal Constitution, but a composition of both"[37] (even though, at the Philadelphia convention, James Madison, James Wilson, and others had vehemently opposed such a compromise as unjust, unprincipled, and incoherent[38]).

After the commencement of the new republic, the unresolved issue resurfaced again and again, under a variety of descriptions and in response to a variety of provocations. Did Congress have authority to prohibit and punish people for seditious speech, or was this a matter within the sovereign domain of the states? Could a judgment of the highest court within a "sovereign" state be appealed to and overturned by the United States Supreme Court? (Although well settled by now, this seemed a hard question because under the logic of sovereignty one sovereign's decision normally cannot be appealed to and overturned by another sovereign.) Did states have the power to "nullify" national legislation that they believed to be contrary to the compact into which they had entered? Could a state that believed the national government had exceeded its authority withdraw from the compact, or "secede"?

All of these questions turned on whether the union was a unified nation with ultimate authority lodged in the national government or, instead, a limited confederation of still sovereign states. Both interpretations mustered the support of a distinguished group of advocates: John Marshall and Joseph Story (among others) for the nationalist position; Thomas Jefferson, James Madison, and later John C. Calhoun (among others) for the federation or state sovereignty side. Advocates on both sides presented their positions as interpretations of the Constitution, and these interpretations forced the advocates to make claims about the nature and the doings of "We the People."

From a distance, we can perceive the arguments evolving in dialectical, point-counterpoint fashion. The "state sovereignty" advocates began by arguing that the Constitution had been formed by the sovereign states as the contracting parties; it followed, these advocates thought, that the states had the ultimate right to fix the meaning of the contract they had made. Thus, Jefferson argued in the Kentucky Resolutions (written in response to the Alien and Sedition Acts adopted during the Adams administration) that the Constitution was a "compact" formed by "the several states"; consequently, "each party has an equal right to judge for itself, as well of infractions, as of the mode & measure of redress."[39] In a report to the Virginia House of Delegates, James Madison elaborated:

> [It is] a plain principle, founded in common sense, illustrated by common practice, and essential to the nature of compacts; that where resort can be had to no tribunal superior to the authority of the parties, the parties themselves must be the rightful judge in the last resort, whether the bargain made, has been pursued or violated. *The constitution of the United States was formed by the sanction of the states, given by each in its sovereign capacity.* . . . *The states then being the parties to the constitutional compact, and in their sovereign capacity*, it follows of necessity, that there can be no tribunal above their authority, to decide in the last resort, whether the compact made by them be violated; and consequently that as the parties to it, they must themselves decide in the last resort, such questions as may be of sufficient magnitude to require their interposition."[40]

On a similar premise, in *Martin v. Hunter's Lessee*,[41] the highest court in Virginia rejected the authority of the national Supreme Court to reverse the state court's decisions. The Virginia court invoked the logic of sovereignty: if both the states and the national government were "sovereigns," as had so often been said, then it followed that neither sovereign's judiciary had the authority to overrule the other's—any more than the highest court of sovereign France would have power to reverse a judgment of the United States Supreme Court (even a judgment based on an interpretation of French law). "The constitution of the United States contemplates the independence of both governments and regards the residuary sovereignty of the states as not less inviolable than the delegated sovereignty of the United States."[42]

The error in this interpretation—at least according to Justice Story, writing for the court in *Martin*—was that the Constitution had been formed not by the states but rather by "We the People." "The constitution of the United States," Story insisted, "was ordained and established, not by the states in their sovereign capacities, but emphatically, as the preamble of the constitution declares, by '*the People of the United States*.'"[43] Three years later, in *McCulloch v. Maryland*, Chief Justice Marshall repeated the claim. "The [national] government," Marshall contended, "proceeds directly from the people; is 'ordained and established' in the name of the people." "[T]he people were at perfect liberty to accept or reject it; and their act was final." And as it happened, the people had opted for ratification. "The government of the Union, then . . . , is, emphatically, and truly, a government of the people. In form, and in substance, it emanates from them. Its powers are granted by them."[44]

Later, during the so-called nullification controversy, John C. Calhoun responded to such arguments with a more sophisticated version of the state sovereignty position earlier urged by Jefferson and Madison. Calhoun now conceded and even embraced one of the central claims made by the nationalists: the Constitution had indeed been formed by "the people," not by the states per se. The contrary position, Calhoun acknowledged, would violate the principle that authority can come only from the consent of the governed. "[S]overeignty is not in the Government," Calhoun explained; "it is in the people. Any other conception is abhorrent to the ideas of every American."

But this concession, far from settling the matter (as Story and Marshall had supposed) only presented the question in starker form. Once it was conceded that authority resided in the people, "the only possible question that can remain is, in *what people*? In the people of the United States collectively, as a mass of individuals, or in the people of the twenty-four states, as forming distinct political communities, confederated in this Union?"[45]

The answer to that question, Calhoun thought, was obvious. The Constitution could not have been the creation of the people of the United States as a whole because there was no such entity. "No such community ever existed, as the people of the United States, forming a collective body of individuals in one nation; and the idea that they are so united by the present Constitution, as a social compact, . . . is utterly false and absurd. To call the Constitution the social compact, is the greatest possible abuse of language." Since the Constitution could not have been the product of the people of the United States, it followed that the alternative proposition must be the correct one. "The sovereignty, then, is in the people of the several States, united in this federal Union."[46]

To be sure, Calhoun's interpretation seemingly ran counter to the language of the preamble. As noted, the Philadelphia Convention had adopted Gouverneur Morris's idea of replacing the language of "We the People of New Hampshire" and so on with "We the People of the United States." But Calhoun responded to this difficulty not only by declaring ratification by the collective "We the People of the United States" to be impossible (since no such entity had ever existed), but also by appealing to Article VII, which provided that the Constitution would be ratified in separate conventions in each state and would be binding only on the states that chose to ratify it.[47] That qualification would make little sense, he urged, if in fact it was "We the People" as a whole that was deciding whether to ratify or not to ratify.

Marshall and Story, therefore, and on the other side Calhoun, were offering conflicting interpretations of the Constitution, which were in turn based on different conceptions of the enacting "people"; and each side could invoke language in the Constitution that seemed consistent with its interpretation and conception. Marshall and Story quoted the preamble; Calhoun invoked Article VII. So, was there—or *is* there—any way in which an impartial observer might examine this debate and determine which side was right and which was wrong? What kind of fact or facts might settle this dispute?

We know, once again, that there were human beings living in the territory that we call the United States: that is a fact. And we can, if we choose, lump those people into an inclusive class ("people of the United States"), or we can group them into smaller classes ("people of South Carolina" and so on). We can also say—this would also seem to be a fact—that *some* among those people argued about the proposed Constitution, that a relative few of them gathered in conventions to debate and vote on it, and that these conventions met in the separate states. In fact, there was never a single grand ratifying convention for the nation as a whole: Calhoun was surely right about that.

But does that fact in itself demonstrate, as Calhoun went on to conclude, that the various convention delegates were deliberating and voting on behalf of the people of their separate states? Couldn't it have been, as Marshall suggested in *McCulloch*,[48] that the separate conventions were nonetheless deliberating on behalf of "We the People" (as regional subcommittees of that People, so to speak), distances and logistics making a single overarching convention not feasible?[49]

Either characterization is possible. Depending on our purposes and the conclusions we want to reach, one or the other characterization will be more appealing to us. But it is hard to see how any mere fact could determine that one characterization is true and the other false.

To be sure, we might investigate or speculate about what the delegates in the various conventions *thought* they were doing, or in what capacity they thought they were acting. And given that the new nation was still in process of being formed whereas the states had been functioning for decades, it seems likely that many or most of those delegates would have conceived of themselves as acting within and for their states, not for the nation as a whole. Or perhaps not: after all, they did vote for a document that ascribed itself to "We the People of the United States." Still, at least for purposes of argument, let us take it as a fact that most of the delegates believed they were acting on behalf of their states. Have we then settled the question—in favor of Calhoun?

No, because further facts obtrude. It is also a fact, for example, that not every human being in New Hampshire or South Carolina or Virginia participated in the proceedings at all, or was permitted to participate. Not even close.[50] Calhoun objected that "We the People of the United States" could not have ratified the Constitution because no such entity had ever existed (except, we might say, as a fictional construction). But it might be objected in response that no such people as "We the People of South Carolina" had ever existed either (except as a fictional construction). Slaves represented a sizable portion of the human beings in South Carolina, for example, and they had no say in the proceedings to ratify the Constitution, or in governance generally.

From this perspective, Calhoun's argument seems cleverly devised simultaneously to exploit and to conceal the fiction lying at the foundation of authority. Calhoun sets up a binary: conceding that the Constitution had been approved by "the people" (as it surely must have been, . . . else how could it have become law at all, . . . as it obviously was?), he then asks, *Which people?* Was it the People of the United States, or the peoples of the separate states? Those, he says, are the alternatives. But the first alternative is untenable because the first entity ("We the People of the United States") is a fiction. And so by process of elimination Calhoun goes on to conclude, with great conviction, that the second alternative must be the correct one.

And yet it would be equally possible, on this logic (or illogic), to reason in the opposite direction. Given the fact of slavery (and other forms of unenfranchisement), the second alternative is untenable—because there is no such entity as "We the People of South Carolina." More generally, as James Wilson, Alexander Hamilton, and others had pointed out in the early constitutional debates, the states themselves were mere "imaginary beings"[51]—or fictions. Therefore, the first alternative must be the correct one.[52]

The basic point is simply this: the furious, recurring debates in the early decades over the nature of the Union were arguments over what some fundamental authority had done when it—or when they?—established the Constitution. But that fundamental authority was in important part fictional. There were to be sure people living in the United States, and in each of the states; but the authoritative "We the People"—whether of the nation or of the separate states—transcended those mere mortals. It was a fictional construction. Advocates on both sides naturally constructed that fictional entity so as to generate the conclusions they favored. And there was no actual fact that could determine which of these fictional constructions was the true or correct one.

The question, at bottom, was not one about truth, or fact. Rather, it was about what sort of nation (or "imagined community"[53]) Americans would imagine for themselves, . . . and would therefore ascribe to the Constitution, ... and would therefore project back onto an authoritative, imagined "We the People" constructed so as to have chosen in favor of such a nation.

Eventually, of course, the conflict was resolved—for most practical purposes anyway—not by arguments or facts, and not in courts, but rather by bullets in places like Antietam and Appomattox. And yet bullets cannot decisively settle an argument of this kind any more than they can settle a controversy in literature or science. And so although in the decades since the Civil War claims of "nullification" and "secession" have had no realistic chance of succeeding,[54] the same basic arguments made in the early decades resurface from time to time with respect to specific issues that are not deemed to have been settled.

When the Supreme Court considered the question of whether a state could impose term limits on its congressional delegation, for example, the justices engaged in a toned-down reenactment of the antebellum debates. Repeatedly quoting Story and Marshall, the majority opinion by Justice Stevens insisted that states had no authority to impose term limits because (among other reasons) the Constitution and hence the national government were created not by the states but rather by the collective "We the People."[55] Concurring, Justice Kennedy agreed that "it is well settled that the whole people of the United States asserted their political identity and unity of purpose when they created the federal system."[56] Conversely, Justice Thomas (joined by Chief Justice Rehnquist and Justices O'Connor and Scalia) argued at length that "[t]he ultimate source of the Constitution's authority is the consent of *the people of each individual State*, not the consent of the undifferentiated people of the Nation as a whole."[57] The dissenters sought to deflect the argument from the preamble ("We the People of the United States") by observing that in earlier times the term "United States" was typically taken as a plural noun—but shouldn't the phrase then have been "We the *Peoples* of the United States"?—and, much like Calhoun, they argued that Article VII's ratification procedure confirmed that it was the people of the states, not of the nation as a whole, who were the parties to the constitutional compact.[58]

Once again, the nationalist interpretation prevailed, again just barely, this time not by bullets but by numbers—five (five justices, that is) being a larger number than four. As with other constitutional decisions, of course, we can ask whether the majority "got it right." But as in the antebellum debates, there is no fact that could answer this question. Because the debate is once again about the character of what is at bottom a fiction.

The (Unsettlable) Debate about Constitutional Interpretation

Although debates about the nature of the union no longer have the central place or the incendiary quality they possessed in the republic's early decades, other issues of constitutional law continue to provoke passionate debate. And beyond specific constitutional questions (about abortion or marriage or voting rights or corporate free speech or capital punishment or presidential powers), recent decades have witnessed a more general and far-reaching debate about the proper method of interpreting the Constitution. What began as an apparently straightforward argument between "originalist" and "nonoriginalist" approaches to interpretation[59] has become ever more sophisticated and complex, as theories on both the "originalist" and "nonoriginalist" sides proliferate and transmogrify and often blend into each other.[60] Far from abating, this debate seems, if anything, to be expanding.

The analysis of this chapter suggests one reason why closure is likely impossible and why neither the originalist nor the nonoriginalist side will ever decisively prevail over the other. That is because the debate over how to interpret the Constitution (like the more specific debate over the nature of the union) is, at bottom, a debate over how to figure out what "We the People" decided or dictated in and through the Constitution. But since "We the People" is a fiction, and since fictions can be fashioned to suit our inclinations and needs, there is nothing to prevent the fiction from being spun out in any number of different ways. And although we will have our reasons for preferring some spins over others, there is no mere fact or facts that can show that one spin is true or correct and the others are mistaken.

Originalisms.[61] Let us start by considering the "originalist" side of the argument. In the movement's early days,[62] the position was often presented as prescribing that the Constitution be interpreted in accordance with the "framers' intent."[63] And in practice, it was often assumed that "the framers" were (or at least primarily included) the delegates to the Philadelphia Convention; originalist arguments might routinely appeal, therefore, to reports of the discussions at that convention.

This position provoked objections that have by now become thoroughly familiar.[64] The "framers' intentions" were and are said to be undiscernible[65] — and hence subject to manipulation in favor of whatever results a particular originalist may prefer. Or, sometimes drawing on comments made by Jefferson, interpreters object to letting contemporary generations be governed by "the dead hand of the past."[66] These and related objections have been asserted and responded to so often by now that the debates have for the most part become thoroughly scripted (although new wrinkles do sometimes appear). And, as we will see, most originalists no longer advocate interpretation according to "framers' intentions" anyway. We should nonetheless pay attention to two particular objections to "framers' intentions"—let us call them the "aggregation objection" and the "authority objection"— because these will come up again with respect to later, more complex versions of originalism, and also with respect to "nonoriginalist" approaches to interpretation. (They will also come up, in the next chapter, with respect to other forms of interpretation, such as statutory interpretation.)

The aggregation objection asserts that it is difficult or impossible to aggregate the intentions of a diverse multiplicity of legal authors— or enactors, or "framers"—into a single intended meaning that could then serve to fix the meaning of a legal provision.[67] A multiplicity of enactors might seem to create no great difficulty if we could suppose that the enactors were all of one mind, so to speak—if they all understood and intended the provision in the same way. But such unity seems unlikely in many real-world situations. Within just a very few years, for example, James Madison, Edmund Randolph, and Alexander Hamilton (all "framers" who had participated in the Philadelphia Convention) were disagreeing vehemently about whether the Constitution authorized Congress to create a national bank.⁶⁸ So if Framer A intended the Constitution to mean X and Framer B intended it to mean Y (Y being different from and perhaps inconsistent with X), how are these divergent interpretations supposed to be combined to produce a single, controlling meaning?

The authority objection is different: it suggests that even if the framers had all been of one mind, they had no authority in any case to adopt the Constitution and should therefore not be treated as having authority to fix the Constitution's meaning. After all, it was only "We the People" who could adopt a Constitution for the nation, so why should a relative handful of men who conducted secretive discussions in Philadelphia have the right to give that document its meaning? This objection can be understood as pointing out an instance of what we earlier called the "separation error." The objection asserts that determining meaning in accordance with "framers' intentions" (with the Philadelphia delegates being treated as the primary framers) separates the meaning of the Constitution from the authority that made that Constitution our fundamental law—namely, "We the People of the United States."

Originalists may acknowledge the force of this objection and attempt to deflect it by arguing that what matters is the understandings and intentions not of the Philadelphia delegates but rather of the delegates to the various state ratifying conventions.⁶⁹ This concession would seem to aggravate the aggregation problem. If it was hard to discern and aggregate and reconcile the intentions of a few dozen delegates who actually met in a single stuffy room and talked with each other for days on end, how much harder must it be to discern and aggregate the intentions of hundreds of different and disparate men who met in thirteen wholly separate gatherings, at different times and in different places?⁷⁰

Moreover, it is not clear that the concession in favor of ratifying conventions overcomes the authority objection in any very satisfying way. That is because, once again, it is not plausible to suppose that the ratifying conventions truly spoke for all of the people—the actual human beings—who lived in America at the time. Again, for example, we have the problem of the unenfranchised—women, slaves, Native Americans. And this is not even to address the problem of how delegates *then* could somehow make decisions binding on people who came to the country (and to the world) *later*, or *now*.

These and other difficulties have led most originalists to move away from the early "framers' intentions" version in the direction of an approach that emphasizes "original public meaning."[71] But does this revision deflect the objections aimed at "framers' intentions"?

The answer may depend in part on what is meant by "original public meaning." Suppose we understand the concept in what we might think of as a factual sense: "original public meaning" would refer to what *actual* flesh-and-blood citizens in, say, 1787 and 1788 *actually* understood the text of the proposed Constitution to mean.[72] This conception, it seems, would aggravate exponentially the aggregation problem. If it was difficult to discover what a few score delegates who met and talked with each other in Philadelphia intended, and if it is likely that those delegates did not always share a common understanding or intent, how vastly greater those difficulties are if we instead ask what was intended or understood by several million Americans who did *not* meet and/or talk with each other and who were utterly disparate in terms of location, education, vocation, disposition, and condition of freedom or servitude.

Still, by asking about the actual understandings of actual citizens, would we at least have solved the authority problem? Because now we would actually be focusing on "We the People of the United States," rather than on some elite pretending to speak for those people? Well, no. Because even if we could ascertain what the Constitution meant to actual citizens, and even if those understandings miraculously distilled themselves into some unified and intelligible interpretation, we would be looking at the people not as the *authors* of the Constitution, but rather as its *subjects* and recipients. If the Queen of Hearts commands that your head be chopped off, the fact that the Queen's order is enforced according to your understanding of her words does not mean that you somehow intended the removal of your head. Same for "We the People."

Thus, if we indulge the fantasy that most or all Americans of the time actually read some constitutional provision (the "necessary and proper" clause, let's say) and formed an understanding of what they thought it meant, and if we make the even more fantastic assumption that these millions of understandings largely converged, it is nonetheless entirely possible that many Americans would have read the provision and thought, "It seems to me to be saying X, and *I don't like X*. X is not something I ever did or would vote for—even though those high-and-mighty self-styled 'delegates' at the ratifying convention did vote for it." In that case, we might say that the necessary and proper clause means what "We the People" thought it meant; but we surely could not say that the clause as thus interpreted reflects or reflected the will of the putative authority—"We the People."

But these reservations may seem largely beside the point, because in fact most originalists of the "original public meaning" party have not favored this sort of factual understanding of "original public meaning" anyway. In the factual understanding, public meaning would be in a sense "subjective": it would inhere in what citizens subjectively understood the text to mean. But most originalists eschew this conception and instead prefer to talk about "objective" public meanings.[73] This is a contested concept, to be sure; there are acute critics who deny that "objective" semantic meaning is a coherent or intelligible concept at all.[74] For present purposes, though, we need not enter into this debate. It is enough to say that *if* there is such a thing as the kind of "objective public meaning" that many originalists invoke, tethering constitutional interpretation to that objective meaning *would* seem to solve the aggregation problem (by stipulation, basically)—but only at the cost of exacerbating the authority problem.

How so? Well, the commitment to an "objective" public meaning deflects the aggregation objection by making aggregation unnecessary. We need not try to combine the understandings of the multitude of drafters, enactors, or citizens because their understandings are not decisive anyway: what matters now is the posited true or "objective" meaning of a provision. It might be that some Americans—*many* Americans? *all* Americans?—subjectively understood a provision to mean something other than its correct or objective meaning. If so, those Americans were simply wrong. Too bad for them.

The point can be clarified, perhaps, if we consider what "objective" meaning is supposed to consist in. "Public meaning" originalists do not naively suppose that particular meanings just attach to particular words as properties of those words in the way that, say, hardness attaches to rocks or coldness attaches to ice. Originalists understand, rather, that linguistic or semantic meanings exist through and for human beings who use language to communicate with each other. They nonetheless explain how meanings are "objective" in one or both of two complementary ways.

First, they may suppose that for a given linguistic community, there are "rules of language" or linguistic conventions (reflected in, for instance, dictionaries of the time) that determine the meanings of particular configurations of letters or words.[75] Such meanings are conventional, not Platonic—no one supposes, for example, that the marks M - A - N would just inherently refer to a male human being whether or not anyone ever used the marks in that way—but the meanings are still "objective" in the sense that they are independent of the semantic intentions or understandings of *any particular speaker* or hearer.[76] Linguistic conventions yield "sentence meanings" or "utterance meanings," as opposed to "speakers' meanings" or "utterers' meanings."[77] Or so goes the argument.

Or theorists may try to explain "objective" meanings by reference to some idealized or hypothetical hearer or reader—one who is thoroughly competent in linguistic usages and who is endowed with some properly idealized knowledge.[78] The hypothetical reader of the Constitution, for example, may be said to be one who reads the entire document with care, and thus is cognizant that the same term is used in particular ways in different sections of the document. He is also someone who is familiar with whatever the relevant modes of linguistic usage or legal interpretation are.[79] It might be that hardly any actual flesh-and-blood human beings would possess all of these qualifications; indeed, maybe *no* actual member of the American public in 1787 fully and perfectly fit the description of the hypothetical reader whose idealized understanding is the criterion of the text's meaning. In theory, therefore, it might turn out that X was the "objective public meaning" of a constitutional provision even though *no* actual human being in 1787 or 1788 in fact read the document with the proper care and linguistic and legal expertise needed to discern that meaning.[80]

In thus objectivizing constitutional meaning, it seems that originalists do overcome the aggregation problem—by stipulation, as it were. Linguistic conventions can be said to yield a unified "sentence meaning," even if the actual human beings who employed those conventions differed as to what that meaning was. On this view, those actual human beings who intended or understood something other than the true or objective sentence meaning were simply mistaken. They were using the language incorrectly—like Andy Sipowicz on *NYPD Blue*, who sometimes talks about his "prostrate" problems. Or the hypothetical reader who is treated as the measure of the text's meaning can simply be idealized as unitary, not multiple: consequently, no aggregation problem arises. One (hypothetical) reader, one meaning.

Differences or conflicts in the meanings intended or understood by actual Americans of the founding period—Hamilton in opposition to Madison, for example—can thus be brushed away as inconclusive with respect to the question of what the text actually meant. Much as with a scientific fact, disagreement does not preclude a correct answer: if the "objective" meaning was what Hamilton thought it was, or what Madison thought it was, the other man was simply wrong.

In thus overcoming the aggregation problem, however, "original public meaning" theories aggravate and underscore the authority problem. It may be true, as we noted already, that the Philadelphia framers were not "We the People" and hence had no authority to enact the Constitution. Even the delegates to the state ratifying conventions could claim to speak for "We the People" only by pretending to a sort of more or less transparently fictional agency. But at least these constitutional actors were real human beings. They were actual members of the empirical class of "the people." By contrast, the idealized meaning-makers of "original public meaning"—whether the impersonal linguistic conventions or the idealized hypothetical reader—are not and were not actual members of "the people." They do not even pretend to be real human beings at all. Indeed, that is the whole point of imagining or invoking them—to escape the embarrassing limitations of actual human beings. But then how can an impersonal sociological phenomenon (linguistic conventions, or "the rules of language") or an imaginary and concocted character (the purely hypothetical reader) possibly claim authority to speak for "We the People"?

In this vein, Richard Kay argues that "[t]he Constitution is binding because it is the expression of the will of 'the people.'" But the original-public-meaning approach separates constitutional meaning from that authoritative source. Consequently, the approach "severs the connection between the Constitution's rules and that authority that makes us care about those rules in the first place."[81] Kay is saying that the original-public-meaning approach commits what we have called the separation error. And it seems that he is right.

In their incisive defense of an "original public meaning" originalism, Gary Lawson and Guy Seidman concede the point, even revel in it. Thus, Lawson and Seidman insist that the Constitution must be interpreted as an expression of "We the People," that "We the People" is a fiction, and that the meaning of the Constitution must therefore be determined in accordance with the understandings of a purely hypothetical author or reader.[82] Faced with the objection that this approach would deprive the interpreted Constitution of authority or legitimacy, however, Lawson and Seidman explicitly decline to contest the point. On the contrary, they explain, repeatedly, that they are talking about the question of the Constitution's *meaning*, not its *authority*. Whether the Constitution has authority, they say—and if so, how—is a question of political theory in which they have no interest.[83]

In the dominant "original public meaning" approach, in short, constitutional meaning is the product not of real people but rather of impersonal linguistic conventions or of an unabashedly hypothetical or fictional interpreter. But if the actual human beings we call "the framers" did not possess authority to enact the Constitution (because "the framers" were not equivalent to "the people"), how could such authority possibly be ascribed to some ghostly, fictional meaning-maker? How could that fictional entity's understanding possibly claim to reflect "the consent of the governed"?

Rule of (meaningless) law? Original-public-meaning theorists may try to justify this move to the impersonal or the hypothetical by invoking the venerable ideal of "government of laws not of men."[84] Framers, delegates, legislators are *men*: these men do not get to rule us, but only to make the *laws* that rule us.[85] Thus, the enactors—the framers or the ratifying conventions or legislatures, ostensibly speaking on behalf of "the people"—have the authority to enact particular *texts*, such as the original Constitution or the Fourteenth Amendment. And these texts constitute "the law." But the enactors are *not* empowered to determine what this "law" means. Rather, whatever the enactors may have intended, the law means what it *really*, objectively means—as determined by the conventions of language or by the hypothetical idealized reader.

There are two problems with this position. First, and most essentially, its central distinction—between the authority to make law and the authority to give the law its meaning—is untenable. Second, the position rests on an unnecessary and indeed extravagant construction of the "rule of law" ideal.

We might start with the second problem. It is one thing to say that lawmakers do not govern directly and personally, so to speak—like the petty despot or Wonderland's Queen of Hearts, whose personal, ad hoc, perhaps whimsical commands ("Off with their heads") are the ultimate authority. Instead, lawmakers govern through the rules they enact—through laws. And having enacted a rule or law, the legislators themselves are subject to it just as everyone else is; nor do they get to determine how the rule or law applies to particular cases as they arise. Fine. But none of this leads to the extreme conclusion that the meaning of the law should be divorced from the meaning intended and understood by the authorities who made the law, and who made it law.

Indeed, that kind of separation results in a strangely distorted "law" and a bizarrely denatured "authority"—which points us to the first and major problem. Is it sensible—is it even intelligible—to separate "the law" from what the law means? As Jeffrey Goldsworthy explains, "A law necessarily means something—nothing meaningless can be a law—and *its meaning is part of what it is*."[86] Cut off from its "meaning," what sort of thing would that "law" even be? Some intrinsically meaningless conglomeration of words[87]—or, more precisely, of marks (because "words" already connotes meaning)? And what sort of authority are we conferring if we tell someone—the convention, the king, whoever—"We confer on you the authority to make our law—but that only includes the authority to enact *words* (or marks);

you don't have the authority to determine what those words (or marks) will mean"? What could possibly be the point of conferring that sort of denuded "authority" on someone?[88]

On the contrary, as we noticed at the outset of this chapter, if we care about a legal text because it is an expression of authority, then it should follow that what we care about is what norm or command or rule that authority was seeking to communicate through the text. If the "framers" or the convention delegates had authority to make the law, surely that authority must have included the authority to endow the texts in which the law is expressed with meaning—a meaning that under the ideal of "rule of law" will be binding on the lawmakers just as it is binding on other subjects.

The separation error, and the bizarreness of this particular originalist conception of legal authority, go mostly unremarked because it seems that unless the enactors were linguistically incompetent, the meanings they intended would usually correspond very closely anyway to the "objective" meanings attributed to their words.[89] Any gap between the "subjective" meanings intended by those deemed to have authority to make law and the original "objective" meanings would presumably be *de minimis*. So we can suppose that enactors would for practical purposes mostly have the mean-making authority that in theory the notion of "objective" public meaning denies them.

Even so, once the "text" is separated from that text's "meaning," and once it is supposed that the "rule of law" entails that enactors have authority to adopt the "text" but not to fix the text's "meaning," there is no longer any obvious reason why the separate capacity to infuse the text with meaning needs to be placed in the same time frame as the enactment. Why might we not say that "the framers" (or the delegates, or whoever) get to establish "the text," but that the text's "meaning" will be determined at some other time—perhaps later, or perhaps on an evolving basis? In this way, the "objective meanings" divorced from authoritative text favored by many "original public meaning" originalists provide a nice opening to their ostensible opponents—or to approaches usually thought of as "nonoriginalist."

Nonoriginalisms. If originalism as a self-identifying movement arose in response to what were perceived as adventurous or lawless decisions of the Warren and Burger Courts, "nonoriginalism" as a self-conscious position arises, as its name implies, as a response to originalism. On the basis of difficulties such as those we have been discussing, and often with a special concern for the "dead hand" problem, nonoriginalists contend that the proper interpretation of constitutional provisions should not be limited to the "original understanding" or the "original meaning." Typically, nonoriginalists are not averse to taking those original meanings into account for whatever useful guidance they may give.[90] But constitutional interpretations should be shaped by other criteria as well—evolving social understandings, contemporary values and needs, political-moral philosophy, and considerations of that sort.

"Nonoriginalism" sounds likely a purely negative or contrary position; but described more affirmatively as "living constitutionalism,"[91] this position has its obvious and powerful appeal. When the choice is put in these terms, who wouldn't prefer a "living" constitution (whatever that means) to the apparent alternative—by implication, a "dead" constitution? Or, to use the metaphor preferred in Canadian jurisprudence, who wouldn't prefer to live under the shade of and to eat the fruit of a "living tree," as opposed to a dead tree?[92] Moreover, because nonoriginalism treats original understandings not as determinative of meaning but merely as a factor to consider, the problems of discerning and aggregating enactors' understandings seem less threatening. If we can ascertain an original understanding, fine: if not, this is not a big problem. Presumably, an undiscernible or unaggregable original understanding will merely count for less, or for nothing, in the interpretive mix.

And yet nonoriginalism has its own serious problems with authority. More specifically, if "original public meaning" originalism falls into the "separation error" in a subtle way, nonoriginalism commits the same error in brazen fashion.

As noted, original public meaning separates enactors' understandings from the meanings of the texts they enact, but the gap between what the enactors intended and what the "objective" meaning is will likely be slight or nonexistent—scarcely noticeable, most likely. Nonoriginalism, by contrast, vastly expands and deliberately calls attention to that gap. We might say that this is precisely where nonoriginalism lives and moves and has its being—in the ostensible gap between enactors' intentions and textual meaning. The whole purpose and point of nonoriginalism is to emphasize that gap. To put the point differently: nonoriginalism makes a distinctive contribution only insofar as there is a practically significant separation of the intentions or understandings of the legal authorities who originally created the law from the "meanings" now ascribed to that law.

But this openly proclaimed separation of the Constitution's operative "meaning" from the understandings or intentions of the enacting authorities (whoever we deem them to have been) underscores and exacerbates the problem of authority. If the enacting authorities did not intend to enact a rule or doctrine of the kind a court proclaims— if the authorities did not intend their text to mean anything like *that* (and, once again, it is only in such situations that nonoriginalism makes a distinctive contribution)—then what *is* the authority on which the rule or doctrine can be justified? (If the enactors had actually intended to "delegate" such authority to future judicial interpreters, as is often claimed, then once again nonoriginalism would be superfluous[93]—but more in a moment on that possibility.)

We might appreciate the question in relation to a recent, celebrated example: *Obergefell v. Hodges*,[94] the Supreme Court decision declaring a constitutional right of same-sex couples to marry. Merely as a matter of justice or sound policy, of course, many Americans heartily approved and others deplored the decision. The average citizen was perhaps less interested in the question of the decision's authority. Still, that question cannot simply be wished away. So, what is, or what was, the authority supporting the Court's much-contested decision?

Insofar as it attempted to provide a legal rationale for this novel right, the decision purported to be based mainly on the Fourteenth Amendment's due process and equal protection clauses. And yet it seems likely that the enactors of those clauses—and for this purpose it hardly matters whether we say that the enactors were the members of Congress who proposed the amendment, the members of state legislatures who ratified it, or the general public at the time—would have been surprised to learn that they had enacted any such thing. More likely, they would have been aghast. (This was, after all, the era in which "Christian nation" ideas were perhaps at their zenith[95] and were endorsed by the Supreme Court itself.[96]) So then, once again, what was the authority for the court's decision?

Probably the most candid response would be that in cases such as *Obergefell*, the authority that supports the law belongs not to the original enactors, but rather to the court itself. Nonoriginalists may commend this answer for its honesty and "realism."[97] Wouldn't we prefer to have important questions decided by sagacious lawyers today than by a collection of upper-class white males who died a century or two ago? Perhaps—and yet this "realistic" position encounters two serious problems.

The first is familiar enough—namely, there is no satisfying explanation consistent with the venerated consent proposition of how or why the courts themselves can claim authority to govern in this way. Constitutional authority in our legal system is supposed to belong to "We the People," not to unelected judges. Consequently, although academic theorists may favor assigning such authority to judges, the judges themselves studiously refrain from claiming lawmaking authority in their own right. Instead, they purport to be agents faithfully finding and enforcing a meaning that is already in some sense there, in the Constitution.

The second problem is less often noticed but perhaps even more challenging. Suppose we were content (as some among us evidently are) to declare forthrightly that courts themselves have or should have authority to make constitutional law or create constitutional rights. Even so, the current practice of constitutional adjudication would seem to be a bizarre way of structuring and exercising that authority. That is because (except perhaps for a few adventurous academics and critics) no one proposes that courts should be able to create rights just on their own, so to speak, without reference to the constitutional text: everyone still assumes that the rights or doctrines created by courts have to be in some way connected with or derived from that text.[98] And yet if we really thought that courts themselves do or should have authority to make constitutional law, what would be the sense or the point of that irksome constraint?

It as if we were to say to some respected collegium of eminent women and men: "We don't want to be governed any longer by the dead hand of our defunct ancestors—by ancestors who, whatever their virtues or shortcomings may have been, lived in a world vastly different from our own. So at least in some of the most fundamental matters, we authorize you, in your wisdom, to govern us. *Except that*—and pay close attention, because this is important—your rulings have to be expressed in the same incantatory language of those same ancestors. That's right: in the language chosen by those dead people by whom we do not wish to be governed. And if it turns out (although this seems unlikely, given your cleverness and ingenuity) that you can't figure out a way to couch some wise ruling in that incantatory language, then—sorry!—you'll just have to forgo making that ruling."

What could possibly be the sense of such a peculiar authorization? And yet this is precisely the sort of adjudication that the proponents of nonoriginalism typically celebrate.

Nonoriginalism thus appears to face a kind of dilemma with respect to the question of authority. Nonoriginalists conceivably might—and sometimes do—just boldly argue that courts have authority to make our supreme constitutional law, unconstrained by the intentions or understandings of some company of long deceased "framers." Some find this position attractive, especially if they believe (as constitutional theorists have sometimes wishfully proposed) that judges are detached and reflective figures who pursue "the ways of the scholar"[99] or who have a talent for moral philosophy.[100] But that conception and logic would suggest that judges should not be constrained by the constitutional text: and this is a position that few theorists and even fewer judges seem prepared to embrace.[101] Conversely, a nonoriginalist who wants to defend current practice presumably should be willing to defend the textual constraint—to explain, that is, why judges should be constrained by the enactors' *words* but not by what those enactors understood the words to *mean*. And it is not easy to see how that defense would work.

But perhaps I have exaggerated the embarrassment? There is in fact a very familiar and comforting response to these objections—a response that both originalists and nonoriginalists routinely resort to—and that I have thus far willfully neglected to notice. So we need to consider that response.

A Constitution of principles? The response, of course, is to view the Constitution and its framers as having enacted a set of lofty political principles. Principles of fairness, freedom, equality, human dignity—that sort of thing. In this vein, Ronald Dworkin proposed that the First, Fifth, and Fourteenth Amendments be read as enacting "abstract moral principles" which should be understood "at the most general possible level."[102] The Bill of Rights as a whole "consists of broad and abstract principles of political morality, which together encompass, in exceptionally abstract form, all the dimensions of political morality that in our political culture can ground an individual constitutional right."[103] In particular, the Fourteenth Amendment's equal protection clause stated "a principle of breathtaking scope and power."[104] In this respect, Dworkin was echoing a distinguished academic predecessor, Herbert Wechsler, who understood the Fourteenth Amendment's due process and equal protection clauses to be "a compendious affirmation of the basic values of a free society."[105]

More recently, Yale law professor Jack Balkin claims that the Constitution "features general and abstract concepts," uses "the vague and abstract language of principles," and embodies principles that are "broad, abstract, or vague."[106] It is for Americans "a source of important values, including justice, equality, democracy, and human rights," which are "objects of aspiration."[107] The Constitution "serves as a kind of higher law—it states ideals of liberty, equality, and democracy that people seek to live up to over time."[108]

But the interpretation of the Constitution—or at least some of its most important provisions—as the embodiment of "principles" is not limited to self-professing "nonoriginalists." In fact, Balkin describes himself as an originalist (while rejecting the conventional distinction between "originalism" and "living constitutionalism"). And other scholars or judges with impeccable originalist credentials routinely interpret particular constitutional provisions as enacting broad principles. Robert Bork, one of originalism's founding fathers, set the precedent: he explained the correctness of *Brown v. Board of Education* by arguing that even though the enactors of the Fourteenth Amendment did not intend or expect the provision to invalidate racially segregated schools, the principle or value of "equality" embodied in that provision nonetheless had that beneficent implication.[109] More recently, virtually identical arguments have been made for the proposition that the original meaning of the Fourteenth Amendment requires recognition of a right to same-sex marriage, even though Americans at the time that amendment was adopted would admittedly have found the proposition "unintelligible."[110]

The appeal of this conception of the Constitution as a repository of principles is understandable enough. The conception allows jurists and advocates to deal with many of the difficulties we have been discussing, in two basic steps. If we suppose that the framers or enactors (whoever we take them to be) intended to embody broad principles in the Constitution, then we can appeal to their decision and their text for *authority* (step one); we can then use the *principle* they ostensibly enacted to reach results that seem indicated today (step two). A huge proportion of modern constitutional law and theory amounts, basically, to the employment of this two-step approach, suitably elaborated and obfuscated.

In this approach, the differences between originalism and non-originalism melt away, as Balkin enthusiastically contends. For personal or political reasons, advocates may still choose to associate themselves with one or the other label. But nothing much seems to hinge on the choice; under either heading the same interpretive moves are available.[111]

The "principled" Constitution and fictional authority. Given this virtual consensus, it may seem almost impertinent to ask whether the Constitution really *is* principled—or, more precisely, whether the enactors of the Constitution, or of particular provisions, actually intended to constitutionalize "principles" of (to quote Dworkin) "breathtaking scope and power." As noted, Herbert Wechsler, in a seminal article advocating "principled" constitutional adjudication, declared the due process and equal protection clauses to be a source of such principles. But Wechsler acknowledged that the enactors of those provisions probably did not intend to create any such grandiose jurisprudential cornucopia; he remarked only that he personally preferred this construction. "I cannot find it in my heart," he shared, "to regret that interpretation did not ground itself in ancient history but rather has perceived in these provisions a compendious affirmation of the basic values of a free society."[112]

Rarely do those who ascribe some broad principle to a constitutional provision attempt to demonstrate with any care that the enactors actually intended the provision to have such a meaning. Often they infer that if a provision, like the due process or equal protection clause, seems indefinite or uncertain in its meaning, the provision *must have been* intended to embody a principle—as if being vague or inarticulate were essentially equivalent to being "principled." This seems an odd inference: we do not normally suppose that someone who is diffuse or inarticulate must therefore be a person of "principle."

And in any case, it is possible—isn't it?—that the apparent indefiniteness of a provision is merely the result of our own ignorance of a more definite meaning that the wording carried for those who originally adopted the text. Thus, legal historians who investigate particular provisions often discover more definite conceptions or understandings that have been forgotten with the passage of time.[113] In this vein, Bruce Ackerman, although an enthusiastic proponent of an expansively "principled" Constitution, acknowledges that what seem to us to be indefinite and thus principled provisions often had more precise meanings when originally enacted. It is only with the passage of years and the "fading of lived experience," Ackerman explains, that these more definite meanings recede from view, thereby permitting later generations to treat the provisions as statements of broad principles.[114]

Still, isn't it *possible* that enactors might choose to enact some general principle, leaving it to later generations to figure out what the principle means in their own circumstances? Enactors *could* do that, couldn't they? Well, yes; and indeed insofar as we regard "We the People" as the author of the Constitution, we can imagine that (fictional) author as having done whatever we need him/her/them to have done. If you doubt that we can do this, just read Jack Balkin's exhilarating "originalist" interpretations of the American constitutional tradition.

Realistically, though, how likely is it that the enactors of a constitution would do such a thing? Think of it this way: on what assumptions would such an open-ended authorization to the indefinite future make political sense? Imagine first a pessimistic bunch of framers—framers who expect that future generations are likely to be less enlightened than their own generation is (or at least than they themselves are). Maybe they believe they have somehow been blessed to occupy a sort of hard-to-replicate moral high ground: providence, for its own mysterious reasons, has favored them with an opportunity to reflect on political matters in a detached and enlightened way, but future political actors are likely to be less detached, less enlightened, or less public-spirited. (In fact there is considerable evidence that the Philadelphia framers *did* understand their situation in something like this way.[115]) On these assumptions, it seems, the framers would not want to enact a set of broad "principles" for later generations to interpret and apply. On the contrary, they presumably would want to protect their descendants by building as much concrete content into their constitution as possible—as a hedge against the more benighted notions and inclinations that they anticipate in their less fortunate successors.

This is, to be sure, a bleak view of things (even if our own founders did hold it). So let us instead be more cheerful and imagine a more sanguine set of framers who believe in the likelihood of moral, political, and philosophical progress. The next generation, they think, is likely to be wiser and more virtuous than the present one, the following generation even more so; and so on. On these more optimistic and progressive assumptions, would a constitution's designers want to entrench in it broad principles "of breathtaking scope and power"?

Well, . . . probably not. What would be the point? What would be the point, that is, of entrenching some currently favored "principle" in a Constitution and then binding succeeding generations to that principle? If the principle is a good one, a more enlightened posterity will presumably embrace and follow it anyway. On the other hand, it is at least possible—isn't it?—that principles cherished by the current generation might turn out in the long run to be misguided or perverse. This sometimes happens: think of once-favored principles like patriarchy or racial hierarchy or religious establishmentarianism. So, given that a principle we like might turn out to be less than ideal, or worse, why would we want to bind our wiser and more virtuous descendants to follow that principle? Or in any case, why put them to the inconvenience and expense of repealing such a principle, or else of interpreting it into ineffectuality, or studiously ignoring it (as modern courts have done with, say, the "no impairment of contracts" clause)?

In sum, the picture on which so much modern constitutional law and theorizing is based—the picture of constitutional enactors who choose to entrench broad principles in a binding and judicially enforceable constitutional text while delegating to future generations the responsibility of deciding what those principles mean—seems both historically dubious and unlikely as a conjecture about what sensible framers would do, whether we imagine those framers either as pessimistic or optimistic about the future.

It may be, of course, that this picture—of the "principled" Constitution—has had good consequences. Your opinion on that point may turn on whether you believe that, on balance, modern constitutional transformations have been a net gain or a net loss. Almost all of us can point to some constitutional decisions that we celebrate and to others that we deplore: what *Roe v. Wade* is to one person, *Citizens United v. Federal Election Commission* is to another.[116] If you think the overall results have been beneficial, then you might join Herbert Wechsler in saying that you "cannot find it in [your] heart to regret" that modern constitutional jurisprudence has chosen to interpret the Constitution as a repository of principles rather than as the mundane framework of government that its merely human drafters intended it to be.

Even so, when you or when I (or Ronald Dworkin, or Jack Balkin, or . . .) make portentous claims about how the framers enacted "principles of majestic generality," we will be trading on a fiction. We will be hypothesizing a "We the People" that we need to justify our current practices and predilections, not a "We the People" that existed as a living, breathing entity in actual human history.

The Constitution as Quasi-Fiction

In this chapter, we have considered two major debates related to constitutional law: the debate about the nature of the union and the debate about whether the Constitution should be interpreted in accordance with its original meaning. We could have focused on more specific debates—about abortion or marriage or criminal procedure or presidential powers or church-state relations. The diagnosis would be different in its details, but in its central point it would be essentially the same.

That central point is simply this: The Constitution is the creation of "We the People of the United States." That is what it says; that is what it *needs to say*; that is what *we need* to take it as saying, in order to square its claim to authority with the axiom that authority must be derived from "the consent of the governed." And so if we are reading the Constitution as an authoritative expression of "We the People," then we need to read it to determine what "We the People" was (or were?) expressing. The problem is that "We the People" is a fiction. It is a truish fiction, perhaps, and possibly a majestic and ennobling fiction; but it is a fiction nonetheless.

Even if "We the People" is a fiction, however, does it follow that the Constitution itself is a fiction? Haven't we already said that the Constitution is surely real—that if you doubt this, you can go to the National Archives and see the thing for yourself?

But once again, the answer (as is typically the case with fictions) seems to be . . . yes and no. No informed person can doubt that there is a real, empirically observable document that we call "The Constitution." But as a comparison, consider this: Is the statement "To be or not to be: that is the question" a fictional statement? In a sense, the statement is surely real. You can open up any copy of *Hamlet* and read it. There it is—as real as your hand that holds the book, or as your eyes that examine it. And yet "To be or not to be" is the statement of a fictional character. In that sense it is a fictional statement, and if we ask what the statement means, we are asking about the intentions or understandings of a fictional character. In that sense, "To be or not to be" is a fictional (even though real) expression. Much like the Constitution, understood as an expression of "We the People of the United States."

And that is what makes constitutional debates unresolvable. It cannot be demonstrated that "We the People" intended this or that.

"We the People" will have intended whatever we need and can bring ourselves to imagine it (them?) to have intended. Nor is there any way to demonstrate that the intentions of "We the People" must be ascertained in this way or that way. We can imagine a "We the People" who wrote a Constitution that was little more than a careful but workmanlike frame of governance—so that its meaning would be ascertained with ordinary, workmanlike, lawyerly tools. Or we can imagine a "We the People" that enacted a Constitution profuse with principles of "breathtaking scope and power"—principles that call on a Dworkinian philosopher-jurist to expound. "We the People" is (are?) obliging: it (they?) will have enacted the kind of Constitution that we want or need to have had enacted.

Just for myself, I would say that the first image—of framers who enacted a legalistic blueprint for governance—is more "truish" than the second: it is closer to what the actual human beings who wrote and voted the Constitution thought they were doing. Gary Lawson and Guy Seidman put the point well: "The actual readers of the Constitution during the time of its creation viewed it as an instruction manual for a form of government. And the Constitution on its face presents itself to the world as an instruction manual for a form of government. It is simply too dry, technical, and boring to be anything else."[117]

But then again, those actual human beings—the ones who wrote and read and voted for the document—were not "We the People." (Even though they purported to act in that name.) Nor is "truishness" the only criterion for judging an interpretation of the Constitution. When we ask about what "We the People" did or intended or thought, we are not asking a factual question; and so there is no fact that can conclusively show that one answer is correct and another answer is mistaken.

IN THIS CHAPTER we have been considering constitutional questions and the Constitution's fictional author as one important area in which the fictional foundation of modern legal authority has important consequences. But is this assessment limited to constitutional law?

The claim that "We the People" is a "fictive entity" (as Professor White put it) may seem relatively easy to accept. But surely no similar claim would be plausible for other legal authorities on which our law is based—for Congress, or the courts, or the president? "We the People" may be a fiction, but those other authorities? Those other authorities are surely real. Aren't they?

We will take up the question in the next chapter.

CHAPTER THREE

Our Quasi-Fictional Government

The previous chapter argued that there is a fictional quality in the Constitution and in the law said to emanate from the Constitution. But then perhaps there is nothing especially startling about that discovery—or especially unsettling with respect to our law generally.

In the American legal universe, after all, the Constitution is a sort of formidable anomaly—crucially important, always hovering over our public deliberations, but also sui generis. The Constitution is foundational, or "supreme." It comes to us from a distant, misty past—almost from another world, a world separated from us by centuries and by vast geographical expansion and wars and depressions and revolutionary political and cultural and technological changes. Perhaps most importantly, the Constitution explicitly presents itself as the expression of an author—"We the People of the United States"—whose self-description already evokes something amorphous, majestic, almost mythic. And, as our discussion showed, it is that quasi-fictional author that gives constitutional law its quasi-fictional quality.

By contrast, most of the laws we routinely deal with—the statutes, the judicial decisions, the executive orders, the ubiquitous local and state and federal regulations—have a much more mundane character. Many of these laws were made by people we ourselves have watched, listened to, voted for (or against), maybe even shaken hands with. Presidents. Senators. City council members. Surely there is nothing fictional about *them*, or about the laws they enact or pronounce?

As it happens, in the neighborhood where I grew up, the owner of the house directly across the street from where I lived got himself elected to be a state court judge. We could watch Judge Thomas — or Boyd, as the adult neighbors called him — mow his lawn or get into his car, a Corvair, to drive to work. Boyd's son Dave was my best friend, and sometimes when Dave's dad wasn't working, he would throw a football around with us. When he *was* working, his rulings from the bench had the status of "law." And it would seem odd — wouldn't it? — to say that Boyd or the law he made was in any sense fictional?

Although, come to think of it, does that description seem any less odd than the assertion that Boyd was a fount of "law"? After all, other neighbors also mowed their lawns and drove their cars to work, and some of them — my own dad, for one — could throw a football a lot better than Boyd could; but no one supposed that what *they* said was "law." Neighbors had known Boyd when he was just a humble lawyer, struggling to make ends meet, and the things he said in those days didn't carry any special weight. And then he happened to get elected, in a vote that most people scarcely paid any attention to, and the next day his utterances suddenly became . . . "law"? Seriously?

Later, when Boyd and his family moved away to a nicer neighborhood, the owner of a local hamburger stand moved into the house, with his wife and his four daughters whose names all began with "P." This man, Gary, had years earlier played quarterback for a college team — a pretty lackluster team, alas — and he also took pleasure in occasionally throwing a football around. Gary was a gregarious fellow, and so after a few years we elected him to the legislature, where he helped to make laws for the whole state. (Actually, *I* didn't elect Gary — I had moved away by then — but my parents and my neighbors did.) Surely there was nothing fictional about Gary, or the laws he helped to make?

Boyd and Gary were pretty humble officials, to be sure. Pretty low rungs on the ladder of legal authority. Once, though, a president (LBJ) stopped briefly at my town's airport, and some people went out and shook hands with him. "How did his hand feel?" I recall someone asking (or maybe I was the one who asked). And the answer (was it from my sister?) was, "Well, it was a fat hand—you know, kind of flabby." LBJ was as high-ranking a legal authority as you could ask for, and yet he seemed to be very real, even if a little flabby. More distant and lofty, and yet every bit as real as Boyd or Gary.

All of these legal authorities—one judicial, one legislative, one executive—appeared to be undeniably real. Even so, I mean to argue in this chapter that our principal lawmakers, though in a sense more real and concrete than "We the People," nonetheless have a quasi-fictional quality to them. As a result, the laws that they make likewise have a quasi-fictional quality—which is one reason why our endless disputes about the meanings of judicial decisions or statutes or executive orders are irresolvable. I will not apply the argument to *all* of our lawmakers or lawmaking institutions; in particular, I will not be asking here whether there is (or *was*, may they rest in peace) anything fictional about Boyd or Gary. It will be enough to confine the discussion to the major governmental institutions or actors provided for in the Constitution—Congress, the Supreme Court, the president (including LBJ—sort of). By the time we have finished with them, it should be evident enough how the analysis would extend to other lawmakers or lawmaking institutions.

At the outset we might note a possible question: is the claim that our major lawmakers and lawmaking institutions are "quasi fictional" a shocking or outlandish one that readers should view with suspicion, or with presumptive disdain? Or, on the contrary, is the claim a perfectly innocuous and indeed tedious one that merely announces what everybody already knows, so that you yawningly ought to agree with the argument of this chapter even without reading it? The question turns out to be complicated, so we will simply note it for now, and then return to it at the end.

The Quasi-Fiction That Is "Congress"

"Last month, Congress enacted 'The Democracy Preservation Act of 2022'": so the news programs and the newspapers report. The statement is perfectly ordinary—similar statements might be made about any of thousands of different statutes—but upon reflection it may also seem just a bit mysterious. What is this "Congress," exactly? And how exactly did it "enact" the named law—so that something that did not exist from the beginning of time up until a month ago now takes its place among the imposing realities of American life, under the proud title of "The Democracy Preservation Act," thus to perdure unless and until it is relegated back to oblivion by the same formidable creative and destructive force (Congress) that gave it being to begin with?

Or maybe nothing here seems mysterious at all. Why make things gratuitously hard? It's basically all laid out in Article I of the Constitution. Under those provisions, as implemented under contemporary demographic conditions, Congress is constituted by the 435 elected representatives and 100 elected senators who gather in the Capitol Building in Washington and who deliberate and vote on laws. And that collection of people enact a law if a majority of the voting members of both the House and the Senate register their votes by voice or ballot in favor of the law. (There is also the possibility of a presidential veto, of course, but we need not complicate the account at this point.) It is all straightforward enough for anyone who has taken a middle-school civics class.

Of course it isn't *quite* as simple as the foregoing description suggests:[1] a few additional stipulations and qualifications would be called for. Maybe more than a few. For example, our description assumed without mentioning that the representatives and senators who voted for a law were sufficient in numbers to constitute a "quorum." If only twenty-five senators showed up for the vote and twenty of those senators voted "aye," we would have a majority of voting members, but the action of those senators would not count as an action of "the Senate," and "Congress" would not be deemed to have enacted the law. Twenty-five senators do not a Senate make—and without a Senate we do not have a Congress.[2]

On the other hand, it doesn't require all 100 senators: that was perhaps an omission in our initial description. Fifty-five senators, or even 51, *can* constitute "the Senate." So 49 of the senators and 217 of the representatives might have been innocently or willfully oblivious to the Democracy Preservation Act; they might have been off campaigning or fishing when the vote occurred. Or maybe they just slept in that day. No matter: the remainder will still count as "the Senate" and "the House," and their votes will still count as the action of "Congress" and will still bring the new law into being.

The math needed to constitute "the Senate," and thus at one remove "Congress," can have its anomalous aspects. For example, if 45 senators show up and they vote unanimously in favor of the Democracy Preservation Act, they will not constitute "the Senate." Theirs will be merely the futile flailings of a gaggle of senators, not an act of "the Senate." Maybe the other 55 senators just didn't care enough to bother to show up, thereby preventing any congealing of senators into "the Senate." Conversely, if 6 of those senators, or maybe 44, *do* care about the law—they are adamantly opposed, let's say—so that they show up and vote *against* the bill, this congregation *will* count as "the Senate." And the bill will be on its way to becoming law. So it seems that the unanimous support of 45 senators combined with *indifference* by the rest is not approval by "the Senate"; the support of 45 senators combined with vehement *opposition* by 44 senators *is* approval by "the Senate." Seriously, does that make any sense?

Well, maybe it does. In any case, it's all there in Article I. With 51 senators you have a Senate; with fewer than 51 you don't—only a bunch of senators. But although this description may now seem accurate as far as it goes, it still does not go quite far enough; or at least it omits to notice some necessary conditions for something to count as an action of "the Senate" or of "Congress."

Suppose, for example, that the vote on the democracy bill has been set for July 15; but as it happens, on July 15 all 435 representatives and all 100 senators are away from Washington, campaigning in their home states or vacationing in the Bahamas. And yet they all care passionately about preserving democracy, and so every single member of Congress goes on television on the prescribed day to manifest his or her unqualified support for the proposed law. "I hereby officially and unreservedly cast my vote in favor of the Democracy Preservation Act": every last representative and every senator conveys this approval to the nation, and to some functionary in Washington who has been designated to watch the television reports and tally the votes.

The proposed law has gained the manifest support of the members of Congress, 535 to 0. It has much stronger support, in fact—much stronger, officially registered support "in Congress," we might say—than would be true in a case where only 51 senators and 218 representatives voted and many of them were opposed. So, do the unanimous but dispersed legislators constitute "Congress"? Has "Congress" acted? Has the bill become "law"?

I'm guessing not. A bunch of representatives and senators scattered around the country probably will not count as "Congress," no matter how unanimous they are in their intentions, and no matter how unequivocally they register those intentions. So it seems we need to supplement our earlier description yet again. Supplement it how? Shall we add that for the legislators to count as "Congress," the requisite number of legislators needs to meet *together* to vote? In one place?[3]

That might be right. Of course, the meeting doesn't have to be in Congress's current gathering place—the Capitol Building. After all, that edifice didn't even exist until more than a decade after the Constitution conjured Congress into existence, and when the structure was damaged during the War of 1812, Congress met for a time in a different building known as the Old Brick Capitol. Still, could Congress meet just anywhere, under any conditions? Or, to be more precise, could the members of Congress meet just anywhere and still count as . . . "Congress"?

Suppose that 55 senators (and, if you like, the vice-president, and even the president, if you think it matters) happen to be refreshing themselves at McGinty's Pub on a raucous Thursday evening. And Senator Gunch is suddenly inspired with the idea of a Democracy Preservation Act, and so he writes it out on a napkin and then passes it around and (observing what appear to be approving grunts and snorts) calls for an immediate vote. "The bleeping media is always complaining—urp—that it takes us forever to get anything done," the senator declares, "so—urp—let's show them." His longtime nemesis, the stodgy Senator Scruple, protests that the proper procedures haven't been followed—there have to be committee hearings and first and second readings of the bill and so forth—but Gunch's friend Senator Slough responds, "Enough, Scruple, with your tiresome procedural nitpicking: I move that the usual rigamarole be waived and that we proceed to vote on Gunch's bill. All in favor?" A resounding "Aye!" roars through McGinty's; and the group then proceeds to vote in favor of the bill, 51 to 3 (with Senator Scruple abstaining).

Has "the Senate" acted? Is the bill ready to be sent on to the House of Representatives for consideration? Imagine that on the same Thursday evening, 250 members of the House have gathered in Section A of Nationals Park, just above the home team's dugout, to enjoy a baseball game against the Dodgers. A legislative intern carries the napkin containing Senator Gunch's newly approved bill over to the stadium, where the representatives pass it around and then, also waiving the usual procedures, vote unanimously in favor, just after the seventh inning stretch. Their vote is captured on the stadium's big screen for all the wildly cheering fans to see. And then, still on the big screen, the president (an avid fan, who had earlier made her way from McGinty's over to the game) reads and then autographs the now slightly beer-stained napkin. A stadium-wide roar goes up, followed by an exuberant "wave." Is the Democracy Preservation Act now "law," binding on the nation's three hundred million–plus citizens?

But of course this is a shameful scenario, unworthy of our nation's leaders. My apologies for even imagining it. Let us shift to something a bit more dignified, and more high-tech. Suppose that legislators decide that Washington is just too stuffy and oppressive in the summer—or maybe there has been an outbreak of the plague, like in the *Decameron* (or, we can now add, like the pandemic of COVID-19)—and so they agree to remain in their respective states and to vote on bills through video-conferencing. Through the miracles of modern technology, they will all be permitted to see each other and to discuss, orate, object, posture, and protest, as is their wont, and then to vote, all in each other's virtual presence. The only difference is that they will do this from a distance—no more contagion-spreading coughs and handshakes. If they approve the Democracy Preservation Act in this way, has "Congress" acted?

Maybe. When this paragraph was initially written the scenario seemed far-fetched; today, after COVID-19, it is much more plausible, and remote deliberations and voting seem more normal and acceptable. But it doesn't really matter what the answer is. The point is just that the "Congress" that has authority to make law is clearly not identical, or reducible without remainder, to the 535 admittedly real persons who are described as the "members" of Congress, or even to a voting majority of those persons. The persons are one thing; "Congress" is something else. Something that is not unrelated to those human beings, surely, and yet that somehow exceeds or transcends them. More than some specified number of legislators is needed for us to say that "Congress" has convened and exercised its authority. And it is not perfectly obvious what all that "more" consists of.

Still, we rarely have any difficulty in practice deciding when and whether Congress has acted or enacted.[4] So the complications we have been considering may seem more theoretical than real. Fair enough. But there is a related difficulty that is *not* fanciful or theoretical—on the contrary, it is perfectly familiar and routine—and that again raises (albeit in a more oblique way) the question: What *is* "Congress," exactly? We need to consider that difficulty.

Interpreting Statutes: The Authority and Aggregation Problems, Again

Whether or not Congress has enacted a statute is not something that typically generates much disagreement. But we do disagree, frequently and sometimes ferociously, about what a statute that Congress has enacted *means*. As I write these words, the Supreme Court has just today heard argument about whether a federal statute's prohibition of discrimination based on "sex" means that discrimination based on "sexual orientation" is illegal: the issue has provoked vehement disagreement.[5] Such disputes pervade our society and our legal system. And those disputes turn out to involve assumptions about what sort of thing Congress is.

Disagreements about what a statute means are hardly surprising, among other reasons because the practical reality behind the enactment of a particular statute is likely to be messy. Some legislators may have intended or understood a contested provision in the statute to mean one thing; others may have intended or understood it to mean something different; still others (and most likely a majority) may have had no opinion one way or the other. Perhaps they paid little attention to the statute at all and registered a pro forma vote in its favor only because their colleagues or party leaders urged them to do so.[6] So, from this potentially complicated mass, or mess, of disparate intentions and inattentions and understandings and omissions, how is an interpreter or a court supposed to extract a unitary meaning that will be the meaning given to the law by *Congress*?

The received (though currently much-contested) wisdom that has been recited over and over again for centuries holds that a statute should be interpreted in accordance with "the intent of the legislature" that enacted it.[7] British treatise writer Matthew Bacon explained in 1736: "Such a Construction ought to be put upon a Statute as may best answer the Intention which the Makers of it had in View."[8] True, hardly anyone today has heard of Matthew Bacon. (I don't remember having heard of him until a week or so ago, when I stumbled on the quote.) A few decades later, though, the hugely influential William Blackstone endorsed a similar position.[9]

And yet that received wisdom still leaves the basic questions to be answered. What exactly *is* "the legislature" that does this intending, and how exactly does it go about "intending" something? And what sort of thing is this legislative "intent"? How is it constituted? Is it something "subjective," or rather "objective"?

The answers to such questions that have come from the courts are diverse—chaotic,[10] we might say—and sometimes comical. In *Kosak v. United States*,[11] for example, the Supreme Court interpreted an ambiguous provision in the Federal Tort Claims Act by relying on a construction presented in an internal memorandum written by a low-level Justice Department attorney who had assisted in drafting the statute—even though, as Justice Stevens pointed out in dissent, "[t]here is no indication that any Congressman ever heard of the document or knew that it even existed."[12] The Court insisted that the internal memo was "significant"[13] but omitted to explain *why* the memo was significant; nor is it easy to imagine what such an explanation might say.

Theorists and scholars and the occasional judge attempt to think about the questions more systematically. And they have tended to gravitate toward three main approaches[14] (each with its manifold variations, of course) that resemble the main approaches we saw in considering constitutional interpretation. One approach, similar to the "framers' intent" position in constitutional interpretation, understands "the intent of the legislature" to refer to the subjective intentions of the legislators or to some aggregation of those subjective intentions. This approach is sometimes described as "intentionalism." Another approach, sometimes called "textualism," is similar to the "original public meaning" position in constitutional law.[15] This approach maintains that statutes should be interpreted not in accordance with the subjective intentions of the legislators, but rather in accordance with the "objective meaning" of the texts enacted by the legislators.

Textualism is sometimes said to be the dominant position today: as Justice Elena Kagan remarked, "We are all textualists now."[16] But its preeminence is challenged not only by intentionalism but also by a third family of approaches which, much like "nonoriginalism," attempt to give judges more leeway, or more distance from the concrete intentions or understandings of the enacting legislature. The most familiar version of this third approach is sometimes called "purposivism": the idea is that a court should implement a statute so as to achieve the legislature's overall purpose, without feeling unduly constrained by more concrete expectations or understandings. In this vein, scholars may propose that statutes be interpreted "dynamically"[17]: the parallel to "living constitutionalism" is obvious. Other members of the same family can be thought of as more "pragmatic" in character.[18] It may be argued, for example, that given modern realities such as statutory overcongestion and political gridlock, courts should feel empowered to "update" statutes (or should defer to and ratify the updating done by administrative agencies).[19]

It is not surprising that approaches to statutory interpretation parallel the positions in constitutional interpretation. The various approaches invoke similar rationales and provoke similar objections. Many authors accordingly discuss constitutional and statutory interpretation together,[20] scarcely distinguishing between them, offering basically the same arguments and rejoinders with respect to each.

Should we then forgo further discussion of statutory interpretation, and instead simply incorporate by reference the discussion of constitutional interpretation from the previous chapter? We *could* do that. But it would be presumptuous to assume that any given reader will have read that chapter or will remember it. In addition, the arguments in the statutory field have some special permutations that deserve notice. Most importantly, we need to see how these thrusts and parries in the field of statutory interpretation point to the overall conclusion for which this chapter is arguing—namely, that "Congress" and the statutes Congress enacts have a quasi-fictional quality. And so, with apologies, we wade again into the issues of interpretation and of aggregation and authority.

Aggregating legislators' intentions? Start with the intentionalist approach, which from the late nineteenth century until relatively recently seems to have been dominant, or simply assumed. In this view, a statute means what it was intended to mean by the legislators who voted for it. The actual, human legislators. As Roscoe Pound explained early in the twentieth century, "The object of genuine interpretation is to discover the rule which the lawmaker intended to establish; to discover the intention which the lawmaker made the rule, or the sense which he attached to the words wherein the rule is expressed. Its object is to enable others to derive from the language used 'the same idea which the author intended to convey.'"[21] Any other approach amounted, as Pound's title put it, to "spurious interpretation."

If all of the legislators somehow possessed a single group mind, or (less exotically) if all of them or at least a majority converged in their intended meanings, this proposal would seem to pose no great difficulty.[22] Pound implicitly but artificially imported such a condition by repeatedly referring to "the lawmaker," in the singular. But of course legislatures, including Congress, are not composed of a single "lawmaker." And it is common that legislators do *not* converge in their intentions or understandings.[23] So in that situation, how is a unitary meaning supposed to be extracted from the legislators' diverse and divergent intentions? Theorists have reflected on the question—obsessed over it, even—but they have not hit upon any satisfying answer. Which is not surprising, because there *is* no satisfying answer. Or so I will argue.

One such situation of divergent intentions, albeit a somewhat unusual one, would be a case in which some legislators (whose support was necessary to a law's enactment) intended and understood it to mean X, while a different group of legislators (whose votes were also necessary) innocently intended and understood it to mean something completely different—Y. Larry Alexander provides a clear hypothetical example.[24] Alexander imagines that by a 2–1 vote, a three-person legislature enacts a statute providing that "there shall be no meetings by the bank." Unfortunately, one of the supporting legislators intends "bank" to indicate the riverbank—she understands the prohibition to be based on concerns about flooding—while the other, supposing "bank" to refer to the town's financial institution, thinks the point of the statute is to avoid interference with people who are trying to deposit or withdraw money. Suppose we have reason to know that each of these legislators supported the law *only* on the assumption that it meant what he or she thought it meant. So then, what does the statute mean?

Alexander's answer to that question is rigorously logical—and utterly untenable as a matter of actual practice. As we saw in the previous chapter, Alexander emphasizes the absurdity of separating the authority to *make law* from the authority to *give the law a meaning*. It is implausible—and subversive of conferred authority—to say that "the law" is one thing while its "meaning" is something different: if the ostensible authorities don't get to give meaning to the law, they are not actually making law (because a "law" divorced from its meanings is not actually "law"), and they are not actually being respected as the authorities they are supposed to be. Alexander also assumes in the "bank" hypothetical that authority to make law has been conferred on the legislature—which, he supposes, is equivalent to the aggregation of human legislators—so that only if a majority of those legislators converge in supporting a law can a law come into existence. In his imaginary case, no such converging majority has formed.

Because the supporting legislators understand the law's words in utterly different senses, they have not converged on any *meaning*; and because a law is not separable from its meaning, they have not converged on any *law*. So the apparent convergence is illusory. Alexander dutifully concludes that there is no law. The "no meetings by the bank" enactment is not law, but merely "gibberish."[25]

This conclusion may be logical enough, but it is almost surely not a conclusion that a court would actually reach if the "bank" statute were invoked in a case. Rather, a court would suppose that a law *has* been enacted, and so the law must mean *something*. How would the court choose between the riparian "bank" and the fiscal one? Who knows? But the court would do its best to interpret the law, somehow, and would attribute the law as interpreted to "the legislature." To a legislature, apparently, that possesses intentions and understandings independent of—and not reducible to—the intentions and understandings of its human members.

To be sure, stark cases like Alexander's "bank" example, in which unbeknownst to each other different legislators innocently intend two definite but completely different meanings, may be anomalous. What seems overwhelmingly likely, though, and much more pervasive, is that laws will be enacted although only a minority of legislators have bothered to inform themselves about what the laws actually say. Take the Affordable Care Act, or Obamacare as it is popularly known. The law was massive and notoriously complicated, and it seems likely that most members of Congress never read through it and had little inkling about much of what it contained. As Speaker of the House Nancy Pelosi famously (and, one hopes, facetiously) remarked, "We have to pass the bill so that you can find out what is in it."[26]

The Affordable Care Act may seem an extreme and unrepresentative instance; but if so, it probably leads to an underestimate of the phenomenon we are considering here. Thus, the vast hosts of laws that, unlike the Affordable Care Act, receive little or no public attention seem even less likely to be read and studied by most legislators. In such instances, we arguably have not two completely different intentions, as in Alexander's "bank" example; rather, we have an intention that may possibly be shared by the subset of legislators who have actually paid attention to a law, together with relative obliviousness (and thus, realistically, *no* semantic intentions) by the majority of legislators.[27] Thus, if the "bank" law is "gibberish," as Alexander argues, because there is no convergence on a unified meaning, isn't it likely that enormous chunks of what we had thought were our laws—most of them, probably—are also "gibberish"?

Aggregation through delegation? That is an unsettling possibility, but maybe an avoidable one. Couldn't we just say that in such cases, a law's meaning is determined by the intentions and understandings of the relatively small subset of legislators who *did* pay attention to it? The great bulk of complacent or otherwise occupied legislators who never bothered to read the bill, we might say, have effectively delegated authority for the law's meaning to the attentive few.[28]

Or, more generally, we might stipulate to some meaning-maker or meaning-making procedure. So although it is true, we might say, that legislators' intentions may often diverge and that in many or maybe nearly all cases most legislators may not have any concrete intentions at all about a law's meaning, this is not a problem. The meaning of the law will be determined in accordance with the understandings of, say, the law's drafters or its principal sponsors, or maybe of the committee in which the bill originated or of the chamber's presiding officer, or in some other way. (Or maybe of some invisible low-level Justice Department attorney who assisted in drafting the bill?[29] . . . Probably not.) The other legislators will be presumed to have delegated mean-making authority to the designated meaning-makers.[30] The possibility might be supported by sophisticated philosophical explanation of how joint intentions or collective agency is possible.[31]

This approach may seem inviting, not only because it purports to offer a solution to the aggregation problem but because it corresponds to an actual process that we often observe in practice. For example, on a law faculty, let's say, it may be that proposed faculty rules and revisions are constantly being put forward by the Dean's Office or by some indefatigably conscientious colleague or committee. Most faculty, busy with teaching and scholarship, may find these incessant proposals tiresome and disruptive and may rarely bother to read them at all. (I'm speaking here of a purely hypothetical situation, of course.) Even so, these inattentive faculty members may vote for the proposals anyway, or perhaps the proposals are deemed to become effective unless someone objects; and if asked later what a newly approved rule means, they might say, "I haven't the slightest idea; it means whatever the dean or the committee intended it to mean." In such situations, it seems entirely realistic—not at all a fiction—to say that faculty members have self-consciously delegated meaning-making authority to the Dean's Office or the committee.[32]

Something quite similar might happen—arguably *does* happen, routinely—in Congress or in a state legislature. So, does this observation solve the problem of aggregating legislators' intentions?

Sadly, no. Delegations of meaning-making authority that might be sensible and perfectly acceptable in many institutional contexts are, it turns out, distinctively problematic in a legislative context. It is not just that there is no settled understanding of who the relevant meaning-makers are in, say, Congress. (Although there isn't, and that *is* a problem.) The more serious objection, rather, is that this sort of delegation seems inconsistent with the assumptions and requirements of legislative authority.

How so? Here is a simple, abstract statement of the point: Both constitutional rules and perhaps the very logic of representative government would seem to require that laws be approved *by the legislators themselves*; legislators are not permitted to delegate their lawmaking authority—or at least not to delegate it *to other legislators*.[33] But if, as argued earlier, it is a misconception to treat a law as something separate from its meaning, and if it is thus an error to separate the authority to make law from the authority to make a law's meaning, then the impermissibility of delegating *lawmaking authority* to other legislators entails the impermissibility of delegating *meaning-making authority* to those other legislators.

Consider an illustration. Imagine that the state of California elects Harry to the Senate. Though garrulous or charismatic enough to get elected, Harry is also obsessively committed to golf, or perhaps to some nobler pursuit—collecting and preserving endangered species of mollusks, maybe. In any case, although pleased and honored to be a member of what is sometimes described as the nation's most exclusive club, Harry finds it unbearably tedious to have to sit through Senate sessions and functions, and he is looking for a way to shift these responsibilities to his senatorial colleagues—or at least to *someone*—so that he can devote his time to more rewarding or worthwhile activities. For centuries, he reflects, many Christian clergy governed their parishes from afar while rarely or never actually showing up in church: why shouldn't this same privilege extend to senators?

Finding that other senators share his sentiments, Harry first proposes the formation of a "Senate Legislation Committee," to be composed of five senators elected by the full body, which shall be assigned power to represent the full chamber in approving or rejecting all bills (subject, let us say, to being overridden by the full chamber). The idea is very similar to what happens routinely in federal courts of appeals, where panels of three judges are authorized to make decisions and ruling for an entire circuit of judges, subject to being overridden by a gathering of the full circuit en banc. In addition to freeing up the senators' time, Harry argues, this measure also will drastically reduce the problem of legislative gridlock: it will be much easier to get five senators to act on a law than to herd five score of felinish legislators into line.

Harry's proposal garners enthusiastic initial support among his senatorial colleagues. And then a killjoy legal counsel quashes the idea by opining that the procedure would almost surely be declared unconstitutional. Under the Constitution, counsel explains, laws have to be voted on by the full Senate (or at least by a quorum).

Disappointed, Harry seeks an alternative, and (again drawing on venerable ecclesiastical precedent) he hits on what seems an inviting possibility: he will delegate to his sister-in-law Sally, in writing, authority to represent him in all Senate business, including voting. Sally herself, who as it happens hasn't been doing much anyway of late, is flattered and excited by the prospect of high-level multitasking—namely, doing her knitting and deliberating and pontificating in Senate hearings. Once again, though, legal counsel puts the kibosh on this plan. "Sally has no authority to legislate," counsel points out. "She was never elected."

Harry responds that if this is the problem, he will delegate his voting authority to his fellow senator from California, who *was* duly elected; he will give her written authority to cast his vote in addition to her own. Much in the way that he gave his lawyer a power of attorney to settle a lawsuit against him or to sign mortgage papers for him. Still no good, counsel explains. "There's just no getting around it: *you* are the only one who can exercise your vote."

Harry is stymied—and then he strikes on an ingenious idea, which he shares with enthusiastic senatorial colleagues. Why not just enact, at the beginning of each congressional term, something that will be called "The Rorschach Act of 20— "? The law will be simple in its terms. Section 1 will prohibit citizens and residents of the United States from committing acts that are "unjust, oppressive, or detrimental to the public interest." Section 2 will command citizens and residents to perform all acts which shall be "necessary to the public interest." Section 3 will provide that "for purposes of this Act, the meaning of the terms 'unjust,' 'oppressive,' 'detrimental to the public interest,' and 'necessary to the public interest' shall be determined by the Senate Meaning-Making Committee, to be composed of five Senators elected by the full body."

The Rorschach Act, Harry explains, will be voted on and approved by all the senators according to the strictest procedural rules. Every *i* will be dotted; every *t* crossed. Of course, the act will also need to be approved by the House of Representatives and signed by the president (or at least not vetoed). Some negotiating might be required; the House's concurrence might need to be secured by amending the law to provide for a comparable procedure in the House, so that House members will likewise be freed up to pursue higher purposes.

Suppose that Harry manages to get the Rorschach Act adopted. Is he now free to pursue his golf game or his mollusk preservation mission?

Despite the notorious difficulties in the "nondelegation doctrine," though, it seems virtually certain that a court would, and in any case should, strike down Harry's law as a gross violation of constitutional requirements for lawmaking. But why? After all, don't we have a "law" (namely, the Rorschach Act), enacted in meticulous compliance with all constitutional requirements? It is only the meaning-making function that has been delegated. If these are separable—if "the law" is separable from its "meaning," in other words—then what exactly is the problem?

But then, of course, that is the point: lawmaking and meaning-making are *not* separable. Once again, separated from its meaning, a string of words is not a law. It is nothing but a conglomeration of meaningless marks, and meaningless marks are not law. And this is true whether the attempted separation of law from meaning is made wholesale (as in the case of the Rorschach Act) or retail (as in the case of any particular statute, if we suppose that many or most legislators have attempted to "delegate" the ability to determine meaning to the smaller number of legislators who actually paid attention to what is in the bill).

Or think of it this way: if a single, omnibus "Rorschach Act" amounts to an unconstitutional delegation, would the conclusion be any different if Congress instead enacted a series of smaller Rorschach Acts for special subject matters? One Rorschach Act for immigration, another one for health care, still another one for taxes, and so on? In each case the statute says something to the effect that "the public interest shall be served" and then delegates the authority to say what the "public interest" *means* to a special meaning-making committee. Legislative inertia is in this way overcome. But if this *formal* meaning-making delegation is a blatant constitutional violation, why is it more acceptable to permit the bulk of senators and representatives *informally* to delegate meaning-making authority to a bill's sponsors or to the small group of legislators who bother to inform themselves?

And so it comes to seem that there just is no satisfactory way to discern the meaning of a congressional statute by aggregating the intentions or understandings (or lack thereof) of the various senators and representatives.

The Turn to Textualism. Precisely! an advocate of the textualist approach (like Justice Scalia) might respond. The impossibility of aggregating legislators' subjective intentions into a unitary meaning is one crucial consideration that points us away from the legislators' subjective intentions and toward something else. Something more objective. *Textual meaning.*[34]

Of course, intentionalists might agree that "textual meaning" is controlling; they might think the proposition that a text (including a statutory text) should be interpreted according to its "textual meaning" is no more than an obvious, albeit useless, tautology. A text is a text and the text means what it means. Right? But of course *they*—the intentionalists—equate textual meaning with the semantic intentions of the actual legislators. So-called textualists want something less subjective. The search, according to Justice Scalia, "is for a sort of 'objectified' intent—the intent that a reasonable person would gather from the text of the law, placed alongside the remainder of the *corpus juris*."[35]

In trying to identify some "objective" criterion, Scalia appealed to a hypothetical "reasonable person" reader. Other textualists refer to linguistic conventions as the source of a law's meaning.[36] Or these devices can be combined: thus, Harvard law dean John Manning argues that a statute should be given "the import that a reasonable person conversant with applicable social and linguistic conventions would attach to the enacted words."[37]

The textualist approach to statutory interpretation reflects basically the same position as the "original public meaning" approach to constitutional interpretation discussed in the previous chapter; it is supported by the same rationales, and it generates the same objections. More specifically, proponents like Justice Scalia argue that textualism rather than intentionalism is required by the ideal of "rule of law not of men."[38] But, as in the constitutional area, this seems an unnecessary and indeed extravagant use of that maxim. For all of their foibles and occasional depravities, it is impossible to separate governance from "men" altogether. Laws do not just magically appear in the statute books or the judicial decisions; they are made by "men"—or by human beings. There is just no getting around that fact. Even so, the "rule of law" ideal expresses the crucial difference between regimes in which "men" rule directly and personally in ad hoc fashion ("Off with his head!" "Because I said so.") and regimes in which the rulers are required to govern through law—through written rules or decrees that are promulgated to the subjects and that are presumptively binding on the lawmakers themselves.[39]

But the fact that such rules are interpreted to mean what the rulers intend them to mean is in no way contrary to this ideal; indeed, it is simply an intrinsic part of such governance (and, one might say, of any system involving communication from some persons to other persons). Conversely, to insist that laws do *not* mean what the enactors or legislators intended them to mean is in effect to deprive those legislators, ostensibly endowed with lawmaking authority, of the very authority that had supposedly been conferred on them. Because, once again, authority to enact words but not to give those words their meaning is not authority to make law. As Jeffrey Goldsworthy explains, "A law necessarily means something—nothing meaningless can be a law—and its meaning is part of what it is."[40]

As in the area of constitutional interpretation, this anomaly may pass mostly unnoticed so long as we assume that the relevant linguistic conventions are relatively stable and clear. In that situation, although in the textualist view the legislators do not technically determine the meaning of the laws they enact, in practice they will be able to set that meaning, because they will know what their words will be taken to mean. But consider the opposite contingency. Imagine that in response to, say, social upheaval and massive immigration and rapid technological change, linguistic conventions spin into a sort of chaotic free-for-all. So there is no telling what words spoken by Jones will mean to Jenson or Johansen, or whether words that mean X in the Alta Rica neighborhood today might not mean Y in the Baja Pobre district ten blocks away, and Z tomorrow. When you say, "That's bad!," some people will take your words to mean "bad"; others will understand the words to mean "good"; still others will take you to be commenting on the state of the weather or the economy or the pennant race.

In these chaotic circumstances, legislators might favor rule X, and so they might enact a statute using words they intend to mean X; but they have no idea whether the statute when enforced will instead be taken to mean Y or Z (or maybe BB, or $M4\#c@w$). And of course it is anyone's guess what Justice Scalia's "reasonable reader" would take the words to mean. Legislating becomes a matter of legislators casting their semantic bread on the waters and hoping that the linguistic currents will bring back something approximating what they hoped for.

Is this actually legal authority in any meaningful sense?

To be sure, linguistic conventions are unlikely to be anywhere near as unstable and unpredictable as the preceding scenario imagined. But that observation should be small comfort to the proponents of textualism. After all, insofar as legislators' "subjective" semantic intentions and "objective" linguistic conventions match up, there is no practical difference between the intentionalist and textualist approaches. So-called textualism makes a difference only and precisely in situations in which intentions and linguistic conventions do *not* match up, but instead lead to different interpretations of statutory language. And in those situations, textualism works to deprive legislators of the authority that the people or the constitution purported to confer on them. Or put it this way: it would be a pretty feeble theory that seems attractive only so long as it leads to basically the same conclusions yielded by the rival theory it purports to reject.

We could put the basic point in terms of the impermissible delegations we considered in connection with the intentionalist approach's aggregation problem. We saw there that both constitutional law and the logic of representative government would seem to prohibit legislators from delegating away their *lawmaking authority*; and because a "law" and its "meaning" are not separate entities, this prohibition in turn entailed the impermissibility of delegating away *meaning-making authority* with respect to the texts the legislators enact. But textualism amounts to a systematic campaign to separate lawmaking authority from meaning-making authority. The latter authority is delegated not to sisters-in-law or to other legislators in a Meaning-Making Committee, but rather to a fictional person (Justice Scalia's hypothetical reasonable reader) or else to an impersonal and nonrational agent (the rules and conventions of language).

In noting these objections to textualism, we might also notice one appealing feature that is legitimate but that does not justify textualism as an overall approach or account. The legitimate "rule of law" concern is for "secret" or "private" meanings; the concern is to prevent the injustices that might occur if subjects are sanctioned under laws that seem to them to mean one thing but that were intended, and hence are interpreted, to mean something different. This might happen, it is feared, either deliberately, if legislators harbor secret intentions that their statutory language fails to communicate, or accidentally, if legislators use language ineptly and thereby fail to communicate what they intended to communicate.[41]

But the concern for the first situation is misconceived, because (as we saw in the previous chapter) the intent that is relevant to legal interpretation, in the intentionalist view, is the legislators' *semantic* intent. What matters, in other words, is what the legislators meant *to communicate*. If a legislator hoped for some untoward or insidious result but cunningly declined to communicate that hope in the statute, that "intent" (if it can even be called that) will not be part of the semantic intent that determines the law's meaning.[42]

The concern is more realistic with respect to the second situation: legislators (like other humans) may sometimes use language ineptly, and may thus fail to communicate what they meant to communicate. And such ineptitude could result in interpretations that are misguided or unfair to subjects. Like the poor, injustices and imperfections will always be with us — at least as long as governance is conducted by fallible human beings. If legislators do their job badly, people may get hurt: that is just a fact of life. Still, the law typically tries to mitigate this kind of injustice with interpretive rules or guidelines — or "canons" — such as the idea that a law can be "void for vagueness," or the maxim that criminal laws should be construed leniently to avoid injustice and surprise.[43] If the existing canons are insufficient to avoid injustice, additional and stronger ones could of course be adopted.[44]

Although textualism is not necessary to avoid the problem of meanings that take people by surprise, the approach actually creates its own more serious problem of surprise. That is because, in the textualist approach, a law can come to have meanings that neither the legislators themselves nor their constituents intended or expected (and quite possibly would not have wanted), and these meanings may result in the imposition of costly liability on parties who could hardly have anticipated such meanings.

Even as I write, the Supreme Court has obligingly provided an almost made-to-order example of this unfortunate possibility. Thus, in *Bostock v. Clayton County*,[45] the Court ruled on explicitly textualist grounds that Title VII of the 1964 Civil Rights Act, in prohibiting employment discrimination based on "sex," also prohibited discrimination based on "sexual orientation" or transgender status. The majority admitted that members of the enacting Congress did not intend or understand their words to have any such meaning or effect, that subsequent courts had not understood the words to have such a meaning, and also that Congress had repeatedly rejected efforts to add sexual orientation to the law's prohibition. Nor was this a case in which a legislature created a legal category that turned out to apply to nonexisting or unimagined instances that developed later, as when a prohibition on the marketing of "poisons," say, turns out to cover a poisonous substance that hadn't been invented when the statute was enacted. On the contrary, the possibility of discrimination based on sexual orientation was entirely real in 1964: members of Congress simply did not imagine that this practice would fall under a prohibition against discrimination based on sex. More than half-a-century later, however, it turned out that the law had a meaning—and indeed, under the Court's reasoning, *always had had* a meaning—that no one in Congress contemplated or favored. And employers who had violated that newly discovered meaning would be subject to liability and serious sanctions.

As usual in such cases, of course, some Americans were elated and others were aghast at the Court's interpretation. Either way, the decision nicely illustrates the possibility of surprise—of surprise that will work to the considerable detriment of those taken by surprise—that textualism creates. Employers who for years had been making decisions on the entirely reasonable assumption that there was no federal prohibition on taking sexual orientation or transgender status into account—they knew, among other things, that such a prohibition had repeatedly been proposed in Congress, and rejected—suddenly woke up to discover that (unbeknownst to them, and to Congress, and to almost everyone else) such a prohibition had been there all along. So employment decisions that had seemed perfectly legal at the time had now been retroactively rendered illegal, and employers who had made those decisions were now suddenly potentially liable for massive damages.

Thus, the very real possibility that legislators' intended meanings will not always be readily apparent to the subjects of their laws is in itself no reason to depart from the Blackstonian and commonsensical view that statutes should be interpreted in accordance with the intentions of the legislators who enacted those laws. And yet that conclusion, attractive enough in the abstract, perhaps, still does nothing to solve the aggregation problem discussed earlier. The upshot, it may seem, is that *neither* intentionalism nor textualism provides a viable account of what statutes mean or of how statutes should be interpreted.

"Congress" as fiction. So it seems we face a conundrum. In interpreting a statute, we might look to the subjective intentions of the legislators, but in the frequent cases in which those legislators did not share a common semantic intention, there is no satisfactory way of aggregating their disparate intentions (or lack thereof) into a single unitary meaning. Textualists like Justice Scalia seize on this conclusion and urge that we should instead look to some supposedly "objective" criterion, such as the objective textual meaning of the statute. But even if there is such a thing (as some astute critics doubt[46]), that criterion would deprive legislators of the basic authority that was conferred on them—namely, the authority to make law. A law is nothing apart from its meaning, and if the legislators do not get to make that meaning they do not get to make the law.

Contemplated here in our jurisprudential dark room, the situation may appear hopeless. And yet we raise the blinds and look out the window, and see to our surprise that the legal world goes on tolerably well. Citizens sue other citizens, or are prosecuted by the state, under statutes whose meaning is sometimes contested. And far from dissolving into gibbering paralysis, judges confidently assign meanings to these statutes in accordance with something they may describe as "the intent of the legislature." And then they proceed to award damages, or throw the case out, or send the defendant to jail, as the thus-interpreted statutes direct.

How can this happen? What is going on? How do judges manage to do something that our discussion has suggested cannot be done?

But then perhaps the answer has been staring us in the face all along? The received wisdom said, once again, that statutes were to be interpreted in accordance with "the intent of *the legislature.*" Not "the intent of *the legislators.*"[47] And *not* in accordance with "the meaning of the text" (which in times past would probably have seemed like a piece of redundant silliness—as in "interpret the text to mean what the text means"). What is supposed to govern, it seems, is the intent of *the institution*—the legislature.

And yet, one might well ask, how is this observation helpful? Doesn't it just land us back in the same predicament we have been discussing? More specifically, how can an institution, in itself, have intentions? *Persons* have intentions; institutions abstracted away from those persons do not. Abstracted away from the humans who compose it, the institution—in this case Congress—seems a mere . . . abstraction. A fiction. And can fictions have intentions?

Actually, yes, they can. We are perfectly familiar with fictions—thousands of them—who undoubtedly have and act in accordance with intentions. Hamlet. Harry Potter. Dirty Harry. The Harry who met Sally. We encounter such intention-endowed fictions every day, on television or in novels or in the comic strips.

But this observation may still seem of no help. To be sure, fictional *persons* can possess (fictional) intentions. But how can a fictional *institution*—like Congress, abstracted away from its human constituents—have intentions?

But we have already seen the answer to that question, haven't we? Persons have intentions, including fictional persons: so Congress can have intentions if we treat Congress itself not as a collection of individual persons, but rather as its own sort of conglomerate person. We personify, or anthropomorphize, Congress.[48] Isn't this what lawyers like Roscoe Pound have been effectively doing all along when they insisted that statutes be interpreted in accordance with the intentions of "the lawmaker," or "the legislator," in the singular?

Described in this way, the personification of Congress might seem like a feat of abstraction and imagination. Again, though, we should not make the matter harder, or more exotic, than it is. Congress, as we have seen, is not identical to the 100 senators and 435 representatives who compose it. Congress transcends those mere mortals. And yet neither is it unrelated to them—far from it. Judging from the "Congress" that courts invoke when they perform statutory interpretation, we might say that this Congress is something like a composite of the collection of senators and representatives, except idealized, with their quirks and omissions and (above all) their differences partly imagined away. The Congress that courts defer to, and that in practice exercises authority over us, is *like* the legislators who inhabit it, only a little bit better—more mindful, more cognizant, more devoted to the public good. More careful in its expressions. And above all, more unified.[49]

We said at the outset that if Congress possessed a group mind, the intentionalist approach could work well enough. As it happens, there is no real Congress that possesses a group mind. But in our interpretive performances, we imagine such a Congress. It is like a photograph that we artificially enhance. Or, to put the point differently, the visible Congress composed of human beings does not have a group mind; but the quasi-fictional Congress that we conjure up to exercise authority over us does.

This is why for purposes of statutory interpretation, the statements made about the statute by the various members of Congress are (a) *relevant* but (b) not *determinative*. Consider first their relevance. Although the Congress that judges and other interpreters appeal to may be partly fictional, and in that way independent of our actual legislators, it cannot be *too* far removed from those men and women that we elected to govern us. Because in that case it would lose the "truishness" that (as we discussed in chapter 1) a viable fiction depends on.

Here is one way to appreciate the point. Fantasizing, we *could* imagine an idealized fictional Congress that would be wholly unrelated to our actual senators and representatives. Freed from that constraining connection, we might proceed to conceive a Congress that is vastly wiser, more courageous, more honest, and more harmonious than the actual members of Congress are. It is an alluring vision, but it has one major drawback: this Camelotish Congress would just too obviously not be *our* Congress. It would lack the connection to reality—the quality of "truishness" or, as Edmund Morgan put it, the "viable relation with fact"[50]—that a fiction must have in order to perform its beneficent function. And so although admirable, this paragon of a Congress, alas, could claim no authority. Not over *us* anyway.

Our Congress—the one we look to as an authority—must be related to our actual members of Congress, even though it is not identical to them. And so the actual facts, including committee reports and statements made by legislators, are relevant to statutory interpretation. We would expect lawyers and judges to support their interpretations by invoking such evidence, and they do.[51] But, on the other hand, such statements will not be *determinative* of statutory meaning. Because that meaning, once again, is supposed to correspond to the intent of *the legislature*—which, as we have seen, is not the same thing as the human *legislators* who act in and through it.

In chapter 1 we saw that the viability of a fiction will depend on two sorts of factors. One factor is truishness, or plausibility. A fiction does not need to be true, exactly—indeed, in many situations (as when watching a movie) we are quite aware, at some level, that a fiction is *not* true in a factual sense—but it needs to be plausible enough to support our exercise in bracketing or suspending that awareness, so that the fiction can perform its beneficent function. Conversely, we will have no motivation to undertake this delicate exercise in bracketing or suspending unless the fiction provides us with some kind of compensation for our efforts—enjoyment, or wisdom, or (in the case of law) authority. That is the other factor: a fiction's ability to provide some benefit sufficient to support the suspension of disbelief.

Both factors are manifestly present in statutory interpretation. Lawyers and judges try to square their interpretations with what the legislators wrote, obviously, and also, often, with what legislators said about a law. But lawyers and judges also try to show that their interpretation is just, or consistent with good public policy. As with other fictions, these factors interact: the more we have of one, the less we may need of the other. So it will be difficult to sell an interpretation, no matter how attractive, if it clearly goes against the manifest intentions of the (human) members of Congress. And yet the more just or attractive an interpretation, the more relaxed will be our insistence on conformity to what actual legislators may have said about the statute: why let a few grubby facts deprive us of an admirable law?

And thus it turns out that although there is plenty of material that lawyers and judges can draw on to argue that different interpretations are better or worse, more or less attractive, there is in the end no fact of the matter that can demonstrate that any particular interpretation is simply correct or incorrect. Moreover, people obviously disagree about the relative merits, in terms of justice or policy, of different interpretations: an interpretation that seems eminently just to one citizen will seem manifestly misguided to another. (As the strongly disparate reactions to the Supreme Court's interpretation of the Civil Rights Act in *Bostock* reflected.) And thus the disagreements will continue, and there will be no way in which one interpretation could be demonstrated to be correct and another mistaken. That is not the way fictions work.

Purposivism and its pragmatic cousins. While arguing that the difficulties of intentionalism and textualism point to the quasi-fictional quality of the "Congress" that these approaches invoke, we have thus far neglected to consider the third overall approach, or family of approaches, which has as a central member what is sometimes called "purposivism." But we have deferred consideration of these approaches because, unlike intentionalism and textualism, purposivist and pragmatist approaches come close to openly confessing that they are appealing to a quasi-fictional legislature. So they do not so much challenge our conclusion as confirm it.

A quick qualification is in order. In enacting laws, legislators presumably have, and act to achieve, "purposes." Such purposes, insofar as they can be discerned, are of course closely relevant to ascertaining the "intentions" that animated those legislators and to figuring out the meaning of the texts they have enacted. In this respect, reference to purposes would not be a third mode of statutory interpretation, but would merely be a central technique within the other approaches.[52] Henry Hart and Albert Sacks, early eminent champions of a purposivist approach, while urging that a court should "[i]nterpret the words of the statute ... so as to carry out the purpose as best it can," also insisted that a court must not give the statute "a meaning [the words] will not bear." Hart and Sacks stressed that "[t]he words of the statute are what the legislature has enacted as law, and all that it has the power to enact. Unenacted intentions or wishes cannot be given effect as law."[53] Although classified as purposivists, Hart and Sacks may have been textualists, or perhaps intentionalists, who merely pointed out the importance of purposes in figuring out textual meaning and legislative intentions.

Purposivism becomes a distinctive approach just to the extent that it is practiced in a more "dynamic" or "pragmatic" spirit, so that "purpose" is invoked not merely as a way of ascertaining legislative intent or textual meaning, but rather as a justification for *going beyond* or *updating* the text of the statute. And that, it seems, is precisely what at least some proponents of purposivism seem to have in mind.[54] If the specific means adopted by Congress to achieve its purposes have come to seem outdated or counterproductive, a court should depart from Congress's choice of means and should fashion its own means for achieving Congress's purpose. So goes the argument.[55]

But of course the authority to make law is the authority not just to choose *ends* (or "purposes"), but also to select the *means* for achieving those ends. Often the means will be more contentious—and will require more legislative deliberation and negotiation—than the ends. Everyone agrees, perhaps, that it would be good to expand the economy and protect the environment and promote education. But people disagree, often vehemently, about *how* to achieve these admirable ends—and also about what tradeoffs to make and what priorities to set among the various ends or purposes. Those are the hard questions that Congress, in the exercise of its lawmaking authority, struggles with.

So if a court departs from or exceeds Congress's choices with respect to means (which will usually involve both instrumentalist judgments and decisions about tradeoffs and priorities) and instead devises its own means, it is clear that the court is assuming lawmaking authority for itself. Whether a court *should* do this is not our question here. Let us stipulate for purposes of discussion that in some cases it is desirable for a court to depart from Congress's choices of means or for the court to update a statute that Congress in its sluggishness has failed to keep current: we are in effect stipulating that it is desirable for the court to have and to exercise legislative authority. That is because, once again, the choice of means is as much within the legislative authority as the choice of ends, or "purposes."

In principle, this partial reassignment of legislative authority might be done candidly and openly. Much in the way that the Merovingian regime was transformed into the Carolingian dynasty as the royal stewards began to exercise more and more authority in the Merovingian kings' name and eventually dropped the pretense and openly declared themselves to be kings, it is imaginable that courts (and agencies) in the American system, dropping the pretense that they are humbly carrying out directives from Congress, might openly assume legislative authority. This effective transfer of authority is already, perhaps, an "open secret."

And yet an "open secret" is still a secret. The explicit declaration of judicial lawmaking authority has not happened yet—except perhaps by an occasional outlier (like Judge Richard Posner).[56] For understandable reasons (based on our assumptions about authority and "the consent of the governed"), it may never happen.[57] For now at least, courts still purport to be carrying out Congress's directives. But insofar as the courts follow "purposes" attributed to Congress while departing from the means that Congress has chosen, or insofar as courts "update" legislation that Congress *could* revise but chooses not to revise (or, perhaps more accurately, does not choose to revise), the courts are not acting on directives from any *actual* Congress. They are acting under a Congress of their own imagining. A fictional, or at least quasi-fictional, Congress.

What Is a Court?

Let us suppose, though, that we wake up tomorrow to find that the Supreme Court has in fact made the Carolingian declaration that we have just contemplated. For a long time, the Court says, we have pretended to be merely interpreting and applying laws made by Congress or (in constitutional cases) by "We the People." And for a long time, everyone with more than minimal intelligence and perception has known that these claims are bogus. Hence the unseemly spectacle that transpires every time a new justice is nominated to the Supreme Court: the nominee will solemnly vow never to make law but rather merely to apply the law as written—to "call balls and strikes"—and anyone who was not born yesterday will know that this performance is a solemn sham.[58] Well, enough is enough, the Court says. We hereby announce that we have—and long or always have had—lawmaking power, and that much (though not *all*) of what we do reflects the exercise of this power.

Some pundits and professors are jubilant, anticipating a new era of governance based on honesty and "reason"; others predict that the Court's authority will collapse (because there is no plausible account of how the Court's newly-proclaimed legislative authority is based on "the consent of the governed"). In fact, both sides are disappointed. Governance goes on pretty much as before: in practice, nothing much seems to have changed.

Would the Court's improbable, hypothetical honesty have the effect of eliminating the fictional quality of our law? Actually, no. True, this imaginary candor might eliminate the need to invoke a quasi-fictional Congress or We the People as authority for what the Court does. And yet, it turns out that the Court itself has its own fictional dimension, and for basically the same reasons that apply to Congress and congressional legislation. In fact, much of our discussion earlier in this chapter can simply be carried over, with a few adjustments, to the Supreme Court.

This might seem a dubious claim, because the Court is supposed to be a fundamentally different kind of institution than Congress is. And it *is* a different institution—in function, arguably, and surely in form. But it will turn out, upon reflection, that these differences do not actually make much difference for our present purposes.

Start with the differences in function. The generally understood function or role of Congress is to legislate—to make law. Conversely, the primary function or role of the Supreme Court is... what, exactly?

A classic description holds that the Court's job is declaratory in character: "It is emphatically the province and duty of the judiciary *to say what the law is.*"[59] By contrast, a more critical but also common view—one that labels itself as a form of "realism"—insists that courts, especially including the Supreme Court, do not merely *declare* law; they *make* it.[60] (This is basically the position that, in my hypothetical variation, the Supreme Court openly owns up to.) On the classic view, the Court's function is different in kind from Congress's; on the more "realist" view, the differences are less stark.

For present purposes, though, we need not decide which of these views, or what combination of them, is more accurate. Even the most stalwart defenders of the "declaratory" view of the judicial function will have to concede that "say[ing] what the law is" is not like a stenographer reading back the trial transcript in accordance with the judge's request. "What the law is" often presents a murky and much-disputed question. Hence all the lawyerly disputations and amicus briefs and concurring and dissenting opinions. And insofar as courts, and ultimately the Supreme Court, are entrusted with the function of giving official answers to such murky and disputed questions, the courts plainly exercise a weighty kind of legal authority, as hardly anyone will doubt. Whether we describe the exercise of that authority as "declaring" or "making" law hardly matters for our purposes. Conversely, even proponents of the more realist view will likely concede that courts make law differently than Congress does. They make law interstitially,[61] perhaps, or using a different process, and they present the law that they make *as if* they were merely interpreting or declaring law that is already there.[62]

Courts, especially including the Supreme Court, also differ from Congress in form—in obvious ways. Congress is bicameral; the Supreme Court has only one chamber. Congress has 535 voting members; the Supreme Court has 9. And unlike members of Congress, who may or may not express their views on the legislation they enact, judges and especially justices feel an institutional responsibility to write opinions carefully explaining and justifying (or, cynics might say, rationalizing and obfuscating) the positions they take. Even if a particular justice does not write an opinion in a given case, he or she will nearly always explicitly join or endorse the opinion of one of the other justices.

Do these differences in form point to a conclusion different from the one we reached with respect to Congress—namely, that Congress transcends its members and thus acquires a partly fictional character? It might seem so. To be sure, aggregation is still an issue—because nine does not equal one. But, conversely, 9 is less than 535, and one (one chamber, that is) is less than two. So perhaps aggregation, which seemed an insuperable challenge with respect to Congress, is manageable enough with respect to the Court? So that there is no need to postulate any institution that transcends the understandings of its human members?

Perhaps. And yet . . . . Just as lawyers and judges often disagree about what a statute means, judges and lawyers routinely disagree about what an earlier judicial decision meant. Often these disagreements will revolve around statements or conclusions that were made in a majority opinion but whose meaning is less than clear. Often the disagreements will lead later interpreters to claim and conjecture about what the different justices intended by what they said or didn't say. In many cases there will be concurring opinions that have to be integrated into the mix and aggregated for whatever they may reveal.[63] Indeed, the justices expect as much: why else would they bother to write concurring opinions? There is no algorithm for doing these aggregations. The interpreters' overall conclusion will nonetheless be presented as the ruling of "the Court"—a court that, as with Congress, is plainly not quite reducible to its human members.

Indeed, the justices quite consciously expect this as well: the majority opinion in a case does not present itself as "the opinion of Justices So-and-So," but rather as "the opinion of *the Court*."[64] Of the institution. Of an institution deemed to possess understandings and intentions not fully reducible to the understandings and intentions of its human constituents.

The distinction between "the Court" and the justices is especially conspicuous in cases in which there is no majority, so that the position of "the Court" has to be constructed through addition and subtraction. In the famous case of *Bakke v. Regents*,[65] for example, four justices basically contended that state-sponsored affirmative action programs were unconstitutional; four justices contended for the opposite conclusion; and one justice (Lewis Powell) argued that affirmative action was permissible only for particular and very limited purposes. The constitutionality of affirmative action of course was—and still is—a contentious and much-litigated question. And later cases were forced to treat Powell's position as "the law" and the position of "the Court," even though only a single justice endorsed it and eight justices disagreed with it. Indeed, not only later courts but the nation's universities dutifully treated Justice Powell's opinion as that of the Court, and thus as "the law" (with devastating consequences for the nation's universities, as Anthony Kronman has recently argued[66]).

The abstracted personification of "the Court" as distinguished from the collection of individual jurists is underscored in the common usage in which an opinion declares, with respect to a decision rendered decades or even centuries ago, that "In *Joe v. Blow*, we held that...." Who is the "we"? Plainly not the actual human beings voting and writing in the present case. (Unless, that is, the justices are asserting some implicit theory of reincarnation, so that, like the Dalai Lama, a current justice is deemed to be a reincarnated embodiment of his or her predecessor. In all the libraries of constitutional scholarship, no one to my knowledge has ever proposed such a theory.) So it seems clear that "the Court" itself is being presented as enjoying a kind of immortality. Not merely of institutional continuity (which in itself could hardly be described as fictional), but of the kind of *personified* continuity that would support statements such as "we ruled" or "we declared." "The Court," in short, is manifestly not the same as the human beings who sit on the Court, and yet "the Court" does the sorts of things that humans do. It speaks, rules, declares.

Just as "Congress" transcends the mere human legislators who occupy and operate the institution, therefore, "the Supreme Court" transcends the individual justices who staff and inhabit it at any given time. And it is this more transcendent Court that the justices present to the world and that the rest of us look to as authoritative. Again as with Congress, this Court is not unrelated to the human jurists that it houses. Like statements made by members of Congress, the opinions of those jurists are (a) relevant but (b) not determinative in later adjudication. Thus, later courts often depart from the most likely subjective intentions of those jurists, but they hesitate to stray too far. If the divergence between *what the Justices said* in a decision and *what a later Court says the decision meant* became too glaring, the fiction to which the Court is appealing—the fiction of "the Court"—would lose its plausibility. It would become too transparently fictional. And it would then sacrifice its ability to perform as a successful fiction does.

The President's Two Bodies[67]

In concluding that both Congress and the Supreme Court are quasifictional entities, we have paid considerable attention to the difficulties of aggregation. Those institutions, after all, are composed of a plurality of human beings—of multiple legislators or judges—and yet we need to treat the institutions as being able to speak with a unified voice. And that necessity may seem to require some sort of aggregation of the votes or views of the various members; so the seemingly insuperable difficulties of such aggregation led to the conclusion that the univocal institution to which we routinely appeal must be some sort of fiction.

But the third constitutionally recognized branch of the national government—namely, the president—does not seem to suffer from this difficulty. After all, there is only one president (at any given time). And unlike the Supreme Court, which says things like "*We held*" with reference to decisions issued long before the current justices were even born, presidents typically do not refer to actions of their predecessors with phrases like "*I decreed*" or "*I declared.*" It would have seemed quite preposterous if President Obama or President Bush had invoked, say, the Monroe Doctrine with the explanation that "In 1823, I declared European interference in American affairs to be unacceptable."

To be sure, the executive branch encompasses many thousands of people; and this multiplicity can present questions similar to those we have been discussing. How does one aggregate the votes of the various commissioners on a federal commission? That sort of thing. Even so, at the top of the sprawling administrative heap there is a single chief executive. *The* president.

So, does this singularity eliminate the need to posit an institution apart from the humans who compose it—an institution that, insofar as it is treated as having the capacity to do human things like speaking and intending, has a quasi-fictional quality? Can we say that whatever the case may be with Congress and with the Supreme Court, at least *the president* is not a fiction?

It might seem so. And might this possibility perhaps contribute to explaining why presidential powers and authority have expanded at the expense of the other branches?[68] Might we say that by contrast to Congress and the Supreme Court, and whatever his deficiencies, at least the president is not some sort of imagined entity or quasi-fiction?

But let us defer the question for a moment and consider an ancient precedent—namely, the king. Notwithstanding occasional disputes about who the rightful king was, the king was typically, it seems, a single man—much like the president. In his classic work *The King's Two Bodies*,[69] though, Ernest Kantorowicz explained that in medieval and early modern thought, jurists frequently distinguished between the king *as a person* and the king *as the king*. The distinction could be expressed in terms of the king's "body natural" and his "body politic." Elizabethan common lawyers elaborated on the distinction in this way: the king's "body natural," they said, was "mortal, subject to all Infirmities that come by Nature or Accident, to the Imbecility of Infancy or old Age, and to the like Defects that happen to the natural Bodies of other People." By contrast, the king's "body politic" was "a Body that cannot be seen or handled, consisting of Policy and Government, and constituted for the Direction of the People and the Management of the public weal, and this Body is utterly void of Infancy, and old Age, and other natural Defects and Imbecilities."[70]

Citing a variety of explanations from Elizabethan judges and lawyers, Kantorowicz showed that these two embodiments of the king were understood to be, paradoxically, distinguishable and yet not exactly distinct. "The King's Two Bodies thus form one unit indivisible, each being fully contained in the other." And yet "[n]ot only is the body politic 'more ample and large' than the body natural, but there dwell in the former certain truly mysterious forces which reduce, or even remove, the imperfections of the fragile human nature."[71]

The distinction between the king's natural body and political body, separate and yet one, had obvious grounding in christological theology.[72] And yet the distinction was not merely a matter of abstract theorizing: it had crucial practical implications and uses—"great and serious advantages," as Kantorowicz put it.[73] The distinction could figure in property and employment disputes, for example. Had a parcel of land been transferred by, or had a courtier been employed to serve, *the king*, or only *the man*?[74] The distinction allowed courts to reach and rationalize what seemed the sensible or prudent results in such cases.

And when a king died—in his "body natural," that is—the "body politic" of the king continued uninterrupted: this idea could be of immense help in maintaining continuity of governance. For example, the idea of the king's two bodies underscored the error of more literal-minded delinquents who claimed that they had not violated "the king's peace" because during the interim between a former king's death and coronation of the new monarch there was no king and hence no "king's peace" to violate.[75] Wrong: "the king never dies."[76]

In the seventeenth century, when civil war broke out, Parliament could act in the name of *the king* to summon armies to fight against Charles *the man*.[77] Eventually Parliament could try and execute "Charles Stuart" without treasonously doing any injury to "the king."[78]

Kantorowicz noted that the eminent historian Frederic Maitland had mocked the notion of "the king's two bodies" as "a marvelous display of metaphysical—or we might say metaphysiological—nonsense."[79] And while noting the practical uses of the idea, Kantorowicz agreed in treating the idea as an intricate and extravagant fiction. This was perhaps too sweeping a characterization. There was nothing fictional, we might surmise, about the king's "body natural": it was a matter of simple, observable fact that there *was* a long series of men and sometimes women who had physical bodies (sometimes very substantial bodies, as in the case of the corpulent Henry VIII) and who were designated as "king" (or "queen"). The fiction, we might say, was in the more transcendent body—in the king who could not err or fall sick or die. And perhaps also in the insistent claim that this more impassible and invulnerable king was somehow one and the same with the more fleshly and tangible king.

From our vantage point, these legal concoctions and maneuverings may seem amusing—the irrational product of a half-theological culture that had not yet arrived at the Age of Reason. "[A]bsurdities," as Edmund Morgan called them.[80] What preposterous things those superstitious, prescientific people could bring themselves to believe! Before scoffing too loudly, though, we might reflect more closely on ourselves and on our own usages. Because although we do not employ—or, for that matter, comprehend—the Chalcedonian terminology that was used to describe the king's two bodies, we do routinely make an analogous distinction in the treatment of our own president. We distinguish, as we sometimes put it, between "the man" and "the office": these, in our usage, are distinguishable and yet one and the same. And, like the old common lawyers, we use the distinction to do essential legal work.

Consider two examples.[81] Since about the mid-1980s, official constitutional doctrine has held that the First Amendment prohibits governments and government officials from doing or saying anything that sends a message "endorsing or disapproving" of religion.[82] Under this doctrine, things like a Christmas crèche in a government building, or a plaque of the Ten Commandments on a courthouse wall, or a state law providing that public school students should be given a "moment of silence" for "meditation or voluntary prayer" have been declared to be unconstitutional.[83]

And yet presidents routinely do and say things explicitly and unmistakably endorsing religion, and the courts turn a blind eye. Presidents end their speeches with "God Bless America." They issue Thanksgiving Day proclamations containing overtly religious language. At their inaugurations they ask priests or pastors to say prayers, they take the presidential oath on the Bible, uttering the words "So help me God," and they solemnly invoke the blessings of the Almighty on their administration and on the country.[84] How could anyone observe these practices and not perceive a message endorsing religion?[85] The violations of constitutional "no endorsement" doctrine would seem to be blatant. And yet legal challenges to such practices have fared dismally in the courts.[86] Why? How?

Judicial decisions have offered no forthright or satisfying explanation. To be sure, the cases say that some superficially religious but rote governmental expressions (like "God save this Honorable Court") may be permissible because over time they have lost their religious quality and now serve mostly to solemnize public occasions.[87] Perhaps the "God bless America" of many presidential speeches can be explained away in this manner. But other religious expressions—particularly those in presidential inauguration ceremonies—are so overtly religious that their religious content can hardly be denied. Kent Greenawalt reports, for example, that "President Obama's inauguration had a lengthy invocation and benediction, with specific references to God and Christ." These expressions, Greenawalt observes, "undoubtedly convey[ed] a degree of approval of the religious ideas expressed."[88] So, why was this endorsement permissible?

Although the courts have provided no clear or satisfying answer, Greenawalt elsewhere suggests what seems to be the implicit rationale. "[W]e need to distinguish expressions of *the government*," he explains, "from the independent expressions of *people who happen to work for it*." Even "leading elected officials . . . often speak in a way that attaches to their position but may not be quite 'for the government.'"[89] Applied to presidential inaugurations, Greenawalt's point suggests that although endorsement of religion surely occurs, it is not *the president* who is endorsing religion. Rather, it is Barack Obama *the man*, or Donald Trump *the man*, who is invoking the blessings of God or commending the nation to the care of the Almighty, or posing ostentatiously with a Bible in front of a historic church.

It is easy enough to understand the appeal, even the necessity, of this distinction. For one thing, the distinction seems commonsensical, at least in some contexts (even if its deployment for particular purposes does not). That hunched-over figure relieving himself in the lavatory: that is the very human, very fleshy George Bush, or Bill Clinton. Right? Not "the president," surely?[90]

To be sure, this characterization may seem less apt for presidential inaugurations: if the man isn't "the president" while and immediately upon taking the oath of office, when in heaven's name *will* he be "the president"? It is an embarrassing question for the "no endorsement" doctrine. And yet it would be profoundly imprudent — wouldn't it? — for a court to prohibit practices and expressions that presidents have routinely engaged in since the republic began. Indeed, wouldn't it violate the free speech or free exercise rights of a man or a woman for a court to rule, in essence, that if they become president they will be constitutionally forbidden to pray or to invoke God — at least in public? Why not drag the "person/office" distinction into service here, however awkward the application? We can just say that *the person* may continue to invoke God, even if *the government* (and hence "the president") cannot?

And yet however necessary, the fiction that in these contexts it is not "the president" who is acting and speaking is still just that — an obvious fiction. Isn't it?

Or perhaps the judgment of fictionality could be avoided if we treated "the president" as nothing more than a sort of abstract Platonic office, and if we avoided anthropomorphizing the office by attributing to it human capacities, such as the capacity to intend, to speak, to decide, to declare. The problem is that doing this would render the office useless for the purposes for which it was created. We *need* the president to be able to issue orders, to stand before and speak to the nation in the State of the Union Address, to appoint and remove executive officials and judges and ambassadors, to direct the armed forces. These actions need to come from *the president*; it is not enough that they come from some *man*, like Donald Trump or Barack Obama or George Bush. And yet these are things that a Platonic, impersonal, pristine "office" just could not do.

In short, "the president" is an office, distinct from the man—and yet *not* distinct. The president-as-office is endowed with capacities that persons have and that abstract offices do not. As with "the king's two bodies," we need to and we do recognize both a person (George Bush, Barack Obama) and an office (the president), and we need to and we do treat these two things as distinguishable (for some purposes) and yet as one and the same. As two natures in one person—or would it be two persons in one nature? The composite is plainly a fiction, and a necessary one: we resort to it much in the way that the Elizabethan judges used the fiction of "the king's two bodies."

Consider another example. In the heavily contested case of *Hawaii v. Trump*,[91] an array of plaintiffs challenged President Donald Trump's executive order excluding persons from several mostly Muslim countries from immigrating to the United States. Although there were also complex statutory questions, the main point of contention among the justices concerned the allegation that the exclusion was based on animus or hostility toward Muslims, in violation of the declared constitutional requirement of religious neutrality. And in arguing against and for this claim, the majority and principal dissenting opinions respectively drew heavily, and just short of explicitly, on the distinction between Donald Trump the man and "the president."

Thus, the majority opinion by Chief Justice Roberts briefly acknowledged a number of statements or tweets made by Trump both before and after his election that might be taken as reflecting animosity toward Muslims. Nor did the majority deny that such statements could be viewed as evidence of animus—of animus, that is, on the part of *Donald Trump*.[92] But the majority downplayed the significance of such statements—statements made by Trump the man—with respect to the legality of "a Presidential directive." The case, the Court emphasized, concerned "the authority of the Presidency itself."[93]

In assessing the exercise of that authority, the majority vacillated somewhat about the proper standard of deference,[94] but behind the different articulations of this standard, the Court's assumption was plain enough: what mattered was not whether the man Donald Trump was biased against Islam, but instead whether *the Presidential directive* could be supported by legitimate national security concerns. If it could be, then the directive would stand as a proper exercise of the power of "the president"—notwithstanding the possibly less admirable motives of the man who happened to be serving as president. *Trump* may or may not have harbored hostility to Islam, but (and this was the crucial point) *the president* was acting to protect national security.[95]

Indeed, in the majority opinion Trump the man almost disappeared. Thus, the majority referred over and over again to "the President," while using the name "Trump" only twice (except when citing case names), and never once making reference to "Donald Trump."

By contrast, the principal dissent, by Justice Sotomayor, in addition to giving a much more extensive recitation of the evidence of animus, honed in on Trump the man. In describing preelection conduct and statements, the dissent over and over referred to "Donald Trump" or just to "Trump." ("Trump justified . . ."; "Trump told . . ."; "Trump told an apocryphal story . . .": "Trump reiterated . . .").[96] With respect to postinauguration developments, the dissent referred repeatedly not to "the President" (as the majority did), but rather to "President Trump."[97] And the dissent made clear that "President Trump" was the same man as the preelection, nonpresidential "Trump." Thus, the dissent emphasized that "President Trump has never disavowed any of his prior [preelection] statements."[98]

In sum, like the Elizabethan-era precedents, the case essentially came down to which of "the president's two bodies" the justices chose to focus on. The majority concerned itself with the body politic, or with "the president," and found that the president's actions were not tainted by the possibly ignoble motives of the man who happened to be occupying the office when the executive order was issued. As the common lawyers might have put it, the presidency "reduce[d], or even remove[d], the imperfections of the fragile human nature" of the man, Donald Trump. The dissent, by contrast, focused on "Trump" and concluded that the bad character and motives ascribed to the man invalidated his directive.

In both the immigration case and the "no endorsement" controversies, in short, actions or statements have been upheld by abstracting "the president" away from the person holding that office. In the endorsement context, it is ostensibly *the man* (who happens to be president) who invokes the blessings of God on the nation. Consequently, it is not *the government* that is endorsing religion. In the context of the exclusion order, by contrast, it was *the president* who acted and whose directive was not to be rendered illegitimate by the "Defects and Imbecilities" (as the common lawyers put it) of the man who happened to be sitting in the presidential chair.

Beyond such specific uses, however, the fiction of "the president" is also useful and perhaps necessary in a more elusive and general sense. Put simply and bluntly: the weight and responsibility and dignity of "the president" are probably more than any mere mortal could shoulder. (At least since the passing of George Washington.[99]) "Every man at his best state is altogether vanity," we are told;[100] and how could such consummate vanity ever command the respect and authority needed to govern a vast nation of people?

Pause for a moment, and just imagine entrusting the sweeping scope of presidential authority to . . . Donald Trump. To the erratic, mendacious, ignorant, petty, narcissistic, delusional, often quite buffoonish figure of the man known as "Donald Trump." Or, for those of a different political persuasion, to the pompous, smug, shallow, and similarly mendacious figure of the man known as "Barack Obama." Or to the rustically charming but prevaricating and lecherous Bill Clinton. Or to Tricky Dick ("I am not a crook") Nixon. Or to the ruthless, exquisitely vulgar LBJ—he of the flabby handshake.

To most of us, at least one of these prospects will seem almost intolerable: to many of us, *all* of them will seem unacceptable. Seriously: Who would willingly consent to turn over the responsibility for important aspects of his or her life and fate to the likes of such men, who are "altogether vanity"? And yet what choice do we have? The military is not going to command itself; foreign policy has to be conducted by *someone*. So, how are we to reconcile ourselves to this humiliating necessity?

To sum up: We need to entrust the vast arsenal of presidential powers and authority to someone or something more worthy and dignified than these . . . men—these flawed, fallible, profoundly finite mortals. We need to entrust authority to something more august and lofty. To "the president." And so that is what we do. Unfortunately, the presidency just by itself is utterly inert. It needs to be rendered operational by some actual person. And so, with trepidation, we appoint Donald Trump or Barack Obama to perform that role. For a time, Donald Trump or Barack Obama will act the part of president. But make no mistake: neither Donald Trump nor Barack Obama is equivalent to "the president." The two are the same, yes, but they are also *not* the same.

The president, like the king, has and needs to have two bodies. And one of those bodies—the one in which "dwell . . . certain truly mysterious forces which reduce, or even remove, the imperfections of the fragile human nature," along with the composite two-in-one body—is a fiction. A fiction that we could scarcely do without.

THE CONCEALED BUT MANIFEST QUALITY OF THE FICTIONS OF AUTHORITY

Our discussion in this chapter has suggested that the principal institutions of our national government—Congress, the Supreme Court, the president—all have a quasi-fictional character. It should be easy enough, for anyone so inclined, to extend this analysis to other governmental institutions—state legislatures or judiciaries, for example. To Boyd and Gary and their associates. So, should this characterization be viewed as shocking and subversive? Or does it merely state the obvious—what everyone already knows and takes for granted?

The answer, it seems—to both questions—is yes. And no. As we discussed in chapter 1, fictions are pervasive in our lives; they serve a variety of valuable functions. And fictions work by inducing us, for a reward, to suspend disbelief—to step into the fictional frame by deliberately declining to notice what we perfectly well know when we are outside of the fiction. They depend, as we said, on a sort of conspiracy between the author or purveyor of the fiction and the audience or participants. While inside the fiction, so to speak, we induce ourselves to believe that what we are being told or shown is true. We treat it *as if* it were true. But then we step outside the fiction, and we are fully aware that what was presented was not *really* true, as we might put it.

Suppose you go with a friend to the movie theater to watch a showing of *Star Wars*. Your friend will consider you boorish if, during the movie, you keeping leaning over and whispering, "This didn't really happen, you know," or "Einstein's theory proves that this sort of intergalactic travel isn't really possible." Conversely, as you enjoy a snack afterward, if you now say, "None of that really happened," your friend will be surprised, maybe even insulted. ("Do you think I'm an idiot?") In short, what is assumed to be true in one frame is perfectly understood to be *not* true in a different frame.

Our fictions of legal authority might seem to be different in this respect. We sit through a movie for two hours and then we leave the theater; but we do not leave the domain of legal authority. Our whole lives are lived within, governed by, that frame. There is no "fictional frame" that we enter and then step out of.

Or maybe there is. At least in reflection, can't we set aside the frame of authoritative fictions? Imagine ourselves in a "state of nature" or "original position" or some such condition? And aren't commitments to things like freedom of conscience or institutional religious freedom—and maybe other rights as well, like the right to privacy—acknowledgments that we recognize and preserve spaces outside the framework of the government's authority?

Or we might try to express the complicated character of a fiction not in temporal terms (*during* the movie and *after* the movie) or spatial terms (*inside* and *outside* the fiction) but rather in terms of cognitive "levels." Even while watching a movie in the theater, we are at one level perfectly aware that what we are seeing is not "actually true," as we might say. Were it not for this awareness, our reactions would be quite different. If outside the movie theater someone deliberately "scared us to death," as we say, we would be outraged; we might sue them for infliction of emotional distress. And yet we pay good money to go to a horror movie, and we complain if the movie is not sufficiently frightening. And when a beloved character in a movie or a novel is killed, we feel a deep and delicious sorrow, but we do not dissolve into stunned and inconsolable sobbing as we would if a real friend were killed. With a fiction, in short, we know all along, at some level, that what we are witnessing is not "really true." And yet at another level, we suspend this awareness in order to enjoy or engage with the fiction.

In a similar way, much of our lives occurs under the auspices of legal authority; but even here there are indications that at some level we are cognizant of the quasi-fictional character of that authority or of the fact that we are participating in a necessary conspiracy of suspending disbelief. Justice Antonin Scalia was perhaps the leading modern proponent of the idea that courts are not supposed to *make* law—that a court's function is merely to *declare* what the law is. And yet, perhaps in a moment of careless candor, Scalia once observed, "I am not so naive (nor do I think our forebears were) as to be unaware that judges in a real sense 'make' law." And then he quickly added: "But they make it *as judges make it*, which is to say *as though* they were 'finding' it—or discerning what the law *is*."[101]

Scalia's comment was offered in criticism of legal realists who question the objective character of law. But notice carefully: Scalia did not assert that the realists were incorrect. He suggested, rather, that they were misbehaving in exposing and thus disrupting the conspiracy on which law is based. He was chastising the realists for spoiling the fiction.[102]

Consider another piece of evidence. It is routine to make a distinction between *persons* and *offices*. We noticed this distinction in our discussion of the president. But the distinction is familiar in other contexts as well. Take Congress and statutes. Don't we describe these laws, at least when we are being careful, as the product *not* of, say, (Congresswoman) Sally Bloke and her colleagues, but rather of *Congress*? Of a governmental entity that we recognize as not quite identical to the imposing or bumbling mortals who inhabit it?

And as long as we are talking again about statutes, we might notice the common use of "canons of construction" that are routinely employed in assigning meaning to statutes. In recent years, the role and significance of such canons has been much discussed;[103] and modern judges are said to make frequent use of such canons.[104] But just barely below the surface, these canons implicitly trade on the notion of a quasi-fictional legislature.[105]

One familiar canon holds, for instance, that a statute should be construed so as to avoid rendering any part of it superfluous.[106] This canon is not just some arbitrary imposition; it has a certain plausibility because it might seem that a careful speaker would avoid repeating himself or herself: most of us have been reproved at some point or other by a writing instructor or a speech teacher for being "redundant." Redundancy, we are thus taught, is a vice to be avoided. And so it might seem that careful legislators would likewise avoid repeating themselves. So if the legislators enacted language that seems on its face to say the same thing in two places, we should nonetheless infer that the legislators meant the second iteration to mean something different from the first. So instructs the canon.

In reality, of course, we human beings are constantly repeating ourselves. (You may have detected such repetition in this very chapter.) Human legislators might do the same thing—out of carelessness, perhaps, or to be sure they have made themselves clear, just as the rest of us do. The canon against superfluity thus instructs interpreters to treat the legislature *as if* it were communicating carefully and economically even if the actual legislators may not have been doing any such thing.[107] The canon instructs interpreters, in other words, to imagine a legislature that is different—more careful, more frugal, more thoughtful—than the collection of actual, human legislators.

In this vein, Abbe Gluck observes that "[s]ome interpretive tools assume Congress is omniscient [and] that statutes are drafted well."[108]

But of course Congress—or at least the visible, human Congress—is not *really* omniscient, and many statutes are *not* drafted well. So interpretation that rests on the assumption of such a legislature is appealing to a Congress that is imaginary. Quasi-fictional.

This sort of fictionalization is routinely assumed in our canons of construction, and in our distinctions between "person" and "office." There seems nothing especially radical or shocking in pointing out this assumption. And yet we do not go around saying or thinking, "Congress is a fiction. So is the Supreme Court—and the president. None of them is entirely real." And it is understandable that we do not often say these things. To do so would risk undermining the fictions—like leaning over to your friend during the movie and saying, "None of this stuff really happened."

Nothing in our discussion, in this chapter or the last one, should be taken as a condemnation of this intricate practice. On the contrary. We *need* authority; we need it, as discussed in chapter 1, to maintain order and to coordinate human interactions. And at least for here and now, the only kind of authority we can have, it seems, is fictional—or quasi-fictional.

Still, there are costs to the pretense—and risks. One cost, perhaps, is the endless, irresolvable contentions about the meaning of constitutional and statutory provisions—debates that proceed on the implicit but mistaken assumption that there is some truth of the matter about what is at bottom a fiction. Or perhaps this contention is not a cost after all. Perhaps it is useful or even necessary to the maintenance of a beneficial fiction. Perhaps it contributes to improving or perfecting that fiction—to making our laws more just or wise than they would otherwise be. Who can say? It is a possibility.

There is also a risk that discourse within the framework of an overarching fiction could degenerate into something less worthy. Into lies. As we discussed in chapter 1, a fiction is not the same as an outright falsehood. And yet the line that separates them can be an elusive one. A fiction, though not exactly a lie, might degenerate into one. A fictional framework of authority might deteriorate into a culture of, as Vaclav Havel put it, "living with lies." We will consider an instance—an egregious instance—of such degeneration in the following chapter.

CHAPTER FOUR

From Political Fictions to "Living with Lies"

Our reflection has suggested that in the American political system, and probably also in other liberal democracies, the authority of government and hence the authority of law is grounded in a fiction, or rather in a family of fictions. This depiction may be mildly embarrassing—because, as Edmund Morgan observed, "it is a little uncomfortable to acknowledge that we rely so heavily on fictions"[1]— but the picture has nonetheless been by-and-large a cheerful one. Fictions are not the same thing as lies, we have said. If not exactly true in a factual sense, viable fictions need to be at least "truish." And they serve to support something we need—coordinating authority. In addition, our particular fictions are mostly attractive and flattering ones: we suppose that we have freely consented to the government's authority over us, that our president and Congress and Supreme Court are more reflective and unified and virtuous than the hard tangible evidence would suggest they actually are. Moreover, at some level we are aware that our fictions are less than factual: so it is not as if we are being total dupes.

In short, we are willingly cooperating in a set of uplifting fictions that work to our benefit. Nothing much to worry about in that, surely!

It has probably been evident all along that a darker depiction would have been possible. Our situation might have been portrayed as one in which an elite class lords it over the rest of us through the systematic practice of deception, or the systematic inculcation of self-deception. Our masters foist on us falsehoods (put forward, ironically, as "self-evident truths") and compel or induce us to believe those falsehoods as a basis for subjecting us to their rule. Even since the writing of this book began, this kind of darker narrative has seemingly become more widespread, with the *New York Times*'s so-called 1619 project[2] and the outrage currently being expressed in reaction to the killing by a police officer of an African-American citizen in Minneapolis.

This darker depiction may or may not be unfair:[3] whether we think so will no doubt depend in part on how fortunate our particular situation is and what we think the alternatives might be. But whichever depiction seems more apt for our own situation—the benign one or the darker one—we can at least *imagine* a regime in which a more grim depiction fits. If you have any trouble conjuring up such a vision, just go back and reread George Orwell's *1984*.

Nor do we need to imagine, or to read dystopian novels, in order to contemplate a legal order in which exhilarating fictions have degenerated into pernicious, degrading lies. To mention just one instance: such a system prevailed in Central and Eastern Europe during much of the twentieth century. The political fictions on which that system was founded were different from ours: they did not look backward to a social contract manifesting the "consent of the governed," but rather forward to a future in which the Party would lead humanity, through revolution, into the classless society—a society in which want and inequality would disappear. The chilling results of this family of fictions were well described for us by some gifted writers and thinkers: Aleksandr Solzhenitsyn, Vaclav Havel, and others (including Hannah Arendt, whose observations about authority and its disappearance prompted our inquiry).

In this chapter, we consider this darker scenario by turning from the liberal democratic West to Eastern Europe of the past century for a sobering look at the consequences of exhilarating political fictions that have deteriorated into oppressive lies. At the end of the chapter we will return to ask how and why—and whether—our own political and legal fictions have turned out to be more benign than the Marxist fictions (or "ideologies," as we often call them) were.

"A Thick Crust of Lies"

Writing in the 1970s,[4] Vaclav Havel, the Czech dissident, playwright, and later president, described how a Marxist government, in order to maintain its authority, forced subjects to endorse, support, or acquiesce in slogans, claims, and propositions that the subjects did not believe. Life under such a regime, in Havel's perception, became a demoralizing and dehumanizing nightmare of mendacity, duplicity, and self-delusion.

By this period, Havel reports, European Communism lacked both the fervor and the ferocity of its earlier, revolutionary stage. The horrors so powerfully described by Aleksandr Solzhenitsyn[5] and, from a greater distance, by Hannah Arendt[6]—the wave after wave of often purely arbitrary arrests, exiles, and assassinations; the imaginatively savage methods of torture; the brutality of the concentration camps—were no longer a familiar part of Czech experience. "[W]hat are people afraid of?," Havel asks. "Trials? Torture? Loss of property? Deportations? Executions?" And he answers: "Certainly not. The most brutal forms of pressure exerted by the authorities upon the public are, fortunately, past history—at least in our circumstances."[7]

And yet, he asserts, the authorities continue to oppress in "more subtle and choice forms." They have constructed a "system of existential pressure."[8]

And what would a "system of existential pressure" be, exactly? As an illustration, Havel imagines a greengrocer who puts up a sign in the window of his shop proclaiming "Workers of the world, unite!"[9] There may have been a time when, for some people, the slogan would have expressed a heartfelt revolutionary imperative, and perhaps also an inspiring prophecy arising from Marxist dialectical materialism. But the days and the decades have passed: the prophecies have not been fulfilled, and the imperative has lost its plausibility. By now, by the 1970s, Havel suggests, it is unlikely that the shopkeeper believes, cares about, or has even given any serious thought to the message conveyed by the slogan.

So then why does the shopkeeper display the sign, which was probably supplied to him from Party headquarters "along with the onions and carrots"?[10] Havel suggests that although the grocer is probably not committed to "Workers of the world, unite!" taken either as an imperative or as a prediction, the words nonetheless convey a "subliminal but very definite" message, which goes like this: "I, the greengrocer XY, live here and I know what I must do. I behave in the manner expected of me. I can be depended upon and am beyond reproach. I am obedient and therefore I have the right to be left in peace."[11]

In short, the grocer indicates his support for the prevailing regime, or at least his acquiescence and conformity, not merely by paying his taxes or voting as he is instructed to vote — though he probably does those things too — but by assenting to the regime's legitimating creed or ideology. He manifests his acquiescence indirectly, by putting up the sign, not in explicit affirmations (which in fact he would be "embarrassed and ashamed" to make).[12]

The grocer offers this barely disguised assent *not* because he sincerely believes the creed but because he wants the authorities to leave him alone. And he knows that if in a rash display of integrity or courage he were to remove the sign, consequences would follow. In the 1970s, it is no longer likely that he would be arrested or sent off to a concentration camp or shot in the back of the head while walking down an empty street. Once again, those days of Communist rigor are in the past. But the grocer's request for a vacation in Bulgaria might be denied. He might be reassigned to a less pleasant place of work. His children might not be admitted to the university.[13] Better just to go along by putting up the sign.

And of course the sign in the window is only one form of tacit assent that the grocer and his fellow citizens are expected to give. Opportunities to indicate one's support (or, if one is careless, to betray one's reservations) are ubiquitous. "[E]very day," Havel observes, "a man . . . solemnly performs ritual acts which he privately finds ridiculous, . . . he unhesitatingly gives answers to questionnaires which are contrary to his real opinions and he is prepared to deny his own self in public. . . . [H]e sees no difficulty in feigning sympathy or even affection where, in fact, he feels only indifference or aversion."[14]

Citizens do all of these things for basically the same reasons that the grocer displays the sign in the window—for reasons of "selfishness and careerism."[15] Or it might be said that citizens act out of "fear"—but, again, not the fear of being arrested, tortured, or imprisoned. "Many of those we see around us are not quaking like aspen leaves: they wear faces of confident, self-satisfied citizens," Havel acknowledges. "We are concerned with fear in a deeper sense."[16]

In what deeper sense? Havel explains:

> For fear of losing his job, the schoolteacher teaches things he does not believe; fearing for his future, the pupil recites them after him. . . . [I]t is fear that carries [people] through sundry humiliating acts of self-criticism and penitence and the dishonest filling out of a mass of degrading questionnaires. . . . Fear of being prevented from continuing their work leads many scientists and artists to give allegiance to ideas they do not in fact accept, to write things they do not agree with or know to be false, to join official organizations or to take part in work of whose value they have the lowest opinion, or to distort and mutilate their own works.[17]

All of this dishonesty or disingenuousness, not so much legally compelled as performed under the weight of "existential pressure," adds up to a way of life that is filled with falsity. To a life that consists of "living with lies."[18] "[L]ife in the system is . . . thoroughly permeated with hypocrisy and lies,"[19] Havel reports. "[A]ll genuine problems and matters of critical importance are hidden beneath a thick crust of lies."[20] Quietly quotidian mendacity and inauthenticity constitute a "hideous spider whose invisible web runs through the whole of society."[21]

Nor is this pervasive mendacity a merely irritating or unseemly feature of life in a late Communist society—annoying, but ultimately not very consequential. Not in Havel's view, anyway. On the contrary, the practice leads to "demoralization" and a "profound crisis of human identity"[22]—to "the complete degradation of the individual."[23] Living within a system of lies produces "paralysis of the spirit, a deadening of the heart, and devaluation of life."[24] The system effectuates a "brutal castration of the humanity of men."[25] Indeed, Havel goes even farther—a regime grounded in and promoting such lies acts on a sort of "death principle." "There is an odour of death even in the 'order' which such an authority puts into practice."[26]

An Excessive Diagnosis?

At this point, though, a critic might complain that Havel is becoming just a bit overwrought. We can imagine that his diagnosis might well be resisted, or flatly and forcefully rejected, not just by the government or the Party that Havel was criticizing but even by many or most of the citizens whom he purported to speak for. Aversion to cognitive dissonance, if nothing else, would presumably lead many or most of Havel's fellow citizens to deny that they are engaged in routine dishonesty. Who is he, after all, to tell them that they do not actually believe many of the things they say or assent to?

Or suppose there *are* numerous small acts or expressions that are less than sincere. Is it really plausible to suppose that such milquetoast dishonesty has the catastrophic consequences that Havel ascribes to it—that it constitutes a "brutal castration" of the citizens' humanity and carries with it an "odour of death"?

Havel's greengrocer might well be among the unpersuaded. Suppose we slip into the grocer's shop during a slow moment—we check carefully to be sure there is no one else around, no police or Party members or eavesdropping customers—and after chatting for a while to gain his confidence, we ask what the grocer thinks of Havel's indictment. What will he say?

"You need to understand," the grocer might tell us. "This man Havel may be a great figure—I don't deny it—but he is an intellectual, an artist, a playwright. He isn't like me, doesn't really understand ordinary people like me.

"So he makes a great fuss about this little sign I put up—'Workers of the world, unite!' It's ridiculous. True, I put the sign up because the Party wants me to. I know that; I admit it. So what? What's the harm? I'm not telling any lies. It would be wonderful—wouldn't it?—if the workers of the world *would* unite. It's probably not going to happen—I know this; I wasn't born yesterday—but still, it would be nice if they did. Am I saying any more than that? How am I being dishonest?

"And in any case, the sign is no big deal. Or the questionnaires either, for that matter, or the other trivial little things this man Havel gets so exercised about. If you really want to know what is a problem for me—a real problem—it's some of these regulations restricting how I can run my business and what profits I'm allowed to keep. That's what *I* care about. Not some silly sign or questionnaire."

And so we need to ask. Was Havel correct in suggesting that the system and its subjects—including the grocer—were being pervasively dishonest? And even if they were, did Havel exaggerate the consequences of such dishonesty for ordinary human beings?

Is the Grocer Lying?

We might start by asking about the accuracy of Havel's diagnosis. When the grocer puts up a sign proclaiming "Workers of the world, unite!," is he being dishonest? Without any close examination, Havel assumes so. But the question turns out to be more complicated than it might initially seem, or than Havel's treatment suggests.

Taken strictly at face value, one might argue, the slogan written on the grocer's sign is not making any claim or assertion at all; it is rather an imperative or command. "Hey there, all of you workers of the world: I hereby order you to unite!" Or perhaps a request: "I *implore* you to unite. *Please*, unite!" A command, however, can be obeyed or disobeyed; it is not the sort of sentence that can be true or false. (The point is made obliquely and humorously in Ring Lardner's "'Shut up,' he explained.") A request, similarly, can be granted or refused: again, it is not the sort of utterance that is true or false. So the grocer might argue that his sign is incapable of being false, and he therefore cannot be dishonest in putting it up.

This initial defense is too facile, though. In context, the sign cannot plausibly be taken as expressing an actual imperative: for one thing, the grocer neither has nor pretends to have the slightest power to issue any such command. Nor is he realistically making any sort of actual request or plea; he knows perfectly well that very few among the "workers of the world" will see his sign, and even fewer will pay any attention. So we need to ask what the sign actually means, performatively, in context. And yet if we do that, a different difficulty seems to arise.

Thus, Havel himself tells us that what the sign *really* means in this context is, basically: "I, the grocer, will follow the directives of the regime; I won't resist or make trouble." That is how both the grocer himself and people who see the sign, including the government's officials, will understand it. But on that interpretation, isn't Havel contradicting himself? Because in fact the grocer *does* intend to follow the regime's directives and to avoid making trouble. And so it seems that the sign is truthful in its de facto meaning—self-corroborating, almost—and the grocer is again off the hook: contrary to Havel's accusation, he is not lying.

And yet this exonerating conclusion still seems too hasty. Let us concede that what the government actually wants is for the grocer in effect to affirm: "I will obey the government and will follow directives." So then why not ask him to say *that*, in plain English—or rather in plain Czech? Or suppose that the grocer understands that what he is communicating is that he will follow orders. Again, why doesn't he say as much, directly and explicitly?

Havel gives the reason: the grocer would be "embarrassed and ashamed" forthrightly to declare his subservience to the government.[27] Perhaps he would even refuse to do this, would find ways to equivocate or to avoid making any explicit affirmation. For its part, the regime understands that the grocer and his neighbors would be reluctant, and might even refuse, to make this forthright declaration of submission. And so the regime allows the grocer and other citizens to indicate their support without quite admitting to themselves what they are doing. They can manifest assent (for practical purposes) without explicitly affirming (thereby avoiding outright embarrassment or shame).

For this exercise to work, of course, it is necessary that both the regime and the citizens understand, at some level, what is going on. And they do understand, at least implicitly.

So then, should we regard this sort of nonaffirming or disguised assent as . . . honest? Or mendacious? The whole exercise involves an expressive version of what George Orwell famously called "doublethink." In "doublethink," one believes and disbelieves a proposition at the same time, or perhaps switches back and forth between belief and disbelief in such rapid succession that opposite creedal states are in effect held simultaneously.[28] In parallel fashion, the greengrocer and his neighbors are manifesting their support for the regime—and they know, and the regime knows, that they are doing this—but they are assenting in a sort of code that allows them at the same time to pretend to themselves that they are *not* affirming something they would be "embarrassed and ashamed" openly to affirm. If not flatly and overtly dishonest, this exercise seems at least deceptive, and self-deceptive.

And then we can ask: How exactly does the placing of a sign saying "Workers of the world, unite!" function to convey this nonaffirming assent? The underlying reality, of course, is that the government asserts, and expects subjects to accept, its legitimacy, or its right to rule. Its authority. And the government's authority is inherently grounded in Marxist ideology[29]—for which the slogan "Workers of the world, unite!" is a kind of effective symbol or synecdoche. By the 1970s, however, it is difficult or impossible for anyone to believe that ideology in any very sincere or earnest way: its predictions and promises have painfully failed realization. So it seems that the elaborated message of the sign, in the Czechoslovakia of the 1970s, would go something like this: "I, the grocer, am indicating that I will sustain the existing regime and obey its orders. I am indicating this by appearing to express my support for the Marxist ideology from which the regime purports to derive its legitimacy . . . although in fact I do not *actually* believe or support that Marxist ideology, and although I understand that the government and its officials do not *actually* believe that ideology either." In this rendition, it seems, both the grocer and the government are implicated in a deep and complex duplicity.

Moreover, the expectation that the grocer will display the sign makes this duplicity virtually impossible to avoid. Genuine honesty becomes an almost unattainable virtue. Suppose, for example, that the grocer happens to be one of those rare citizens who are somehow impervious to disillusionment and who have accordingly retained the revolutionary faith of former days. He really *does* believe in the Marxist vision; he yearns for the workers of the world to unite and thereby to bring about the end of class division and private property. Even so, the grocer will understand that in this context, putting up the sign at the Party's insistence does both less and more than affirm this belief.

It does less because most people who see the sign will suppose, incorrectly in this atypical case, that the grocer has simply conformed to Party pressure; they will not take the sign as expressing any sincere conviction. How is the grocer to make his real meaning clear? Should he scrawl in just below "Workers of the world unite!" something like "*And I really mean it!*"? The sign also does more than affirm the grocer's support for *Marxism*; it will be taken as expressing his support for *the present government*. And it offers that support on the premise that the government is genuinely committed to the Marxist ideology. This is a premise that, unless he is seriously deluded, the grocer will know to be largely false: *he* may still believe in the Marxist vision, but he knows that government does not.

And so even the sincerely Marxist grocer is engaging in deception or misrepresentation. Or, as Havel would say, he is lying. And he is lying not in a trivial matter ("Well, Mrs. Brown, since you ask, I think your new hat is ... lovely!"), but rather with respect to the foundations of the political and social order. Moreover, given the climate of mendacity that prevails, it will be difficult for the grocer to avoid such misrepresentation, because it is simply not feasible for people to add "And I *really mean* this, and nothing more than this" to all of their sincere statements. And even if that practice did become commonplace, it would soon become self-defeating, because presumably people would just start routinely adding that sort of verbal confirmation to their statements—*not* to add it would be a tacit admission of insincerity—and the confirmation would become just as conventionalized and inauthentic as the unconfirmed statements were.

Or perhaps we are being too severe on the hapless grocer? Suppose the grocer—the one who is still a true believer—explains: "Although I understand that my neighbors and the government itself will take the sign in my window to be expressing support for the present unworthy government, that's not what *I* mean by it: *I* mean what the sign explicitly signifies and symbolizes. I'm declaring my commitment to Marxism, in other words—no more and no less. If other people take the sign to mean more than that, it isn't my fault; that's *their* problem."

Let us be charitable, taking the grocer at his word and giving him whatever theory of linguistic meaning is implicit in his defense. In that case, we might amend the charge. Now, it seems, the grocer is not exactly "lying." He is merely . . . knowingly misleading the government and his neighbors. Whether or not he wants to mislead them, that is what he *is* doing—and can hardly help doing. Is there any real practical difference between lying to people and knowingly misleading them?

We might also consider the citizen who consciously thinks (or at least tells herself) that she *does* believe many or most of the things she is expected to affirm, but who is also reflective and self-critical and acquainted with the phenomenon of cognitive dissonance. This citizen might come to have doubts about her own honesty, and indeed about what her real beliefs actually are. "I *think* I believe the things the government asks me to affirm," she might tell herself. "Those things *seem* right. But then again, I don't have much choice, do I? I would have to affirm those things even if I didn't believe them, . . . which would put me in an uncomfortable position, . . . which I would likely try to avoid by convincing myself that I really do believe. Is that what is happening to me? How can I be sure that I *really* believe the things I'm required to do and say?"

The bottom line is that the regime must assert and maintain its authority—that is one essential thing political regimes do—and this authority is inextricably grounded in an ideology that for most people is no longer believable. Consequently, the government must assert, and must expect citizens to assent to, what neither it nor they can any longer fully and truly believe. It achieves this result by developing a whole network of equivocal practices and of multiple or indirect meanings—ways of allowing itself and its subjects to affirm while maintaining a kind of "plausible deniability."

It is hard under this regime to say that any particular affirmation is simply and flatly a lie in the straightforward sense in which a little boy tells a lie when he insists to his mother that it was his sister who broke the cookie jar, even though he knows perfectly well that he was the culprit. But this shadowy, duplicitous realm of untruths and half-truths and equivocations and deceptive "subliminal" meanings—this "whole mendacious structure,"[30] as Havel put it—is perhaps even more inimical to genuine truth-telling, or to "living in truth," than a simpler "either true or false" approach would be. The very notions of truth and falsity begin to slip away, to lose their sense.

Hannah Arendt suggested that totalitarian regimes in fact cultivated precisely this sense of alienation from both truth and falsehood. "The ideal subject of totalitarian rule is not the convinced Nazi or the convinced Communist," she argued, "but people for whom the distinction between fact and fiction (i.e., the reality of experience) and the distinction between true and false (i.e., the standards of thought) no longer exist."[31] Ironically, the more numerous and obvious the government's lies are, the more receptive subjects become, not because they take the lies to be true in any robust sense, but because truth and falsity are notions that no longer seem meaningful or relevant: it is "easier to accept absurd propositions . . . because nobody could be expected to take the absurdities seriously."[32] In such a system, "the difference between truth and falsehood may cease to be objective and become a mere matter of power and cleverness, of pressure and infinite repetition."[33] And hence a "mixture of gullibility and cynicism is prevalent in all ranks of totalitarian movements."[34]

And of course, as Havel explained, central to this deluge of propositions that everyone gullibly purports to accept but no one any longer takes seriously is an "imposing facade of great humanistic ideals" made up of "bombastic slogans about the unprecedented increase in every sort of freedom."³⁵ And thus the noblest human ideals come to elicit not reverence or commitment (or, for that matter, forthright rejection), but rather cynicism.

FALSITY AND DEHUMANIZATION

So it seems that, once we cut through complications, Havel's characterization of the Communist regime as one in which subjects are compelled to "live in lies" does capture a fundamental feature of the regime. No one could regard this feature—this pervasive mendacity—as praiseworthy or desirable. Even so, does it deserve the harsh, overwhelming condemnation that Havel heaped on it? Aren't there violations of human rights that would be far more oppressive—the arrest, torture, and execution of innocent citizens, for example, along with their spouses, parents, and children? One can imagine a cynically candid regime that engages in such practices and makes no effort to hide or lie about them. Wouldn't that brutally honest, honestly brutal regime be far worse than one that prevaricates and that pressures people to put up disingenuously idealistic signs in their shop windows?

The answer to that question will come in two parts. The first part takes note of a kind of philosophical anthropology—an understanding of what it is to be a human being—that is implicit in Havel's criticism. Havel implies that to be human is to stand in a certain relation to truth—to seek to know truth, affirm it, and live in accordance with it. There is, he asserts, a "human disposition to truth." Living in accordance with this disposition is essential to "authentic existence."³⁶

This disposition, he might argue, is distinctive to human beings among the animals, and is the basis of what we call "human dignity." Thus, we share with other animals the need for nourishment—for the greengrocer's onions and carrots—and for other physical necessities or satisfactions like warmth, safety, and companionship. In seeking to satisfy these needs and desires, we share as well with other animals a necessary orientation to *reality*. Neither the cat that cannot distinguish between a dog and a mouse nor the peasant who tries to plant his carrots in October will fare well in the world. But beyond these shared qualities is another feature exhibited only by humans among the animals (because we are not talking here about angels or gods). Only human beings consciously seek to understand and express reality in *truth*. Only humans try to articulate truth, formulate it in philosophies and theories and creeds, attempt to live in accordance with it. It is this "disposition to truth" that is our species' distinctive essence and glory.[37] And also our distinctive shame or degradation—when we dissemble support for things we do not believe to be true.

This truth-oriented anthropology is contestable, to be sure.[38] But it is broadly consistent both with classical philosophy and with classical religion, as well as with some more modern conceptions. Man, said the older philosophers, is the "rational animal"—rationality being the faculty for discerning and following truth. "Ye shall know the truth," commanded the Gospel, "and the truth shall make you free."[39] Or, as Thomas Aquinas put it, "[t]he ultimate end of the universe must . . . be the good of an intellect. This good is truth. Truth must consequently be the ultimate end of the whole universe, and the consideration of the wise man aims principally at truth."[40] To be sure, it might be more natural in a religious context to say that the destiny of human beings is to contemplate and commune with God. But then, in Aquinas's explanation, God and truth are basically one and the same.[41]

The modern secular scientist or philosopher might find much to disagree with in these ancient dicta. And yet he or she would likely concur on the necessity and nobility of the human quest for scientific and philosophical truth.

Indeed, the totalitarian regimes themselves arguably understood and accepted the centrality of truth at the essence of humanity. This fact would help to explain otherwise puzzling features of their administrations in which governments showed a perverse respect for truth even as they tortured and distorted it. For example, the Soviet government famously went to great lengths to force or induce the people it persecuted to make public confessions of its righteousness and of their own spectacular crimes and betrayals—even when these confessions were not and could not possibly have been correct. Leszek Kolakowski, the Polish philosopher and historian of Marxism, reports that "the police insisted on people signing their own confessions, and as far as is known they did not forge signatures." The police did this, using torture to procure the confessions, even though "both the torturers and their victims knew perfectly well that the information was false."[42] The spectacular "show trials" of the 1930s, memorably presented in Arthur Koestler's *Darkness at Noon*, were a dramatic instance of this compulsion to obtain and proclaim such (false) confessions.

But *why* did the government expend the considerable resources required to extract such confessions when it could much more easily have simply issued false reports of the subjects' guilt or, more efficient still, have quietly sent such people off to imprisonment or execution without public comment? Kolakowski explains that the Soviets understood that total power had to include power over truth. If humans are essentially oriented to truth, then a government with complete power would need to have such power over truth itself. Consequently, it was not enough that the government be able to control its subjects' bodies; the government needed to control *the truth*. So although everyone "knew perfectly well that the information was false," the authorities nonetheless "insisted on the fiction, as in this way everyone helped to build an unreal ideological world, in which universal fiction took on the guise of truth."[43]

Moreover, the authorities took special care to eliminate all of the old Bolsheviks who had helped to achieve the revolution, along with anyone else who appeared actually to believe, sincerely, in Marxism. This may seem paradoxical, Kolakowski acknowledges, but in fact the policy was perfectly logical. Someone who genuinely believed in Marxism accepted a supposed truth that was independent of the Party. Such a truth might be used to judge actions taken by the Party. And so the sincere Marxist was a potential threat to the Party's power over truth and needed to be eliminated.[44]

In *1984*, George Orwell powerfully captured this dimension of totalitarian society. Attempting to resist the regime of Big Brother, the protagonist Winston Smith writes in his journal that "freedom is the freedom to say that 2 plus 2 make 4. If that is granted, all else follows."[45] Understanding the point, the Party is determined to extinguish this freedom. Its leader and representative, O'Brien, accordingly mixes torture and sophistical reasoning in order to bring Winston to the point of affirming that 2 plus 2 is 5—at least if that is what the Party dictates. Indeed, it is not enough for Winston to *say* that 2 plus 2 is 5; he needs to, and ultimately does, actually *believe* that 2 plus 2 is 5 (at least to the extent that he is still capable of actual belief at all).[46]

But if the essential feature of humanity, or of "human dignity," is a relation to truth, then it follows that a government that forces human beings on a pervasive and daily basis to "live with lies" has not merely injured them; it has deprived them of that feature that constitutes their distinctive humanity. The government seeks—and, insofar as it is successful, achieves—a "permanent humiliation of their human dignity,"[47] Havel declares. The system "draws everyone into its sphere of power, not so they may realize themselves as human beings, but so they may surrender their human identity in favour of the identity of the system that is, so they may become agents of the system's general automatism."[48]

To be sure, the overall goal (or at least the ostensible goal) was to mold human beings into components of a system in which human needs for food, clothing, shelter, and fulfillment could be satisfied more efficiently and equitably than was possible under more modest and complacent governments. That goal was notoriously not achieved under Communist regimes. Quite the contrary: millions of people starved, and millions more stood in long lines on a daily basis in order to obtain the basic necessities of life. And these failures necessitated further dishonesty. Leszek Kolakowski reports that outputs under Stalin's economic plans "were sometimes half, a quarter, or an eighth of what they were supposed to be. The cure for this was to arrest and shoot statisticians and falsify their findings. In 1928–30, Stalin closed down almost all economic and statistical journals, and most statisticians of importance . . . were executed or thrown into gaol."[49]

But suppose that the goal *had* been achieved—that the system had produced an efficient and prosperous economy in which material goods were equitably distributed. Insofar as this prosperity was achieved on the basis of lies, Havel's analysis suggests that the real result would have been not genuine human flourishing or fulfillment but instead, to borrow a phrase, "the abolition of man."[50]

That is because, once again, to be human is to stand in a relation to truth. Conversely, if forced or induced to "live with lies," even secure, well-fed, well-housed women and men become dehumanized. Which is why even in the "order" that Communist governments managed to achieve there was an "odour of death."[51]

Beyond Propositions

This dehumanization is part of the answer to the criticism suggesting that even if Havel was right about the pervasive mendacity of Communist regimes, the consequences would not have been as destructive of basic humanity as he maintained. And yet this response, grounded in a philosophical anthropology that identifies humanness with a propensity to "truth" as articulated in theories, philosophies, and creeds, may still seem directed more to the intellectual and artistic class of people—to the class to which Havel himself belonged—than to the grocers and factory workers and farmers and custodians who may care very little about explicitly formulated creeds and theories.

Havel sought to extend his observations, however, by emphasizing that truth is not to be understood merely as a matter of correct propositions and theories. It encompasses, rather, living itself—or living in accordance with what he called "the aims of life."[52] Thus, Havel repeatedly contrasted the mendacity of a way of life directed by Party ideology with the truthfulness of living in accordance with "the real aims of life," or "the genuine aims of life."[53] Truthfulness would consist in living "a life that is in harmony with its own aims."[54] And the project he favored would seek to "serve truth, that is, to serve the real aims of life."[55]

Havel's repeated identification of "truth" with "the real aims of life" is intriguing but also puzzling. What are "the real aims of life"? And how are those "real aims" equivalent to "truth"? It might seem that Havel must have had some worked-out account—some natural law theory, perhaps[56]—prescribing what the "real aims of life" are, and that he believed the Czech government was preventing its subjects from pursuing these aims. In other writing, he did sometimes hint at some sort of natural law.[57] But in the writings we are considering here, Havel referred freely and repeatedly to "the real aims of life" but did not support or elaborate those references by articulating any such account. On the contrary, he indicated that the aims of life are likely diverse, varying with the individual.[58]

So then, at the other extreme, did Havel mean that a society and government committed to truthfulness would allow everyone to pursue without restraint *his or her own aims*, whatever those might be? That would be a recipe not for honesty but for anarchy.

Attempting to understand Havel's point, we might start by observing that our various choices and actions implicitly convey some belief or judgment about what is right and good, or at least about what we desire. But these implications might be misleading, or simply false. They might be the product of self-deception.

Suppose you attend the opera regularly, and you talk avidly with other opera-goers about whether Verdi was a greater master than Wagner and whether the tenor in the recent production of *Rigoletto* is a greater talent than the celebrated alto who performed last month in *Madame Butterfly*. Your behavior implies that you derive great enjoyment from operatic music. And perhaps you even believe or suppose that you do—and then one day you reflect and realize that in fact you are usually bored at the opera. You go mostly because at some point you somehow came to assume that this is what people like you do—what cultured, sophisticated people do. We might say that insofar as you have been pretending—to others and to yourself—that you enjoy opera, you have been living inauthentically. You have been living in a sort of lie.

But why would you do this? Why would you invest time and money in opera if you don't actually enjoy it? Perhaps because of social pressure or influence: the friends you have made, or other people you admire or envy, seem to enjoy opera, and so you suppose that you should enjoy it too—even though you really don't. Or perhaps because of laziness or lack of self-examination: at one time you actually did get real enjoyment from attending opera, and so you formed a habit of attending, and then time passed and you didn't pause until now to notice that you were no longer experiencing the former enjoyment.

In other matters, you might behave inauthentically because of a theory or a creed or a philosophy (or, to use the term so often employed in Marxist contexts, an "ideology"). You are committed to a creed that tells you to do X—to cheer at political rallies, to eat only vegetables, or whatever—even though you don't really enjoy X and at some level you don't even believe that X is commendable or mandatory. Why then would you persist in adhering to such a creed? Again, you might do this because of social pressure or influence: other people you regard as important appear to adhere to the creed, so you embrace it as well even though you have no genuine belief in it. Or perhaps you once did believe in the creed, and so you adopted it as a guide to living, and you haven't paused to notice that as time has passed your former belief has lost its vitality.

These observations pertain to arguably inauthentic living on the part of individuals. And it might seem that this sort of inauthenticity should be nothing to worry about: if you don't enjoy opera anymore, or if you no longer really believe in the creed, then at some point you will probably realize this fact and adjust your behavior accordingly. Or maybe this conjecture is overly optimistic regarding human rationality, self-knowledge, and adaptability; maybe we are capable of unconsciously persisting in inauthentic behavior for years, even indefinitely. But in any case, when the scope of focus is expanded from individuals to society in general, and when the governing creed or philosophy or ideology is backed by the power of government, correction becomes more difficult.

It might be that a government committed to a particular ideology compels subjects to act in ways and to pursue ends that the subjects believe to be contrary to their real desires and interests, or to "the real aims of life." But a subject cannot just wake up one day and realize "This isn't how I want to live" and then begin to live more in accordance with his real beliefs and aims. Because if he does that, as Havel observes, there will be adverse consequences.

Still, when people act contrary to their beliefs and interests out of fear of adverse consequences, their interests may be harmed and their freedom restricted; but it would seem odd to say that they are acting "inauthentically" or dishonestly. To take a famous example that will become more important in the next chapter: If you hand over your wallet to a gunman who says "Your money or your life," someone might conceivably criticize you for being cowardly, but no one will fault you for being disingenuous. ("Why would you give your wallet to that reprobate when you didn't really want to? You need to be more honest with yourself!") And if someone did make this criticism, you would have a cogent rejoinder: "Actually, given the alternative (death), I really *did* want to hand over my wallet." By the same token, if subjects obey an oppressive government out of fear of sanctions, they may be acting against their ideal preferences or interests, but it would seem unfair and off-base to say that they are acting dishonestly.

The problem arises, though, because the government does not want subjects to obey merely out of fear of sanctions—it wants their allegiance, or at least their acquiescence—and many of the subjects in the kind of Marxist regime described by Havel are induced to give that acquiescence, albeit in the indirect and equivocal ways discussed above. Without explicitly affirming, they assent: they place the sign in their shop windows and answer the questionnaires and in a hundred ways offer a kind of tacit assent to the regime. Exercising a kind of doublethink, they half-convince themselves that they *are* living in the way they want to live, or at least that they *do* support the regime that requires them to live in this way. The regime in turn promotes policies based in part on an ideology that neither it nor its subjects believe in any earnest way.

And thus both the regime and its subjects are drawn into or complicit in ways of living that are dictated by ideology—by the fictions of political authority—but are not in tune with the "real aims of life." Something like this, it seems, is Havel's indictment.

Which brings us back to the greengrocer who doesn't care about creeds and ideas. Now we can appreciate that the grocer's inauthentic acquiescence is not limited to propositional affirmations—even to indirect and equivocal assents—but rather extends to a whole range of daily activities and expressions and withholdings of expression. This is not, Havel suggests, "authentic existence" in accordance with "the real aims of life." And thus both the intellectual and the laborers, the playwright and the greengrocer, are "living with lies."

Beyond Czechoslovakia

Havel's witness suggests that life in Communist Czechoslovakia in the 1970s was pervaded with lies and that this system was deeply demeaning to human dignity. But was this depressing state of affairs distinctive to the time and place in which he was writing? Testimony of other observers indicates that the pervasive dishonesty discerned by Havel extended to other Communist regimes of Eastern Europe and the Soviet Union, and beyond.

Thus, Leszek Kolakowski's massive history of Marxism leads him to conclude that the Soviet Union subsisted on the basis of a "system of universal mendacity."[59] Aleksandr Solzhenitsyn supported this assessment. In a chapter in *The Gulag Archipelago* called "Our Muzzled Freedom," Solzhenitsyn discussed *"The Lie as a Form of Existence."*[60] Citizens in the Soviet Union, he recalled, "simply cannot believe the stupid and silly images of themselves which they hear over the radio, see in films, and read in the newspapers." Nonetheless, they feel compelled "to applaud madly, and no one requires honesty of them."[61] In this way, "[t]he permanent lie becomes the only safe form of existence." This mendacity is pervasive. Just as Havel described the questionnaires and other instances eliciting constant duplicity, Solzhenitsyn described the "shrill meetings and trashy lunch-break gatherings where you are compelled . . . to be glad over what distresses you."[62]

> [E]very word, if it does not have to be a direct lie, is nonetheless obliged not to contradict the general, common lie. There exists a collection of ready-made phrases, of labels, a selection of ready-made lies. And not one single speech nor one single essay or article nor one single book—be it scientific, journalistic, critical, or "literary," so-called—can exist without the use of these primary cliches.
>
> There is no man who has typed even one page . . . without lying. There is no man who has spoken from a rostrum . . . without

lying. There is no man who has spoken into a microphone . . . without lying.⁶³

This culture of lying created a serious dilemma for parents, Solzhenitsyn reported:

> Your children were growing up! And if the children were still little, then you had to decide what was the best way to bring them up; whether to start them off on lies instead of the truth (so that it would be easier for them to live) and then to lie forevermore in front of them too; or to tell them the truth, with the risk that they might make a slip, that they might let it out, which meant that you had to instill into them from the start that the truth was murderous, that beyond the threshold of the house you had to lie, only lie, just like papa and mama.
>
> The choice was really such that you would rather not have any children.⁶⁴

Years later, in 1974, Solzhenitsyn published an essay entitled "Live Not by Lies!" (He was exiled the next day.) In the essay, he acknowledged that the brutalities of past years were no longer practiced. "[I]t is not every day and not on every shoulder that violence brings down its heavy hand: It demands of us only a submission to lies, a daily participation in deceit—and this suffices as our fealty."⁶⁵ Such participation might consist in the mundane activity of attending "a meeting where a forced and distorted discussion is expected to take place" or a "session, meeting, lecture, play, or film" devoted to disseminating propaganda.⁶⁶ Solzhenitsyn exhorted his fellow writers and citizens against being complicit in such "spiritual servility," and he pronounced a sentence on those who might collaborate in the mendacity: "And as for him who lacks the courage to defend even his own soul: let him not brag of his progressive views, boast of his status as an academician or a recognized artist, a distinguished citizen or general. Let him say to himself plainly: I am cattle, I am a coward, I seek only warmth and to eat my fill."⁶⁷

Writing in the 1950s about the situation in Poland, the poet and essayist Czeslaw Milosz described a similar phenomenon but in somewhat different terms. In the Communist society he knew, Milosz thought that citizens learned to be constantly acting, or performing. To Westerners he explained:

> It is hard to define the type of relationship that prevails between people in the East otherwise than as acting, with the exception that one does not perform on a theater stage but in the street, office, factory, meeting hall, or even the room one lives in. Such acting is a highly developed craft that places a premium on mental alertness. Before it leaves the lips, every word must be evaluated as to its consequences. A smile that appears at the wrong moment, a glance that is not all it should be can occasion dangerous suspicions and accusations. Even one's gestures, tone of voice, or preference for certain kinds of neckties are interpreted as signs of one's political tendencies.[68]

In this perpetual performance, a person may be required "[t]o say something is white when one thinks it is black, to smile inwardly when one is outwardly solemn, to hate when one manifests love, to know when one pretends not to know . . . ."[69]

Like Havel, Milosz explained that people are induced to engage in such acting for careerist reasons, among others. For young people embarking on a career, "[t]he road before them is open, open but guarded: their thinking must be based on the firm principles of dialectical materialism."[70] Unlike Havel and Solzhenitsyn, however, who sometimes seemed to suppose that they and their neighbors were fully conscious of their cultivated dishonesty, Milosz described an internalization that would prevent people from being aware of their implicit mendacity. Thus, he explained that in pursuing a career, a person would likely absorb the ideology or orthodoxy of the regime quite naturally and gradually, and hence would usually not face any conscious or painful choice contrasting "what I am *supposed to* believe" with "what I *really* believe." Most citizens would manage to believe what they were supposed to believe.

Good actors may lose themselves in their characters; in Milosz's experience, subjects in a Communist society managed much the same thing. "After long acquaintance with his role, a man grows into it so closely that he can no longer differentiate his true self from the self he simulates."[71] In achieving this performative unity, moreover, people typically experience a kind of peace. "There is an internal longing for harmony and happiness that lies deeper than ordinary fear or the desire to escape misery or physical destruction":[72] people achieve this harmony by bringing their opinions into line with the regime's.

Subjects might thus avoid internal dissonance, but they did not, in Milosz's view, avoid dehumanization. He described one writer, initially a traditional Catholic, with whom he had at one time been close friends but who gradually shifted over to the Party's perspective and thereby achieved great acclaim: "In his desire to win approbation he had simplified his picture to conform to the wishes of the Party. One compromise leads to a second and a third until, at last, though everything one says may be perfectly logical, it no longer has anything in common with the flesh and blood of living people."[73]

Unlike Havel and Solzhenitsyn, therefore, Milosz did not describe the "actors" of Communist Poland as "lying," exactly. And yet he discerned a loss of individuality, and indeed of humanity. Under Communism, the streets all acquire "a stiff and institutional look." Crowds of people are "uniformly gray." And the system "paralyzes individuals and makes people adjust themselves as much as possible to the average type in their gestures, clothing, and facial expressions."[74]

The combined testimonies of Havel, Kolakowski, Solzhenitsyn, and Milosz thus suggest that pervasive mendacity or at least inauthenticity was typical of Communist regimes. Hannah Arendt's study indicates, however, that this quality was not unique to Communism; it extended to totalitarian regimes generally, notably including Nazism. Arendt discerned many common features in Stalin's Soviet Union and Hitler's Third Reich. Among these features was a pervasive reliance on "the Big Lie." She was thus struck "[n]ot [by] Stalin's and Hitler's skill in the art of lying but by the fact that they were able to organize the masses into a collective unit to back up their lies with impressive magnificence."[75] Totalitarianism generally operates through "[s]ystematic lying to the whole world."[76]

In sum, it was evidently not just Czechoslovakia, and not even Communist regimes, that lived and breathed dishonesty. The situation extended to totalitarian regimes generally.

But was, or is, the phenomenon limited to political systems that we describe as "totalitarian"?

Back on the Western Ranch

In this chapter we have considered how under the twentieth-century totalitarian ideologies of Central and Eastern Europe, political fictions degenerated into imposed but unbelievable falsehoods, resulting in societies constituted by pervasive mendacity—"living with lies"—in a way that was demeaning and dehumanizing. This nightmarish situation, it seems, contrasts with the beneficent regimes of Western liberal democracies founded on the fiction of "the consent of the governed." So, how to account for the comparatively happy results of one family of fictions and the miserable product of a different set of fictions?

It is a hard question. And it is hard to be confident in the possible answers.

One possibility is that fundamental political or societal fictions follow a sort of career or life course and that the "living with lies" condition discerned by Vaclav Havel and others is characteristic of one late, degenerating phase of that course. In its youthful vigor, perhaps, a fiction sustains wholehearted acceptance. It is not perceived as a fiction at all. Jefferson feels no qualms in announcing his "self-evident truths"; Lenin or perhaps Trotsky or at least the soldiers of the revolution really believe in the imminent workers' paradise. Much later, in its dotage, the ideology or fiction has come to seem frankly unbelievable and is thus unable to perform its legitimating work. But there will presumably be a transitional period, during which the fictions are no longer credible to a critical or discerning participant but are still widely invoked and acquiesced in to support the legal authority. During that transitional period, the sort of pervasive disingenuousness described by Havel would prevail.

In this vein, we might say with benefit of hindsight that the Marxist regimes of the Soviet Union and Eastern Europe followed a career from revolutionary fervor to tepid subsistence to, by the late 1980s and early 1990s, dissolution. Writing in the 1970s, though, Havel happened to be situated during the transitional phase of ideological senescence. The ruling ideology was no longer genuinely believable—to either subjects or government and Party officials who actually thought about it (as many presumably did not)—but it was still recited and enforced and largely acquiesced in. That, perhaps, is why the malady of *his* time was ubiquitous dishonesty.

On this view, we might ask whether the Western liberal democracies, grounded in fictions of social contract and "the consent of the governed," are following a similar career course. And if so, what phase do we find ourselves in at the moment?

It also seems plausible to suppose that different fictions will work differently, with different consequences, fortunate or grim. All *men* (or all human beings) may be created equal—that is another of our self-evident truths (or founding fictions?)—but not all *fictions* are created equal. And any given political fiction will have a logic that will influence matters, for better or worse, and quite possibly contrary to the interests or intentions of those who invoke the fiction.

Thus, Edmund Morgan explains that in the seventeenth-century British struggles between the king and the House of Commons, "both were acting out a fiction, [and] neither king nor Commons was what each pretended to be."[77] The Commons, for example, were not ordinary folks; they were in reality gentry intent on protecting and enhancing their own privileged position in society. As demanded by the political fictions of the time, though, "[t]hey claimed indeed to represent all other subjects." This claim was a fiction, but "like other fictions it could restrict the actions of those who espoused it."[78] More specifically, "[t]he Commons' assertions of universal rights were thus in a manner dictated by the premises from which they started. The fiction of their own status as representatives and the fiction of the king's status as God's lieutenant required them to speak in universals if they were to speak at all."[79]

In a similar way, the logic of "the consent of the governed," however fictional that consent might be, has arguably had its beneficent effects in the development of American and other liberal democracies. The logic would seem to dictate an expansion of voting rights, for example—not, as we discussed in chapter 1, because a subject's exercise of the vote is actually equivalent to consent to be ruled, but because denial of that right would seriously undermine the plausibility or "truthiness" of the founding fiction. How can a government plausibly claim to be based on "the consent of the governed" if the governed are not even allowed to vote? And thus we have experienced a steady expansion of the franchise over the course of American constitutional history.[80] Likewise for the freedom of speech. The exercise of this right does not amount to consent to be ruled (and indeed, a subject may exercise the right to assert that he or she does *not* consent); but denial of the right would cast open and obvious doubt on the government's claim to enjoy such consent.

A different legitimating fiction (such as, perhaps, the proposition that the Party is the vanguard of the proletariat, working to achieve the classless society) would not have these salutary and democratic implications. So perhaps we in the West have simply been fortunate to have inherited a relatively ennobling family of fictions.

More generally, it might be that the idea of "the consent of the governed" as the basis of authority is keyed to an ideal of individual freedom or autonomy that naturally works to limit the scope of government. The author of the official version of the consent proposition seems to have thought so, in any case: Jefferson also ostensibly declared, in a similar spirit, that "that government is best which governs least."[81] And whether or not we today believe such limited government to be desirable in terms of justice or public policy, we might acknowledge that the more limited the presence of government in life, the less conspicuous and significant in the lives of the subjects will be the fictions on which that government rests. The fictions will still have to be affirmed on select occasions, but most of life can be lived beyond their purview—and thus beyond the deception that such fictions entail.

In this vein, Orwell's protagonist Winston Smith surmised that if there was any hope of escaping the vicious and mendacious domination of the government and the Party, that hope lay in the proles.[82] In the people whom for the most part the government and the Party didn't care about, and who accordingly lived outside the government's domain of close rule and indoctrination.

Conversely, in more comprehensively totalitarian regimes, government is present everywhere. The imperative of affirming or at least acquiescing in the government, and hence in the government's supporting fictions, will accordingly be pervasive. And the society thus devolves into the condition of "living with lies" described by Havel.

So maybe we in the West have simply had the good fortune of living under benevolent and self-confining fictions?

Is the West Really So Different?

Or then again, maybe this is all wrong—unduly complacent and self-congratulatory. Doesn't living in a fictional framework make it difficult for us—for anyone—to give a reliable judgment? Even a healthy fictional regime depends, as we have seen, on a suspension of critical examination. It depends, we might say, on an ample measure of Orwellian "doublethink." And one careful observer who traveled to postwar Germany and lived with and carefully interviewed a set of ordinary Germans reported that even the subjects of the Third Reich "thought they were free"—that they looked back to the years under Hitler as the "best time of their lives."[83]

> As we know Nazism, it was a naked, total tyranny which degraded its adherents and enslaved its opponents and adherents alike; terrorism and terror in daily life, private and public; brute personal and mob injustice at every level of association; a flank attack upon God and a frontal attack upon the worth of the human person.... These nine ordinary Germans knew it absolutely otherwise, and they still know it otherwise. If our view of National Socialism is a little simplistic, so is theirs. An autocracy? Yes, of course, an autocracy, as in the fabled days of "the golden time" our parents knew. But a tyranny, as you Americans use the term? Nonsense.[84]

Surely, our own judgments could not be as grotesquely warped as theirs were? Could they? Even so, can we trust our judgments?

Here is a still different and sobering possibility. Perhaps the beneficent workings of our own governing fictions are ascribable not to their inherent logic, but rather to historical contingencies that might have been different—and that today *are* quite different. For various reasons, the original proponents of the consent proposition, like Jefferson, also happened to favor a highly limited role for government. But the "freedom" to which "consent" is connected in its logic and purpose is an elastic notion, coming in a range of "negative" and "positive" varieties.[85] So if Jefferson believed that freedom and "the consent of the governed" were inherently conducive to small, narrowly limited government, he was quite plainly mistaken, as the spectacular growth of government in modern times (often under the head of promoting one or another kind of "freedom") demonstrates.

Moreover, in the American founding narrative, "the consent of the governed" is not the only "self-evident truth" and not the only basis of legitimacy. Another such fundamental "truth" is that "all men are created equal." And it also seems to be deemed a self-evident truth that these two self-evident truths are inextricably connected, so that a legitimate government not only must claim the consent of the governed; it must also treat all of its subjects with "equal concern and respect." Indeed, in some contemporary theorizing, the equality proposition seems to have displaced the consent proposition as the primary basis of political legitimacy.[86] For many, "equality" has become the fighting faith of our time.[87] And that faith—or, if you like, that fiction—can have enormous and expansionary implications for government, as again we have witnessed in recent decades.

The expanding role of government has naturally brought with it the ever-more-pervasive propagation of and insistence on the assumptions on which the government's authority is ostensibly based—consent (and its core or companion value of autonomy) and the equality (or "equal dignity" or "equal moral worth") of all persons. These propositions, however, will not spontaneously seem self-evidently true to *everyone*—for some, the contrary may seem closer to the truth—and so the propositions have been buttressed by swelling bodies of coercive law, by proliferating bodies of supportive scholarship or theorizing, and by educational or indoctrination campaigns. And these supportive measures may place citizens for whom these "truths" do not seem "self-evident" in a situation similar to those described by Havel and others.

Thus, Havel complained of "questionnaires" that were calculated to elicit affirmations of the prevailing ideology. Are there equivalents in Western liberal democracies?

Possibilities come to mind. Here is just one: in many institutions, employees are required to receive annual instruction in how to treat others with sensitivity, egalitarian respect, and "inclusiveness." The instruction may consist in part of "mandatory" online tutorials. Mandatory how? Would you be fired for refusing to take the course? Who knows? Better just to comply. And once you log on to the course, you will be presented with unsubtle instruction accompanied by a series of multiple-choice questions asking about how you should respond to a variety of situations. You might actually think that the answers to some of these questions are debatable, but there will be no opportunity to discuss or question: only the "correct" answer will be accepted. Refusal to give that answer will prevent you from proceeding to the next question or section or module, and thus from completing the instruction, and thus from being certified as having satisfied the "mandatory" requirement. In order to keep your job, in short, you will be required to affirm all sorts of specific things that you may or may not believe. Specific things that implicitly suggest or entail other more general things that you may or may not believe.

Here is another instance. Solzhenitsyn noted the disingenuousness of "meeting[s] where . . . forced and distorted discussion[s are] expected to take place." Is there any counterpart of such meetings in academic or other institutional settings in the West? You can answer that question for yourself; but if, like me, you work in a university, the answer is pretty obvious, isn't it? Solzhenitsyn complained as well of the supply of "a collection of ready-made phrases, of labels, a selection of ready-made lies." Discussions were organized around "primary cliches." Once again, is there any similar collection of "ready-made phrases" and "primary cliches" in academic or other institutional settings?

Milosz observed that in speeches or conversations, "[b]efore it leaves the lips, every word must be evaluated as to its consequences": an ill-advised word or expression could have disastrous consequences for one's career or well-being. How many academics, politicians, and media persons today feel under a similar constraint? How often do we read of someone in the academy or the media—or in politics or business—who is sacked or demoted or "canceled," or at the very least forced to issue a series of abject apologies and self-abasing recantations—because of an ill-advised expression of unacceptable opinion? Or even because of an ill-phrased expression of acceptable position? Usually the offending statement will consist of some deviation from the currently prevailing constructions of the fundamental commitment to "equality" in the areas of race, gender, or sexual orientation. A slipup in substance or phraseology and . . . canceled![88]

In a similar vein, Milosz described how for young people starting out on a career, opportunities were available but conditional on holding the right views: "The road before them is open, open but guarded: their thinking must be based on the firm principles of dialectical materialism."[89] Substitute for "dialectical materialism" something like "egalitarian progressivism": Would the same observation hold for a young person today contemplating a media career, or an academic career in the humanities, social sciences, or law?

Recently some astute or perhaps eccentric observers have begun to describe aspects of life in Western societies in terms that sound strikingly like Havel's. In matters of race, sexuality, and gender roles, "we are asked to agree to things which we cannot believe," Douglas Murray argues. "We are asked to believe things that are unbelievable and being told not to object to things (such as giving children drugs to stop them going through puberty) which most people feel a strong objection to."[90] These mandatory affirmations, Murray argues, are traceable back to "legitimate human rights campaigns"—Murray, who self-identifies as a gay man, seems to support those campaigns—but the campaigns have mutated into a new social justice religion whose tenets are relentlessly enforced by condemning anyone who deliberately or carelessly deviates as "'[b]igot,' 'homophobe,' 'sexist,' 'misogynist,' 'racist,' and 'transphobe.'"[91]

Sounding much like Havel, Murray thinks the consequences of this imposition are disastrous. Havel argued that the mendacity created by the "existential pressure" of Marxist ideology led to a "paralysis of the spirit, a deadening of the heart, and devaluation of life." Murray does not cite Havel, but he describes the consequences of the currently imposed ideology of equality in similar terms.

> [T]here is something demeaning and eventually soul-destroying about being expected to go along with claims you do not believe to be true and cannot hold to be true. If the belief is that all people should be regarded as having equal value and be accorded equal dignity, then that may be all well and good. If you are asked to believe that there are no differences between homosexuality and heterosexuality, men and women, racism and anti-racism, then this will in time drive you to distraction. That distraction—or crowd madness—is something we are in the middle of and something we need to try to find our way out from.[92]

Anthony Kronman, longtime professor at and former dean of the Yale Law School, perceives a similar mandatory conformity of opinion that threatens American higher education under the appealing heading of "diversity"—meaning, as Kronman explains, "diversity of race, ethnicity, gender, and sexual orientation."[93] Commitment to such diversity, Kronman observes, is not optional. Faculty and students are often required to take "diversity training," and "[a]pplicants for faculty positions are routinely required to affirm their commitment to diversity and to explain how they intend to promote it."[94]

As it happens, Kronman himself favors affirmative action programs for the purpose of combating societal injustices. The problem, he thinks—and one he traces back to the rationale elaborated by Justice Lewis Powell in the famous *Bakke* case—is that universities have not been legally permitted to justify such programs honestly on social justice grounds. Instead, they have been forced to pretend that "diversity" is an essential academic value in its own right, and they have also been required to pretend that they treat racial or ethnic diversity as only one factor in admissions decisions rather than admit that they in fact are operating under "quotas." Powell's rationale, Kronman thinks, "drove the truth underground and made it illegal for our colleges and universities to address their students with the honesty that the search for truth requires."[95]

This dishonesty becomes difficult to contain. The dishonest rationalization of what Kronman himself believes to be just and necessary programs creates a "climate of mendacity" in the universities. "It breeds dishonesty in an environment where honesty should be at a premium."[96]

These are provocative claims, obviously, and a great deal might be (and has been, and will be) said about them. And one might surely wonder whether the sort of blunt "honesty" contemplated by Kronman would be realistically possible, or desirable. Could a university actually say to its minority students or faculty: "The honest truth is that your credentials in many cases do not measure up to those of your white classmates and colleagues: we have lowered our standards in order to admit or hire you. Without that lowering of standards, some of you would be here anyway; many of you would not be. We have done this because we are committed to remedying the social injustices that have been committed against you or your ancestors." And even if that offensive truth were openly proclaimed, would it actually do much to alter the ways in which racially or ethnically based or gender-based admissions or hiring work to create what Kronman and others perceive as a "climate of mendacity"?

But perhaps these are impertinent questions. It is true, perhaps, that human society does depend, and always will depend, on standardized phrases, labels, and "primary cliches." And any society will have its central tenets or "truths"—the "truths" that constitute it as a society—and will punish deviation from those "truths" with social disapproval, or worse. That is simply the nature of human beings and human societies. But *our* tenets and cliches ("equality," "diversity," "inclusion," "consent"), unlike those described by Havel, Solzhenitsyn, and Milosz, are good and just ones. And so we really, authentically believe them. Don't we?

So it is true, perhaps, that a person who openly advocated, say, traditional gender roles—the kind that her parents or grandparents believed in—could forget about any number of academic or media or political careers. Same for someone who openly opposed any sort of affirmative action or "diversity" program. But that is because such notions *really are* archaic and pernicious; and no one today, or at least no reasonable person, does or could believe them. Today we *really do* believe in all of the prevailing views of gender and sexuality and equality and . . .—the list goes on. Indeed, that is in a sense the whole point and purpose of our prevailing commitments—to allow every person to live freely and authentically in accordance with their true self. Isn't it?

To be sure, as Havel pointed out, the Marxist lies were also routinely presented behind an "imposing facade of great humanistic ideals" made up of "bombastic slogans about the unprecedented increase in every sort of freedom."[97] But *those* "slogans" represented a false "facade"—one that hardly anyone could really believe. *Our* "truths," by contrast, reflect genuinely noble ideals that we really *do* believe and embrace. So here there is no "daily participation in deceit."

How fortunate we are that it is so. *If* it is so.

CHAPTER FIVE

Authority and Faux Authority

We began this book with Hannah Arendt's startling claims that "authority has vanished from the modern world," that "[p]ractically as well as theoretically, we are no longer in a position to know what authority really *is*," and that this absence "is tantamount to the loss of the groundwork of the world."[1] Nor was Arendt alone: other thinkers, we noted, have made similar claims about the disappearance of authority from the contemporary scene.

Our subsequent chapters have circled around these provocative claims without quite confronting them head-on. In sympathetic parallel with these claims, our discussion has suggested that authority in the modern world has a problematic status. In Western liberal democracies, we have observed, political authority has been somewhat precariously grounded in a family of fictions. The American constitutional order purports to get its authority from the quasi-fictional "We the People of the United States"; even our principal institutions of legal authority—Congress, the president, the Supreme Court—have a quasi-fictional quality. And in the previous chapter, we saw how the implementation of supposed authority grounded in classic Marxist ideology led to the nightmarish condition that Vaclav Havel described as "living with lies"—a condition that (to put the point gently) may not be wholly without pertinence to life in contemporary Western societies.

So it may seem that authority has been battered and bruised, or at least subjected to embarrassing interrogation. Even so, nothing in our investigation thus far has purported to show that authority has "vanished," or that we no longer understand what authority is, or that we have somehow lost "the groundwork of the world."

And indeed, the discussion in chapter 1 explicitly contended that a fictional foundation can support real practical authority—if, that is, the fiction is widely enough embraced. That conclusion would seem to indicate—wouldn't it?—that authority has *not* vanished, that (for better or worse) it is still very much with us. Moreover, the fact that we have been talking about authority for many pages now and with respect to a whole variety of issues might suggest that we *do* know what authority is, or that we at least have a tolerably clear working conception. How could we examine the thing, dissect it, argue about its foundations and its consequences, if we had no idea what it is?

So then were Arendt's more audacious claims simply mistaken?

Not necessarily. True, we have been discussing political phenomena that are plainly real—we experience them on a daily basis—and that we often describe using the vocabulary of "authority." As noted, though, Arendt and like-minded critics surely did not mean to deny the existence of those phenomena—of governments and laws and coercive enforcement and such. So if these critics believed that authority has vanished from the modern world, then it seems that they must have thought that these governmental and legal phenomena, whatever vocabulary we might use to describe them, are not truly "authority." They are something else. The counterfeit of authority, maybe, or the simulation. *Faux* authority.

This is a more complicated and subtle claim—one that is hard to get hold of. Still, the claim could be right, couldn't it?

Well, no, it couldn't, someone might contend. The claim, it may seem, is flawed on its face. After all, language is conventional: so if we conventionally use a term to refer to something, then that just is what the term means. If we all describe the liquid material that flows out of faucets as "water," then that is what the word "water" refers to; and it would be merely obtuse for someone to come along and say, "Ah, but you are all mistaken: that stuff isn't *really* water. It's just an imitation of water. *Faux* water." The stuff *is* water: our saying it makes it so. Similarly, if the phenomena of governments and laws and coercive enforcement are real (as they surely are), and if we use the word "authority" to describe those phenomena or some part of them (as we do), then what could be the sense of saying that this isn't "real" authority or that we no longer know what "authority" means?

And yet.... Imagine a situation in which, due to some sort of epidemic virus, say, cattle become extinct, so that the only substance that can be put on a bun with ketchup, mustard, and pickles is one of those artificial "veggie burger" meat substitutes. People continue to call these concoctions "hamburgers," perhaps; as the years pass, not many people even remember what the genuine article tasted like. But then some white-haired ancient of days appears and tells people, "Those aren't *real* hamburgers. They're just an imitation." Others respond, "You're mistaken. These *are* hamburgers. The meaning of words is given by convention, and that is our convention for the word 'hamburger.'"

The conventionalists would have a valid point, perhaps. But the hoary elder would have a valid point as well—and a more penetrating point than the conventional one. Because in an important sense, it would be true that hamburgers had disappeared from the world and that although the word continued, hardly anyone would any longer understand what a hamburger *really* is—or, as we might say, what a *real* hamburger is.

Arendt seems to have been saying something like this about "authority." Could she be right? It is a challenging question, and one that we have accordingly postponed—but it is a challenge we now need to take on.

How to proceed?

We will start with a famous instance in which one of the most respected legal theorists of the twentieth century, the Oxford philosopher H. L. A. Hart, made basically the same kind of claim: Hart contended that something that had been described as authority by a major legal thinker of the previous century, John Austin, and that is often thought of as authority, is not *really* authority. (I am rephrasing slightly but, I hope to show, defensibly.) Reflection will confirm, I think, that Hart's claim was both intelligible and correct. Further reflection will show, in fact, that Hart was more correct than he knew—or, probably, than he wanted to be.

That is because Hart's objection to Austin's account of authority will turn out to be applicable to most other contemporary accounts of authority as well (including the consent and coordination accounts that we considered in chapter 1). Hart hoped to develop a more adequate conception of obligation and authority than Austin had provided; his biographer reports that in his later years he became almost panicky because he feared he had not succeeded in this project.[2] I will suggest in this chapter, however, that Hart's failure, if it was a failure, is attributable to his earlier success: his criticism of Austin, it will turn out, was not containable.

So the argument now will be different from those in our earlier discussions. The problem now is not, as we said then, that these accounts are based on fictions (although they are), but rather that the thing they attempt to explain and justify, though perhaps real and imposing enough, is not really *authority*. It is something more like simulated or *faux* authority. As Arendt suggested.[3]

AUTHORITY AND THE GUNMAN

Austin's influential jurisprudence depicted law as a set of commands issued by a political superior or sovereign to political inferiors or subjects.[4] In filling out this picture, Austin subjected the key terms in this account—"law," "command," "superior," "sovereign," "inferior," and so forth—to relentless (and tedious) analysis in order to distinguish "law properly so-called" from a variety of related or analogous phenomena, such as "imperfect" commands or mere wishes or morality. In Austin's analysis, a "command" is an order or wish expressed to another and backed by the threat of a punishment or sanction, and the result of such an order is an "obligation" or "duty" imposed on the recipient of the command.[5] Such commands might issue from a variety of sources, including God—and Austin spent a whole chapter discussing God's commands and how we can discern them—but the human or positive law that is the subject of jurisprudence comes from a human political superior. From a "sovereign," defined as a person whose commands are habitually obeyed and who is not in the habit of obeying orders from any outside or higher source.[6]

Hart in his turn discerned a variety of deficiencies in this account,[7] but his most elementary objection asserted that Austin had misunderstood the nature of "obligation" or "duty." To make this point, Hart relied on a simple and celebrated scenario—the case of the gunman or mugger. Let's say you are walking through St. James Park, and a mugger steps in front of you, puts a gun to your head, and says, "Give me all of your money or I'll kill you." The situation would seem to fit Austin's account precisely: there is an order, a threatened sanction, and a resulting "duty" or "obligation." Except that, as Hart objected, we would not typically think of this as a case of "duty" or "obligation" at all. Asked by friends why you had given your money to this belligerent stranger, you might say that you were "obliged" by the gunman to do so; but you would probably *not* say that you had an "obligation" to give him your money.[8]

In these discussions, Austin and Hart were explicitly talking about "duty" or "obligation"; but they were also talking about "authority," albeit at one remove. That is because "duty" or "obligation" and "authority" are correlative terms—like "parent" and "child." If you are Joseph's son or daughter, then it follows that Joseph is your parent: that is just what it means to be a son or daughter to someone. Likewise with "obligation" and "authority." Joseph Raz observes that "[i]t is common to regard authority over persons as . . . correlated with an obligation to obey on the part of those subject to the authority."[9] So if we say that someone's command imposes an obligation on you, that is tantamount to saying that the person has "authority" over you. Conversely, if someone lacks the capacity to impose an "obligation," as Hart argued the gunman did, then that person does not possess "authority"—but rather something else (such as, in this instance, the power to "oblige" or compel).

For some purposes, to be sure, the correlative relation between authority and obligation can be pulled apart. But the relation is typically assumed,[10] and neither Austin nor Hart seems to have been attempting to dissolve it. On the contrary, Hart seems explicitly to have followed the usual assumption.[11] So we can say that in Austin's account, "authority" is what a superior has who can issue commands backed by sanctions. For his part, in denying that the gunman's order imposes any "obligation" on you, Hart was in effect denying that the gunman has "authority" over you. The capacity to back up one's commands with sanctions is not enough to constitute "authority."

But why not? We might imagine a revived Austin responding to Hart's example with the same conventionalist challenge we noted earlier. "Look," Austin might protest, "*I say* that the gunman's command backed by a sanction creates an 'obligation' to comply and that this sort of sanction-backed command is characteristic of what we call 'law.' That's how *I* use the words. Other people take a similar view: Oliver Wendell Holmes, for example, with his 'bad man' approach to law.[12] Indeed, the very fact that my jurisprudence has been so influential for over a century would seem to demonstrate that my understanding of these things—of law and command and duty or obligation—resonates pretty widely. And if I and others use the words in this way, then that is just what the words mean. Now, of course, you, Professor Hart, are perfectly free to substitute a different word—'obliges' instead of 'obligates.' You may even be right that the typical English speaker of your time would be more likely to use your term than mine. So what? Shouldn't earnest thinkers like ourselves refrain from this sort of semantic quibbling?"

And, seriously, what exactly *is* the point of Hart's attention to the particular word people would likely use—"obligates" or "obliges"—in describing the gunman situation? As it happens, Oxford philosophers in Hart's day had the curious notion that paying close attention to ordinary linguistic usage might yield important philosophical insights.[13] That day has passed, mostly. So, is there anything more substantial in Hart's analysis of the gunman situation?[14]

Actually, it seems that there is: Hart's attention to the words we would typically use in this situation seems to indicate a deeper point. If we would use the word "obliges" to describe what the gunman did to you, or (more importantly) if we would find it odd and wrong to say that the gunman imposed an "obligation" on you, then that usage suggests that we have some underlying sense of what an "obligation" is—and that we do not perceive any such thing in the gunman situation.[15] And that initial observation might in turn lead us to look and ask more carefully. What *do* we understand an "obligation" to be (and by implication, insofar as these are correlative terms, what do we understand "authority" to be)? Why would we think it a mistake to describe the gunman situation using the terms of "authority" and "obligation"?

One initially tempting response should be noted, if only so that we can appreciate its insufficiency. Someone might say that we use the term "obligation" to refer to "moral" reasons or "moral" duties.[16] And although you surely have a very powerful reason to comply with the gunman's command, that reason is one of prudence or self-interest; it is not a "moral" reason. That is why you have no "obligation" to do as the gunman commands.[17] If you are a prudent person, then you will hand over your money to the gunman in order to save your life. Even so, if you somehow managed to distract him, knock his gun into the bushes or the lake, and then run away, people might commend you for your bravery, or they might say that you acted recklessly; but no one would say that you had violated an "obligation."

Probably there is some truth in this suggestion, and yet it does not fully capture our intuitive understanding of why the gunman situation does not present an "obligation" and why he accordingly lacks "authority." To see why, imagine that Norris is a swaggering, Ramboish, risk-relishing character, consummately skilled in the martial arts; and until recently he would never have handed over his money to a mugger. Even at significant risk to himself, he would have tried to disarm the assailant. But as it happens, a year or so ago Norris married, and he now has a spouse and a child who depend on him for support. So although Norris's first impulse when confronted by the gunman is to fight back, that impulse is promptly followed by a contrary thought: "I really, really hate to give anything to this cowardly creep. But I can't take the risk of getting wounded or killed, because then who would take care of my spouse and child?" And so, biting his tongue and cursing his luck, Norris meekly hands over his wallet.

In this case, we would likely agree that Norris's reason for complying with the gunman's command has a "moral" quality. We might even say that the gunman's order triggers or implicates a "moral obligation" to comply and that if instead Norris recklessly resists he will have violated that obligation. And yet we would still not think that *the gunman's order* imposed an obligation. Norris's moral obligation came from a wholly different source. And so the gunman still would not have authority. It is not enough that Norris had an "obligation" to comply: for there to be "authority," the obligation would need to come from the order, or *from the gunman*.

So we need to reflect more closely. What *do* we think "authority" is? And why exactly is this authority missing in the gunman case?

"Just Because" Authority

Start with the first question. What do we think "authority" is? In fact, there is a familiar, commonsensical (but, upon reflection, puzzling) response to that question—and, as it happens, one that sometimes appears in more scholarly discussions as well. A person has "authority," we sometimes say, if you have to do what they tell you to do "just because they told you to."

By contrast, a friend or sibling might admonish you to do something and explain some reasons why you should do it, and if you are persuaded by those reasons you might follow the admonition. But in that case, you wouldn't say that you acted "just because she told me to"; nor would you say that you acted out of respect for the "authority" of the admonisher. Rather, you acted because of the reasons that were given you; if all on your own you had thought of those reasons, you presumably would have done the same thing. Your doctor tells you to stop eating avocados, maybe, and explains that you have a condition in which avocados may cause a fatal allergic reaction. You may follow the doctor's orders—but not just because she told you to do something, but rather because the reasons she offered were persuasive. You would have done the same thing if you had self-diagnosed using an online program. But authority comes into play only when you act "just because" someone told you to.

Let us call this everyday notion the "just because" conception of authority. In fact, theorists sometimes invoke a similar formulation in their accounts of legal authority. Jules Coleman suggests that "the law purports to govern our conduct by telling us that we have an obligation to act in a certain way *for no reason other than that the law commands it.*"[18] In a similar vein, Richard Friedman observes that "we describe such situations [of authority] by saying that an order is obeyed or a decision is accepted *simply because* X gave it or made it."[19]

For all of its easy familiarity, though, the "just because" conception is also elusive. In particular, three phrases in the formulation call for clarification. Those clarifications will lead us toward a clearer understanding of what "authority" is (or at least what it would be, if it exists at all).

The First Qualification: Prima Facie Reasons

The first of these clarifications is relatively simple. The "have to" in "you *have to* do what they say just because they said to" should not be interpreted too strictly; it should not be interpreted to require something like deterministic compulsion. Thus, the fact that you might disobey or escape, or that in some extraordinary cases you might even be justified in disobeying or escaping (to save your life, maybe, or to save the life of your spouse), does not necessarily defeat or negate authority. Authority is consistent with (and arguably even assumes) some freedom of choice and action on the part of those subject to the authority.[20]

It has traditionally been supposed, for example, that a father has authority with respect to his children or that God has authority over us. We will raise questions about these examples later, but for now let us take the traditional suppositions as correct. To say that your father or God has authority over you is not to say that you are compelled to—or that you literally "have to"—do what they tell you to do. It is perfectly possible to say that these worthies have authority but that you are still free to obey their orders or to disobey them.

So "have to," it seems, in the context means something like "have good reasons to." Someone has authority, in other words, if their telling you to do something in itself gives you a good reason—a prima facie reason, as philosophers sometimes say—to do as you were told.

This first qualification or clarification, however, does not yet tell us why the gunman lacks authority over you. The gunman's order does give you a prima facie reason to comply; conversely, the gunman does not exactly compel you in the strong deterministic sense to hand over your money—not in the sense in which, say, gravity compels you to move toward the ground if you step off your roof. You *could* refuse the gunman's order and take the risk of dying. Our second and third qualifications, however, will shed more light on the gunman's lack of authority.

The Second Qualification: *Personal* Reasons

A second necessary clarification of the "you have to do what they say just because they said so" formulation focuses on the "they." "They" refers to a *person* or *persons*. There are all sorts of things or facts in the world—the physical terrain, the weather, the stock market, the condition of your body—that give you prima facie reasons to act in particular ways. Insofar as these facts are impersonal, however, we do not treat them as having or exercising "authority."

Normally, perhaps, you go for a walk in St. James Park each afternoon at five o'clock, even on rainy days. But on a particular day a ferocious storm is raging; the thunder booming all around resembles a military bombardment, and trees are surging and snapping in the wind and torrential rain. So you prudently decide to stay indoors. The lightning storm is a natural fact that, given your aversion to death or serious injury, provides you with a reason to do or forgo doing something. And yet you would not describe the storm as having "authority" or as imposing "obligations" on you. No person, no authority.[21]

To be sure, our usage is flexible: when we are subject to someone's order, we may describe *the person* giving the order as having authority, but we may also sometimes describe *the order itself*, or *the law*, as having authority. The title to this book refers to "the authority of law." Even so, we suppose that the order or law has authority because it comes from someone—some person or persons (the legislature, the judge, the general)—who has authority.[22] We cannot imagine a statute book just appearing, for example, except as the product of some person or group of persons who have authority; and if the book somehow did just appear—or more plausibly, if it appeared but as the work product of someone who lacks authority (an eccentric grad student, maybe)—we would treat it with the indifference it deserves.

The requirement of personal reasons may help to explain why Hart was correct about the gunman situation. At first glance, this may seem a surprising observation, because the gunman surely *is* a person. And yet upon reflection, it seems that his status as a person is purely incidental; it does not give his order the personal quality characteristic of authority.

Think of it this way: Aren't the cases in which there is a lightning storm in St. James Park and in which there is a gunman in St. James Park equivalent in their essentials? In each case, we might say, your reason for acting is to avoid death or bodily injury, and some outside fact—the storm, the gunman—just happens under the circumstances to implicate that reason. To be sure, the reason arising from the gunman's threat, unlike that arising from the storm, *does* emanate from a person. And yet, for purposes of your decision, that fact is pretty much beside the point. *To you*, as you decide whether to hand over your money, the gunman with his order and his gun and his threat are more in the nature of external facts from which you predict the likelihood that death or injury will occur if an action is not taken. They are equivalent to the ominous sounds of thunder that lead you to infer that if you go out into the park there will be a risk of serious injury.

So although the threat does indeed emanate from a person, *what matters to your decision* is not the fact that it comes from a person but rather your assessment of its evidentiary value in predicting whether bad consequences will follow if you do not act in a particular way.[23] The mugger *is* a person, but only incidentally so: it is not his personal quality that matters to your decision.

Or think of it this way: Suppose you decide to stay indoors because there is a riot going on outside; people are throwing rocks and shooting guns. Now the reason for your staying indoors is surely associated with persons. But for you, that fact is pretty much irrelevant: the rocks thrown by and the bullets fired by persons are no different for your considerations than the lightning bolts and driving rain.

We could underscore the point by imagining scenarios in which the same kind of threat comes not from a person but rather from, say, some sort of robot whose wiring has short-circuited and thereby caused the robot to become a menace. If you believe the robot will inflict death unless you place a green piece of legal tender in its gleaming mechanical pincers, the fact that the robot is not a person will have no apparent relevance to your decision. But you would not say that the robot has "authority." Or imagine that some highly sophisticated and powerful vending machine has gone seriously haywire and is about to explode, and the only way to avert the danger is to keep pumping quarters into the slot. (A menacing red light on the machine keeps flashing, "INSERT MORE COINS.") In this situation, you have the same sort of reason to "hand over the money" as you have in the mugger situation: you want to avoid the imminent risk of injury, and the way to do that is to transfer money to the source of the danger. The fact that this source of danger is a person in one case and a metal machine in the other does not alter the type of reason that induces you to part with your money. But again, you would not say that the vending machine is exercising "authority" over you.

In order to have authority, in short, it seems we need to have personal reasons—not just reasons that happen to be associated with persons, but reasons for which what gives the reason its force is that it issues from a person. As Joseph Vining observes, "[A] search for authority presupposes the personal."[24]

The Third Qualification: Intrinsic versus Indirect Reasons

If this second requirement seems subtle and a bit elusive, the third qualification will be even harder to pin down: but we must try. So, what does it mean to do something—or to have a prima facie reason to do something—"just because" someone told you to do it?

Read in a void, the phrase might seem to suggest that the authority's command is *by itself* fully sufficient to produce the prescribed response—that no other facts or considerations or conditions are needed. The authority's say-so *by itself and without anything else* is sufficient to cause you to do something. But this seems an impossibly demanding requirement. Indeed, our discussion of "have to" has already suggested the inadequacy of this conception of "just because." If authority is consistent with or even presupposes the freedom of subjects to comply or not, in other words, then it seems that a command will not be sufficient just in itself to produce a desired action: at the very least it will have to interact with the subjects' own desires, interests, values, or commitments.

Can we even imagine a situation in which someone acts "just because" someone else so ordered in the strictest sense of "just because"—a situation in which the order by itself, without anything else, is sufficient to produce the action? Well, maybe. Suppose some technologically advanced totalitarian government implants electronic chips in its subjects' brains, such that without any choice or thought on their part, they automatically comply with orders—much in the way that characters in a video game automatically respond to signals from the player's controller. In that case we conceivably might say that subjects do things "just because" the government commands them to. Even so, it would seem odd to say that the government has "authority" over those subjects. On the contrary, we would have entered a domain (like a video game) in which notions like "authority" and "obligation" no longer seem to apply at all. If you approach a group of gamers and ask whether a person playing the video game Zelda has "authority" over the character Link, or whether Link is "obligated" to obey the player's commands, your question is likely to produce uncomprehending stares.

But if "just because" does not mean that the authority's orders are by themselves fully sufficient to produce the prescribed actions, then what *does* the phrase mean?

We might look for help, as Hart did, by thinking about how people ordinarily talk about their reasons for doing what they do. We are often asked by friends, family, bosses, or others to explain why we did something; and in response, we say, "I did it because of X." But the X will sometimes seem to be a sufficient explanation ("Oh, *that's* why you did it. Now I understand."), while in other instances

X will seem nonresponsive just in itself, and hence will require further explanation. "Well, okay, but I still don't understand. How was X relevant to what you did?" And in accounting for why some explanations seem sufficient while others call for further explanation, it may be helpful to distinguish between what we could call "intrinsic" goods and "indirect" or instrumental goods—which in turn are the basis of intrinsic and indirect or instrumental reasons.

The distinction is familiar and commonsensical enough. We like or want some things for their own sake; we like or want other things only because they will be instrumental in getting something else that we care about for its own sake.

This distinction between intrinsic and indirect goods—and thus between intrinsic and indirect reasons—is one that we routinely use in accounting for and understanding why people act and that we may express with the language of "just because."[25] You have a friend, Sarah, who is a passionate lover of classical piano music. Her favorite composer is Scarlatti. As it happens, Horowitz is playing Scarlatti tonight at the concert hall, and so Sarah goes to the concert. Asked why she went to the concert, she might say, "Because Horowitz was playing Scarlatti," and that would seem to be an apt and sufficient explanation of her decision.

Other factors were in play, of course—the price of the tickets, the availability of transportation, and so forth. Someone might insist that a full explanation would need to list these other factors: "I went because I like Scarlatti and the tickets were affordable and I had no other conflicting commitments and . . ." But the typical explanation would not need to list all of these factors. Sarah's unadorned "just because Horowitz was playing Scarlatti" seems apt because it indicates that for her, the music was an intrinsic and not merely indirect or instrumental good.

By contrast, you have another friend, Melinda, who is tone deaf and wholly oblivious to the charms of music, but she enjoys Sarah's company. Melinda might attend the concert with Sarah. If asked to explain, though, it would be misleading for Melinda to say, "Just because Horowitz was playing Scarlatti." True, the fact of the pianist playing Scarlatti was a factor in the aggregate of circumstances that led Melinda to attend the concert. Scarlatti was, as tort law scholars say, a "but for" cause of Melinda's decision: but for the playing of Scarlatti, Melinda would not have been in the concert hall that evening. Even so, Melinda went because Sarah went; she would have been just as happy to attend a baseball game or a lecture on Heidegger if that had been what Sarah wanted to do.

The relation between Melinda's action and Scarlatti was not a "just because" relation, but rather a contingent and indirect one. So she could not accurately say she went "just because Horowitz was playing Scarlatti." She perhaps *could* say, however, that she went "just because" Sarah was going—because, for her, friendship with Sarah is an intrinsic good, and thus the source of intrinsic reasons.

"Just because," in short, is an understood way of distinguishing between intrinsic and indirect or instrumental goods, and thus between intrinsic and instrumental reasons for acting. And that seems to be the sense of "just because" in the common formulation which says that someone has authority if "you have to do what they say just because they said to." Their command in itself, and just because they gave it, implicates something that for you is an intrinsic good; the command thus gives you an intrinsic and not merely instrumental reason for acting. A "just because" reason.

We can now return to the gunman situation and observe another reason why the gunman does not have "just because" authority. Even though the gunman's threat provides you with a compelling reason to act, that reason is only contingently related to things that you regard as intrinsic goods. "Preserve my life" is likely an intrinsic good for you. If you say, "I gave him my money in order to save my life," no one will answer with "I don't understand. Okay, you saved your life. And so . . . ?" By contrast, obeying muggers is not something you regard as an intrinsic good or an intrinsic reason. Sarah might actively seek out a Scarlatti concert; you do not actively seek out muggers who will demand and accept your monetary contributions. Rather, the connection between the gunman's threat and anything you regard as an intrinsic good is indirect and contingent. If you happened to know that the mugger's gun was not loaded, or if (unbeknownst to the gunman) you happened to be wearing a bulletproof outfit, then you might have decided *not* to pay. Consequently, it would be misleading to say "I gave him my money just because he asked me to."

And if that sort of "just because" is the mark of authority, then we can say that the gunman lacks such authority. What he has is something else. Something that *resembles* or simulates authority in the sense that it gives you a prima facie reason to do what he says, but not actual authority in the sense that it directly implicates your intrinsic goods or gives you intrinsic reasons to act.

A Further Condition: Verticality

In order to have "just because" authority, therefore, we need to have a command or request issuing from a person, directed to someone for whom compliance with that person's command or request is an intrinsic and not merely indirect or instrumental good. But we might wonder: could this sort of personal "just because" reason ever actually occur? Could we ever regard it as an intrinsic good to do something "just because" another person ordered or asked us to?

Actually, yes: we have already seen that the conditions of a personal and direct reason to act are often satisfied in the context of friendship. Thus, as a musical illiterate Melinda could not say that she went to the concert "just because the pianist was playing Scarlatti." But she *could* aptly say that she went "just because Sarah asked me to." She could say this if friendship with Sarah is something she values for its own sake, and not just instrumentally. That is because part of what makes a relationship one of friendship is an understood prima facie desire to do things that will please one's friend.

To appreciate the point more clearly, vary the example just slightly: Suppose that Melinda has had more than enough social interaction just lately and would prefer to spend a quiet evening at home, but Sarah wants to go the Scarlatti concert and does not want to go alone, and so she asks if Melinda will go with her. It sounds like a tedious evening to Melinda. Scarlatti? Seriously? But then again, Sarah *is* her friend. And Melinda is not the sort of crass, opportunistic person who uses other people just for personal benefit: friendship is to her an intrinsically valuable thing.[26] "Maintaining friendship" or "helping out friends" is for her an intrinsic good—something she values for its own sake. In that case, she might go, and later explain, "I went *just because* my friend asked me to." And for people who know her, this would be a perfectly understandable and sufficient explanation.

In this situation, it seems, we have not only a prima facie reason that emanates from *a person* in the essential sense, but we also have the proper "just because" kind of reason. The requirements for authority that we have discussed thus far all seem to be present. So then, have we stumbled upon an instance of genuine, "just because" *authority*?

It seems not. It would be very odd and misleading—wouldn't it?—to say that Melinda's friend has "authority" over her or that she went to the concert in obedience to the friend's "authority." So it seems that something is missing—that some further condition is still needed in order to have "just because" authority. But what is that condition?

In this case, though, the answer may seem obvious. A relationship with a friend is an association among persons who are presumptively social equals, we might say, or who are on the same social plane.[27] Friendship is a horizontal relationship. "Authority," on the other hand, occurs in hierarchical settings; it entails a relationship that we think of as vertical in nature. People exercise authority *over* other people. The king rules over his people. The principal presides over the school. Austin was right about that much: authority is something that "superiors" exert with respect to "inferiors"—"superiors" and "inferiors" within the chain of authority, that is, though not necessarily in other respects. Without that kind of vertical or hierarchical relationship, we do not have "authority"; we have something else. Like friendship.

In sum, and consolidating the first and third of our clarifications, we might say that in order to have authority, three things are required. There must be (1) a *person* who (2) stands in a *vertical or hierarchical relationship* with one or more other persons for whom (3) complying with the hierarchically superior person's wishes is an intrinsic good, or something that the persons on whom those wishes are imposed value for its own sake. They comply not just for instrumental reasons or from fear of sanctions, but because "doing what So-and-So orders" is something they intrinsically want or need to do. If all of these conditions are satisfied, we have "just because" authority.

These are demanding requirements, to be sure. Can they ever actually be met? It is a challenging question, but we can defer it for the moment. Our first priority will be to see that, whether or not this sort of genuine authority *can* exist, it does *not* exist under the typical accounts of political authority. Or at least those accounts do not give any satisfactory explanation or justification for it. Not even if we assume that the factual premises of those accounts are true. If the premises are true and the logic is sound, those accounts will give us *something*—reasons for subjects to comply with laws or orders. But that *something* will not be authority. Not real authority.

Consent and the Simulation of Authority

Given its centrality in our own political tradition, we should start with the consent account. Authority, once again, is supposed to be based on "the consent of the governed." A common observation, as we discussed in chapter 1, is that this consent, and the "social contract" by which it was supposedly given, are fictions. But let us set aside that difficulty and imagine that all of the subjects really *do* consent, much in the way the Levelers (unsuccessfully) sought to establish consent with a written Agreement of the People during the English Civil Wars.[28] Suppose a consortium of lawyers and political philosophers gets together and writes up a proposed social contract conferring a defined set of powers on a proposed government, and all of the inhabitants of the land gather, inspect the contract, discuss it for as long as they like, and then freely and spontaneously put their John Hancocks on the document. In doing so, they explicitly and voluntarily agree to support the new government (so long as it honors the terms of the contract, of course). Do we now at long last have genuine political authority?

It might appear so, but the appearance is deceptive. Suppose that a few months after the signing ceremony, the government assesses a tax for the building of roads, and one of the citizens of the newly formed state—call him Charle—refuses to pay. Charle doesn't deny signing the contract, nor does he deny that the contract gives the government power to tax. It's just that he thinks the proposed roads are unnecessary, and so he doesn't want to pay for them. The government in its turn threatens to put Charle in jail unless he complies with the tax law.

Do we have just a repeat of Hart's gunman scenario? Would we say that Charle is "obliged" to pay the tax (by the threat of imprisonment) but he is not "obligated" to pay?

Probably not. This situation seems manifestly different from the gunman scenario: that is because, once again, Charle has freely consented to be ruled by the government, and he consequently has an "obligation" to obey the law. Let us set aside potentially vexing complications about personal identity (i.e., is Charle now the same person who signed the contract several months ago?) and about the capacity to bind one's future self. We might then conclude that Charle does have an obligation. After all, he promised to obey the government's laws.

But then that is the crucial point: Charle has an obligation, yes, but *not* "just because" the government ordered him to do something. He has an obligation because he independently promised to do what the government ordered. It is after all a prima facie good to keep promises: Charle will likely acknowledge this, and in any case we would think that he *should* acknowledge it. But then the intrinsic reason that applies to Charle is *not* "obey the government and its laws" but rather "keep promises."

Thus, if Charle had at the outset held out and refused to promise, he would *not* have an obligation (not on the consent account anyway), even though it would be the exact same government imposing the exact same law. Conversely, Charle might have promised almost anything: he might have promised his spouse, say, to follow the advice of the astrologer (who writes a daily column in the newspaper) or of Miss Manners (who does the same thing) or of the Dalai Lama (who gives advice through books and interviews). And we could then say that Charle has a prima facie reason—amounting to an obligation—to follow the counsels emanating from those sources. But it would seem odd to say that the astrologer or Miss Manners or the Dalai Lama has "authority" over Charle. Indeed, none of them even knows of his existence or makes any attempt to address him at all.

As it happens, Charle did not promise to obey those sources; instead, he promised to obey the government and its laws, and so those are what trigger his obligation. What is doing the obligation-creating work here, though, is the moral obligation to keep promises. *Not* the government's authority. The government's commands or laws come into play only contingently and incidentally, in the same way Miss Manners's advice might if Charle had promised to follow *that*.

We can generalize the point. In the idealized social contract scenario, subjects do have an obligation to do what the government tells them to do. But they have this obligation not "just because" the government has told them to do things, but rather because they have made promises and (we can assume) they have an obligation to keep those promises. The government's commands just happen to be something that they have picked out to include in their promises.

In chapter 1, we considered Robert Paul Wolff's argument that authority cannot be reconciled with our commitment to autonomy as the basis of personhood and dignity. We said then that the one account that might avoid Wolff's objection would be the consent account: if we consent to be ruled, then our autonomy is not violated by our recognition of the government's authority. But it now appears that the consent account did not really answer or defeat Wolff's argument after all, but merely did an end run around it. If the only reason we are obligated to obey the government's law is that we have voluntarily promised to do so, then we are not really recognizing or consenting to the government's authority: rather, we are exercising *our own authority*, or our own will, in a way that just happens to pick out the government's laws as something that we choose and promise to follow. And so we still have not encountered genuine or "just because" authority.

Authority and Coordination

Or consider the other main account of authority that we discussed in chapter 1—the coordination account. Articulating this account, John Finnis argues that authority arises from two things: our *need* for directives or rules to coordinate our social interactions, together with the *power* of some person or persons or institutions to provide and maintain such coordinating directives or rules. This seemed a plausible account, and at the time our main point was only that in our own legal tradition, the government's *power* to provide effective coordination is linked to the *perception of authority*, which is in turn linked to the official fiction of "the consent of the governed." Now, though, we can appreciate a different complication: even if the coordination account gives us reasons to comply with the government's coordinating directives and rules, those reasons sound in some combination self-interest (it serves our own interest to uphold mutually beneficial rules) and, perhaps, respect or concern for our fellow citizens, or for the common good. We do not comply "just because" the government tells us to do so.

"Promote your own interests" and "respect and help your neighbors" may be things that we do or should regard as intrinsically valuable or obligatory. The same may be true for "Promote the common good." By contrast, "Obey the government" probably is not an intrinsically valuable good or obligation. (If it were, our whole problem would be solved *ab initio*, so to speak. Why should we obey the law? Because we intrinsically want to, or ought to: beginning and end of discussion.) So we may have prima facie reasons to obey the government and its laws; we may even obey out of a sense of obligation. But our obligation runs to ourselves and our fellow citizens. It does not run to the government.[29]

In this respect, the reason for complying with government directives seems closely analogous to the reason for complying with the gunman's directive in the "Rambo" situation discussed earlier—the situation in which Norris, the victim, complies not out of respect *for the gunman* or for the order itself, but rather because of an obligation to spouse and children. In that situation, as we saw, Norris might plausibly be said to be "obligated" to comply. But because Norris's obligation is owed to someone other than the person issuing the order, and because the order is only contingently related to that obligation, it would seem implausible to say that the person issuing the order thereby acquires "authority."

The same analysis would seem to apply to Finnis's coordination account. Thus, a compliant citizen might explain, "I obeyed the law because I wanted (or was morally obligated) to promote the common good, and the government's directive was a fact that led me to conclude that acting in accordance with the directive would achieve that objective." The reason for following the law—the "obligation," even—derives from an independent obligation to which the law is contingently related.

Indeed, Finnis himself (following Aquinas) carefully explains how in the case of *unjust laws*, subjects are not obligated by the laws themselves; but they may nonetheless have a moral obligation to obey those laws so as to avoid injury to fellow citizens.[30] But although just laws surely have a stronger claim on us than unjust laws do,[31] insofar as the *obligation to obey* derives from a general duty owed *to our fellow citizens*, there seems to be no difference in this particular respect between just and unjust laws. In neither case does the law provide the "just because" sort of reason that is the mark of authority.[32]

THE SERVICE CONCEPTION OF AUTHORITY

Perhaps the most widely discussed account of authority in modern legal theory is Joseph Raz's "service conception of authority."[33] Raz suggests that practical authority can be understood in terms of three basic ideas, or theses. The "dependence thesis" asserts that authoritative directives are "based on the other reasons" that would guide a person or agent in any case, operating "to sum [those reasons] up and to reflect their outcome."[34] The dependence thesis is supplemented by "the normal justification thesis," which explains our rationale or justification for obeying authority: we do what the authority says because we are more likely to comply with the reasons that already apply to us by following the authority's directives than by acting on our own independent judgments. In that case, we do not so much *add* the authority's directives into the mix of reasons we act upon—this would be a kind of double-counting—but rather treat those reasons as *replacing* or *preempting* other reasons.[35] Raz describes this last idea as "the preemption thesis."[36]

These are abstract propositions; a clarifying example may be helpful. Suppose your stockbroker advises you to sell your stock in IBM. She is presumably acting on the basis of the same profit-making objectives that led you to consult her in the first place and that would motivate you if you did not have a broker. *Her* profit-directed advice derives from—is dependent on—*your* profit-making purposes (the dependence thesis). And if you think your broker understands the stock market better than you do, you may plausibly conclude that you will achieve your own investment goals more effectively by following her advice than by acting on your own amateurish judgments and guesses (the normal justification thesis). In that case, your broker's directives will provide you with reasons that are not so much "in addition to" the profit-making reasons you already have, but that in an important sense "replace" or "preempt" those reasons (the preemption thesis). You would not say, "I sold my shares because I wanted to make a profit, *and also* because my broker advised me to." That would be redundant, and misleading.

Raz provides a sophisticated explanation of a particular kind of reason for acting. His account has been criticized,[37] but let us suppose that it is persuasive in describing a familiar form of *practical reasoning*. On that charitable supposition, does Raz give us "authority" of the sort we have been looking for?

It seems not. On the contrary, if offered *as an explanation of authority*, or of obligation, Raz's account seems to invite the same kind of criticism that Hart made against Austin and that we have been considering with respect to the consent and coordination accounts. That is, Raz's account may explain why you have good *reasons* to do as your stockbroker advises; but those reasons are not reflective of any *authority* that your stockbroker has over you.

Thus, speaking loosely, you might say, "I sold my stock in IBM because my broker told me to." But even though your broker is a person (our first condition for authority), and even though within the investment hierarchy the broker arguably stands in a vertical relation to you (our second condition), our third condition is plainly not met. The "because" in this statement does not reflect the kind of personal and "just because" reason needed for authority. In fact, you follow the broker's advice for purely instrumental reasons. "Make profits" may be a principle of action for you; "obey my broker" almost surely is not. So the more complete explanation of your sale of the IBM shares would say, "I sold the stock because I want to make a profit in the market, and my broker's advice led me to believe that the best way to achieve this goal would be to sell. Did I have an 'obligation' to do what my broker told me to do because she told me to? Of course not!"

In fact, closely considered, it wasn't the broker's *order* at all, but rather her *expert opinion*, that was relevant to your decision to sell. If you had known (by, say, overhearing a phone conversation between the broker and some other client) that the broker believed IBM was going to plummet, you would have had the same reason to sell even without any actual instruction from her. And, conversely, if you had known that the broker *didn't* actually believe IBM would drop, you presumably *wouldn't* have sold even if she had advised you to do so (by mistake or misfeasance of some sort). The broker's advice was an evidentiary fact, and you would have had the same reason to act if you had encountered the same kind of evidence from some impersonal source.

Nor is the problem that our stockbroker example is dealing with an area of self-interest rather than of "moral obligation." The same conclusion follows if we suppose that the ostensible authority is mediating moral rather than merely prudential reasons, so that your choice is a matter of "moral" obligation. Commenting on Raz's account, Kenneth Himma explains:

> Suppose that right reason demands always that we comply with moral standards. Suppose further that A is infallible in determining what is required by moral standards and is morally impeccable in the sense that A always directs what is required by those standards. And suppose that there is no other fact that might legitimate A's authority apart from A's impeccability. While I am morally obligated to comply with the correct moral judgments that are expressed in A's directives, it is false that I am morally obligated *by* A's directives. If A's directives always demand what is required by morality, I am morally obligated to do as A says — but not for the reason that A says it.[38]

We might put the point simply: in Raz's "service conception of authority," the putative "authority" stands to us basically in the role of expert adviser—whether in prudential or moral matters. And we do often have reason to follow the advice of experts. But not because they have authority over us, or "just because" they advised something; rather because it often serves our interests or aids our judgment to make use of their expertise. This conclusion does not show that Raz's theory of authority is mistaken; it merely shows that it is not a theory of *authority*—or at least not of the kind of authority we have been looking for.

OTHER COMMON ACCOUNTS

Other familiar accounts of authority focus on duties grounded in obligations of gratitude, reciprocity, or fair play.[39] One such account emphasizes duties ostensibly arising from *what government and law do for us*. If someone does you a favor or confers a benefit on you, you are morally obligated, perhaps, to return the favor or to bestow a benefit in return. Government and law confer benefits on us (protection against violence, for example), and we are obligated to reciprocate by accepting the law as authoritative for us.

This reasoning provokes a variety of objections, but for our purposes we only need to consider one. So let us suppose that we are all net beneficiaries of government, and also that we have duties of gratitude to our benefactors (even if we did not request the benefit). In some cases, it might be proper—indeed we might even have a moral "obligation"—to express this gratitude by doing what our benefactor asks us to do. But does it follow that this obligation meets the conditions for authority, thereby turning our benefactor into someone with "authority" over us?

It seems not. Suppose your rich Uncle John, out of the kindness of his heart, gives you a major present—a Mercedes, let's say. You are presumably obligated to feel and express gratitude to Uncle John. Perhaps you are also obligated to reciprocate by doing something nice for him. One possible way of doing something nice and hence expressing gratitude—but only one way, and only a possible way—might be to comply with requests he makes, or with directives he issues.

Suppose you are a celebrated song writer and John says, "Please, my child, write me a song": gratitude and reciprocity may imply that you ought to do this. And you might explain, "I wrote the song because Uncle John asked me to." Even so, the "because" seems indirect and contingent. The more complete account would say something like this: "I wrote the song because I wanted (or felt obligated) to do something nice for Uncle John—he did after all give me a Mercedes—and the fact that he asked me for a song led me to believe that this would be a way of doing something nice for him." But there might well be other ways of discharging gratitude-based duties.[40] You might surprise him with tickets to the Super Bowl or with a basketball autographed by Michael Jordan. Conversely, if your one true love has just left you and you know that in your current forlorn and embittered mood any song you might write would bring your uncle more sorrow than joy, you might sensibly conclude that your duty of gratitude to Uncle John means that you should *not* comply with his request for a song.

In sum, you may well have a good reason to do what Uncle John says to do in a particular context. Even so, it would be a misstatement to say that you act "just because" John told you to, and hence a mistake to say that John has "authority" over you.[41] Even if you have an "obligation," that obligation derives from some other normative source—the duty of gratitude, perhaps—and not from any authority possessed by Uncle John. Substitute "law" or "government" for Uncle John, and the same conclusion obtains: gratitude may give you reasons to act, but nothing that upon close inspection appears to satisfy the specifications for "authority."

A related approach emphasizes the obligations of "fair play" that we owe to our fellow citizens or subjects. In an early article, Hart himself suggested that legal obligation arises from the obligations we owe to our fellows in what is taken to be a sort of common venture. "[W]hen a number of persons conduct any joint enterprise according to rules and thus restrict their liberty, those who have submitted to these restrictions when required have a right to a similar submission from those who have benefitted by their submission. The rules may provide that officials should have authority to enforce obedience and make further rules."[42]

Hart's "joint venture" or "fair play" rationale has generated extensive discussion.[43] Once again, however, we need not enter into the merits of those debates: for our purposes the important point is that, whatever its virtues, the "fair play" account seems subject to the same reservations noted earlier with respect to the coordination account. Even if we have a moral obligation to comply with the rules of the joint venture, this is an obligation that we owe not to the rules or the rulers but rather to our co-venturers. Indeed, Hart himself emphasized the point.[44] And so the "joint venture" account may supply us with reasons to obey or conform, but it does not yield "just because" authority.

Authority: The Impossible Dream?

Theories of authority are legion, and it would be impossible to examine them all individually. So is our conclusion inherently insecure? The theories we have considered fail to yield genuine authority, perhaps, but the next theory down on the list might succeed?

Maybe. But our consideration of some leading theories makes this seem unlikely. It is not just a matter of inductive inference—not just that if five or six leading theories have failed to give us authority, the seventh will probably fail as well. Rather, we can see why these efforts by their nature seem incapable of yielding authority. The very structure of the arguments seems to portend failure.

How so? Look at it this way: The accounts attempt to give us reasons why we should comply with the laws promulgated by governments. And the reasons that they give us will appeal either to our own interests (as in our stockbroker analogy) or to moral duties such as the duty to keep promises, to manifest gratitude for benefits conferred, or to act for the common good. Or of course they may appeal to both kinds of considerations (as the coordination account does).

This is not a mere coincidence. The theories have to appeal to *something*, or else they will supply us with no reasons to obey the law.

And it is difficult to see what else the theories *could* appeal to, other than our interests and our moral commitments and duties.

But if we obey the government and its laws because we think this is in our own interest, then it seems we are not obeying "just because" the government has told us to do so. We are obeying, rather, because we expect to benefit by obeying (much in the way that the victim hands over money to the gunman in order to preserve his life). Alter the calculation of interests, and our reasons to obey will disappear. We are like shrewd prodigal sons who do as our father commands not because he commands us but only because and only so long as we believe we will come out ahead by doing so.

Conversely, if we obey because the government's directives and laws connect to some other independent moral duty that we have, such as the duty to keep promises or to show gratitude, then once again we are not obeying "just because" the government told us to do so. We are obeying, rather, because we have an independent moral duty that happens to connect with something the government has ordered us to do.

Consider a different instance. Maybe we also believe we have a moral obligation to help the poor. If so, then we may act to satisfy a beggar's request, for food or shelter or whatever—but not because the beggar has "authority" over us. We do what the beggar asks not "just because" he asked, but rather because an independent moral duty instructs us to do so. Same for the government in the more duty-based accounts based on promises, or gratitude, or "fair play."

John Simmons explains the basic point. For many laws, Simmons observes, such as laws prohibiting murder, theft, and fraud, "it is perhaps plain in these cases that there is a moral duty or obligation to do . . . what the law requires." Even so, "this duty should not be seen as equivalent to a duty to *obey* the law." That is because "[a] moral duty to obey the law would be a duty to do as the law requires *because* it is required by valid law, . . . a duty to obey the law as such, not to do as it requires just insofar as it happens to overlap with independent moral duties."[45]

In sum, it seems that either consequentialist, interest-based or more deontological, duty-oriented accounts of authority may or may not succeed in giving us reasons to conform to the law; but either way they fail to deliver genuine authority. Nor is it just that prevailing accounts happen to fail to explain and justify authority. Given their structure, it is hard to see how they *could* succeed in this task. Hart's argument that the gunman gives us reasons to comply but does not have actual authority over us expands to encompass other common accounts as well. The argument seems to be uncontainable.

Our discussion has focused on the authority of law—and of government. And yet it may seem that the problems we have observed are not limited to political and legal authority; they may seem to apply more generally. Take the extreme case—God. The objections we have been making to legal authority may seem to apply with equal force to God's authority (stipulating, for purposes of argument, that there is a God in the classic sense—omnipotent, omniscient, omnibenevolent).

Actually, the argument is familiar enough, tracing back at least to Plato.[46] Why should we do what God commands us to do? Maybe because God will bless us for our obedience, and punish us for our disobedience? But then it seems we are really just pursuing our self-interest, not respecting God's authority. Or maybe the answer is that God commands us to do what is right and morally obligatory—on its own, so to speak. God tells us not to kill or tell lies because, independent of what God decrees, it would simply be wrong in any case to kill or tell lies. But in this case, again, it seems that God is at most some kind of moral expert:[47] God is in moral matters much like (although more reliable than) your stockbroker in investment matters. And we have already seen that experts are basically sources of evidentiary facts or information; they do not truly exercise "just because" authority over us.[48]

If anyone possesses genuine authority, one might think, it would be God (if there is a God).[49] So if even God lacks genuine "just because" authority, the search for such authority might as well be abandoned. Or so it may seem.

Lingering Questions

So, has our discussion vindicated Hannah Arendt's assertion that authority has "vanished" from the modern world? Not exactly. Because in order to "vanish," it seems that something needs to have existed to begin with. Whereas our analysis has seemed to suggest that genuine authority—"just because" authority, as we have been calling it—is in principle beyond justification. Authority in that core sense *couldn't* exist, or at least so our discussion thus far has suggested: not even God could have it. And if something couldn't exist, then it never did exist; and it accordingly cannot have "vanished." Just as Hart's objection to Austin's account of obligation and authority turned out to have implications beyond those Hart contemplated, Arendt's verdict on authority seems not to be limited in its application to "the modern world," as she thought. Tentatively seeking to support Arendt's claim, we have overshot the mark. Or so it may seem.

For the same basic reason, however, our discussion has also fallen short of supporting another of Arendt's claims—her claim, namely, that in losing authority we have lost "the groundwork of the world." Because if "the groundwork of the world" is connected to authority, as she suggested, and if genuine authority does not and could not exist, then again it seems that we have not "lost" any groundwork of the world. There never was any "groundwork" to begin with—not of the kind she was contemplating anyway—and so there was never anything we could lose.

Should we be troubled by these (tentative) conclusions? Maybe not. As we noted at the outset, authority is not something we instinctively welcome. It bosses us around, restricts our liberty, orders us to do things we may not want to do. So if it turns out that there is not and never was any real authority, maybe that is cause for celebration. True, most of us do not yearn for anarchy. But that is not a worry, it seems, because our discussion has shown that *reasons to comply* with the government's laws arguably *can* be justified, on more than one account. What more do we need, really? If the reasons for compliance do not add up to genuine "authority," so what?

And yet it seems puzzling—doesn't it?—that so much reflection by so many major and estimable thinkers could have been devoted to exploring and expounding on something that doesn't and couldn't exist. Not just Arendt and Hart and more contemporary theorists like Raz and Dworkin and Finnis, but thinkers throughout the ages like

Plato and Aquinas and Locke. Did all of these worthies somehow allow themselves to be led on a fool's errand? And if there can be no such thing as genuine authority, then how did not only these thinkers but also the rest of us somehow come by the notion to begin with? How did we come to have views and intuitions about what is and isn't authority—intuitions of the kind that Hart invoked in criticizing Austin's jurisprudence? If genuine authority is practically inconceivable, how did we come to conceive of it?

Maybe our discussion has taken a wrong turn, or at least overlooked something important? So we might check our reasoning by asking again: Can we imagine how genuine "just because" authority *could* exist (whether or not our present governments and laws actually possess it)? What assumptions might need to be changed for that to become a real possibility? And what might have happened to bring about our current situation—a situation in which authority, which might once have been more readily accessible (at least as a concept if not as a practical reality), has by now "vanished" from the world? We will pursue these questions in the next and concluding chapter.

CHAPTER SIX

Is Genuine Authority Possible?

Our previous chapter finished anticlimactically, with two basic carry-over questions. First, can we point to or at least conceive of a relationship that satisfies the conditions for genuine or "just because" authority? If we can, then, second, what has happened to make this sort of authority opaque to people today—so opaque that astute observers like Hannah Arendt and like-minded critics would be led to lament that authority has "vanished from the modern world"?

Suppose we manage to identify answers to these questions, or at least the beginnings of possible answers. We might then go on to ask whether Arendt was right in saying that the disappearance of authority would be tantamount to the loss of "the groundwork of the world." What might that claim even mean? What would it be to lose "the groundwork of the world"?

A Preliminary Complication: Authority and Servility

In the previous chapter, reflecting upon H. L. A. Hart's famous analysis of the gunman scenario, we concluded that the possibility of genuine or "just because" authority, as opposed to various sorts of authority substitutes or counterfeits, seems to depend upon three conditions being met. There would need to be (1) a *person* or persons (2) standing in a *vertical or hierarchical relationship* with one or more other persons for whom (3) complying with the hierarchically higher person or persons' wishes or orders is an intrinsic reason for action—something that directly implicates an intrinsic good—and not merely a means to achieve some other end or a fact that happens to implicate some independent duty. Can we find, or at least imagine, any instances in which these conditions are satisfied? That was our principal carry-over question.

At the outset, though, we now need to add one further qualification. In order to have "authority," it seems, we would need to find an instance in which these conditions were met *in a normatively attractive way*. Without this additional qualification, our search for authority might be too easily but disappointingly concluded. That is because in fact we often observe situations in which, for some people, obedience to some ostensible superior seems to be intrinsically satisfying, or an end in itself—but this satisfaction strikes us as degraded or perverted, not as admirable or ennobling.

Thus, on old news reels we observe crowds of hysterically cheering people for whom carrying out the will of the Führer or Il Duce appears to be their driving passion. In his study of mass movements such as fascism, Eric Hoffer provided a grim description of the mentality:

> To the frustrated, freedom from responsibility is more attractive than freedom from restraint. They are eager to barter their independence for relief from the burdens of willing, deciding, and being responsible for inevitable failure. . . .
>
> The frustrated follow a leader less because of their faith that he is leading them to the promised land than because of their immediate feeling that he is leading them away from their unwanted selves. *Surrender to a leader is not a means to an end but a fulfillment. Whither they are led is of secondary importance.*[1]

These examples—Naziism, fascism—are extreme and, perhaps, distant. But we may observe similar if somewhat more muted features in political or religious or nationalist movements today. And there are, arguably, more mundane instances all around us.² Indeed, we may sometimes discern a similar mindset up close . . . in, say, a law faculty.

Thus, in a faculty meeting discussion of proposal X, Professor Bah stands up stoutly for the dean's ill-considered, manifestly misguided position. Professor Bah is surely intelligent enough to see the flaws in this position. So then why does he insist on defending the indefensible? If we are charitable toward Professor Bah, we may interpret his stance as being at least rationally self-serving: he hopes that by demonstrating his allegiance to the dean, he will receive in return a better committee assignment or a larger salary increase, maybe even a professorship or a chair. This interpretation *might* be right. And yet, observing Bah over the years, we have to admit that he doesn't seem to be so calculating, or so foresighted. He may not actually be contemplating any tacit quid pro quo. Rather, his reward seems to be more immediate and more intrinsic: he seems to derive satisfaction, or to feel smugly at peace with himself, so long as and just because he is lining up with an authority figure. The dean. Or rather . . . The Dean.

Such cases would seem to meet the "just because" conditions we discussed above. We have a political or organizational hierarchy, a person at the top giving orders or instructions, and people below who find it intrinsically satisfying to follow those orders or instructions. So, should we say that with our search scarcely commenced, we have already stumbled upon genuine authority—in leaders like, for example, Il Duce? Or The Dean?

We *could* say that. Insofar as we regard authority as a potentially valuable or admirable thing, however, as Arendt seems to have done, the servility described by Hoffer and more dimly reflected in Professor Bah surely does not qualify. Such servility, we might say, is a manifestation not of a relation of "authority" but rather of a perversion of that relation. We sometimes use the pejorative term "authoritarian" to distinguish such perversions from the genuine article.³ Theorists work to distinguish these things. Joseph Vining, for instance, devoted a longish, searching book to reflections on the difference between "the authoritative" and "the authoritarian."⁴

It is possible, of course, that the "authority/authoritarian" distinction is a false dichotomy—that, with all due respect to Vining's probing reflection, there is ultimately no difference between "the authoritative" and "the authoritarian." Perhaps servility, subservience, submission, and obedience are just different words—and there are others, like "cringing," "groveling," "self-abasing"—for the same basic phenomenon of self-degradation. Philosophical anarchists (like Robert Paul Wolff, whom we considered in chapter 1) suggest as much. Wolff invokes the hefty authority of Immanuel Kant, with some plausibility: in his celebrated essay "What Is Enlightenment?" Kant described submission to authority as "laziness," "cowardice," "barbarity," and "self-imposed immaturity"[5]—without attempting to distinguish between good "authority" and degrading "authoritarianism."

Maybe the philosophical anarchists, and also Kant, are right. Before (submissively?) acquiescing in their judgment, though, we ought to proceed a bit further with our inquiry. Perhaps we can find hierarchical relationships that satisfy the "just because" conditions but in a normatively attractive or admirable way? If we can, then any blanket indictment coming from the likes of Wolff or Kant would be at best overbroad.

Friends

So, where to look? We might begin with a relation that is comfortably familiar and that we typically regard as attractive and admirable—namely, friendship.

Friendship and intrinsic reasons. In the previous chapter, we saw that friendship—genuine friendship, that is, as opposed to the opportunistic or instrumentalist kind in which one uses "friends" in the pursuit of more purely self-serving interests—would seem to satisfy two of our three conditions for authority. So even if friendship will not get us all the way to authority, it might at least start us off in a promising direction.

Thus, friends make demands on each other—or if "demands" seems too severe a term, they express requests or manifest wants or needs to each other—and they often act to satisfy these requests or wants or needs. Friendship gives us reasons to do things for each other. These reasons meet the first of our conditions: they come from a person, and in an essential, not merely incidental, sense. It is of the essence of what we might call "reasons of friendship" that the requests or needs that friends seek to satisfy are the requests or needs of *persons*: they are not like the "Check Oil" command that comes on in a car and that elicits our prompt obedience (or, for some of us, our procrastination).

These reasons also satisfy our third requirement: for those in a relationship of genuine friendship, meeting the needs or desires of a friend seems to be an intrinsic and not merely an instrumental reason for acting. Asked why you did something that someone asked you to do, you might answer, "Because she's my friend," or "Because my friend asked me to," and this would be a perfectly satisfactory, if summary, answer. The answer would not seem nonresponsive (in the way that, say, "Because it was Wednesday" would) or a mere gesture toward some other more satisfactory explanation.

Other factors would be involved, of course—your ability to do what your friend needed, for example. You don't *always* do what your friends ask. Sometimes you say, "Sorry, I can't. I'm busy," or whatever. And yet "Because my friend asked me to" is prima facie a satisfactory explanation; it does not need to be understood as shorthand for something like "because in helping her I expected to gain some advantage," as might be true in a purely business relationship. Having and being a friend is, for most people, an intrinsically and not just an instrumentally valuable good.

Friendship as a constitutive good. Indeed, to say that friendship is an intrinsic good understates the point, and it will help us move forward to see why. It seems too weak to say that there is a person for whom having a friend is a "good" in the way that having a tasty meal or seeing an exciting movie or even landing a lucrative job is a "good." We often feel, rather, that our friendships help to make us the people we are. Deprived of your friends, you would not merely be the same basic person except a little a bit less happy or fortunate (as would be true if, for example, you lost your job or had your car broken into).

Without your friends, rather, you would be a lesser or less complete person. Not as fully yourself.

And so we might say that friendship is not merely an "intrinsic good"; or at least it is a distinctive and particularly valuable kind of intrinsic good. We might describe it as a "constitutive good." Friendship is a good because it helps to *constitute* us as persons.

The impression or experience of being constituted as the people we are by our relationships with our friends is familiar enough. But it also challenges or undermines the conception of personhood that is implicit in the pervasive modern commitment to autonomy. Appreciating how it does this will be important in our effort to identify genuine authority.

Persons and relations. Thus, the conception of persons as autonomous beings implies what we might call a "freestanding" or "free-floating" notion of personhood. Or, if you like, an atomistic conception of personhood—one which assumes, as Alistair MacFayden puts it, "the ontological priority and independence of the individual from relations."[6] I am the person I am just in and of myself; you are the person you are just in and of yourself. Our relations with one another may make us better or happier persons, much in the way that a college education might make us a better person or a good and fulfilling job might make us a happier person. But these things—an education, a job, a friend—do not alter our status *as persons*: that is something we just have in ourselves, so to speak.[7]

In this common conception, our status as persons floats free of our various interests and relations. Those interests and relations attach to our personhood as adjectives attach to a noun. To use the old philosophical terminology: our personhood is the essential substance, our various interests and relationships are the accidents that attach to that substance.

The experience of friendship as constitutive, however, suggests a different conception. We are not truly persons "all on our own," so to speak: we are constituted as persons, rather, by a variety of ingredients or components, and one of those ingredients or components is our relationship with others—especially with our friends. Alistair MacFayden observes that "we are what we are only in relation to others."[8]

John Macmurray presents that idea by saying that "the unit of personal existence is not the individual, but two persons in personal relation; and . . . we are persons not by individual right, but in virtue of our relation to one another. The personal is constituted by personal relatedness. The unit of the personal is not the 'I,' but the 'You and I.'"[9]

Consider an extreme instance (or perhaps a close cousin, or maybe a perversion?) of friendship—namely, romantic love. The sort of thing that is celebrated in a million popular songs and movies and novels. The very ubiquity of such productions surely indicates that they express an experience that humans are widely familiar with, or at least that many aspire to. And an endlessly recurring theme in such productions is, you fulfill me, you complete me, I'm not myself without you. As often as not, of course, the idea is conveyed in the negative (and often in maudlin form): Now that you've left me, my life is empty or meaningless. I'm not myself anymore. But whether conveyed positively or negatively, and whether expressed poetically or pathetically, the point is clear: such a relationship is not merely an instrumental good, and indeed not merely a "good" at all in the sense in which a nice car or lucrative job is a "good." The relationship, rather, is something that is somehow essential to one's very personhood.

Personhood as a potentiality. If these common reports of friendship and romantic love challenge the "freestanding" or "free-floating" conception of personhood, they also challenge our standard conceptions in another way. They suggest that, contrary to our usual assumption, personhood is not an all-or-nothing thing that one just has or doesn't have, but rather some more-or-less mix of actuality and potentiality. Personhood is not something that you just have completely and fully if you have it at all (which you do, it seems, if we can address you as "you"). Rather, personhood is something more like a potentiality that you can actualize in varying degrees.

This suggestion is counterintuitive, because we typically think that any individual just *is* a person (at least upon reaching adulthood?)—at least up to the point that he or she dies, upon which (bracketing questions of life-after-death) he or she is *not* any longer a person. We do not typically talk about "partial persons" or "protopersons." Being a *person* is like being a *citizen*: you either are one or you aren't. (Although, again, if you aren't a person we will have trouble talking with or about or especially *to* "you.") And yet experiences with friendship and romantic love imply a different conception. If your friendship "completes you" or "makes you the person you are," the implication is that before or without the friendship you would be a lesser or less complete person.

So being a person is *not* like being a citizen—a status that you either just have or just don't have—but more like being an athlete, say, or a musician, or a scholar. The earnest undergraduate is a scholar, perhaps, . . . but not in as full a sense as the grad student, . . . who is herself not as fully a scholar as the assistant professor, . . . who is not as fully a scholar as the person who has devoted decades to the mastery of her subject. And it is not just a matter of becoming a *better* scholar. With two academicians of equal seniority and dedication to their subjects, we may say that one is a better scholar than the other. But the senior and devoted professor is not merely a better scholar than the undergraduate; she is more fully and completely a scholar. And she is more fully and completely a scholar than she was when she was a grad student—even though she *was* a scholar even then.

Perhaps being a person is more like being a scholar: it is not something that you just have in full upon being born or upon learning to speak or upon turning twenty-one, but rather something that you have in partial or inchoate form and that you aspire to and achieve (or don't achieve) over time. And one of the ingredients that form you into a person—into a more full and complete person—is the relationships that you have with others. Especially with your friends.

Thus, to the person who says, of a friend or a lover, "He completes me" or "I wasn't myself until I met her" or "I'm not myself without her," we might ask: "Hmm. Well then what were you before you met her? Surely you weren't just an automaton, or a blob of protoplasm. It seems you must have been . . . a person." And the answer might be: "Yes, I suppose I must have been a person: what else would I have been? And yet . . . I wasn't fully the person I am now. It's not just that I'm happier. I'm a different person. A more complete person." In this way, your friendship helps to constitute you as a person—as a more complete person than you are or would be without the friendship.

Friendships, in sum, are not merely enjoyable or pleasant, or advantageous; rather, they help to constitute us as persons, or as more complete persons, in the ways we have just been noticing. And if friendship or romantic love can be constitutive goods, and thus sources of "constitutive reasons," and if these are a particularly important kind of "intrinsic reasons," then it seems that relationships of friendship or romantic love would satisfy two of the three conditions for genuine authority. They thus provide help in conceiving of the *kind of intrinsic and personal reason* that would be needed for authority.

The missing element. Even so, we have not yet arrived. Friendship still does not give us authority because, as we noted already, it fails to satisfy the requirement of a *vertical or hierarchical relationship* between the person who issues and the person who complies with a request or command. Friendships and romantic relations are horizontal relations, rather, occurring among persons who are presumptively equals, or who treat each other as equals.

To be sure, friendships and romantic relationships can sometimes devolve into unequal partnerships in which one party dominates the other. Insofar as this happens, though, we think of the change as contrary to, or as a perversion of, the relationship. And the reasons of friendship or love accordingly lose their force.

Knights and Lovers

Or do they? Romantic love in particular may at least point us beyond horizontal relationships and gesture in the direction of something that looks more vertical in character. It is common, in other words, in a romantic relation for one partner to present himself or herself as subordinate to the other: the lover declares that he is the "slave" or the "servant"—or, as Shakespeare put it, the "slave and vassal"—of the beloved.[10] This theme was especially conspicuous in the cult of "courtly love" that flourished during (or perhaps was later invented and projected backwards onto[11]) the Middle Ages and in the ethos of chivalry.[12] The knight kneels before his lady, declares his servitude to her, asks her to command him to perform some heroic or impossible deed. Such submissiveness is for the knight an intrinsic and indeed constitutive good: it is part of the essence of being a knight. "Why did you set off on that dangerous and seemingly hopeless quest?" we might ask the knight, and he replies, "Because my lady commanded me." Within the ethos of chivalry, no further motivation or justification is necessary.

In such a relationship, it may seem that all three requirements for "just because" authority are present. The command comes from a person (the beloved, or the lady); the knight regards fulfilling the command as intrinsically valuable and indeed essential to his identity as a knight; and the relationship is hierarchical in the sense that the knight declares himself to be in a kind of servitude or vassalage. The example thus suggests that we *can* at least conceive of a relationship of authority satisfying all three of our conditions—or at least we can discern such a relationship in another, distant era.

But have we found an example that satisfies our additional condition of being admirable or normatively attractive? Or is the sentiment of chivalric subordination that is exalted in such ideals a perversion of real human dignity and well-being?

From our twenty-first-century vantage point, it is hard to say. Unquestionably the ideals of courtly love and of chivalry have exercised a powerful influence: these things have *seemed* attractive and ennobling to millions of people and have thus inspired countless songs and legends (and even modern movies and musicals, like *Camelot* and *Man of La Mancha*). And stories of knights and chivalry continue to have their appeal—for some people at least: you can easily find a few movies or series enthusiastically depicting the age of knights on Netflix.

And yet, as Edmund Burke observed, "the age of chivalry is gone," and unlike Burke, most of us do not mourn its passing. We find chivalry to be a quixotic ideal, so to speak—something out of another age that we are not sure whether to regard as admirable or ridiculous.[13] The most familiar example is indeed a quixotic one—Don Quixote, with his slavish devotion to the harlot he named Dulcinea: and Don Quixote is a ridiculous figure. Isn't he? And even when we remember the time of knights with admiration or nostalgia, we may pick out the features that seem to portend our own more horizontal values—the egalitarian quality of King Arthur's Round Table, for example, or the convention- and hierarchy-defying feminist courage of Joan of Arc.

In sum, whether the ideal of courtly love should be taken as reflecting a relation of genuine authority or rather of abject irrationality is debatable. We can mark the instance as a possible but contestable case, therefore, and proceed with our inquiry.

Vertical Friendship?

Even so, the cherished and admirable experience of genuine friendship at least suggests what we need to look for. Friendship *would* satisfy the criteria for authority, we have said, except for its horizontal character. So what we would need, it seems, is a kind a *vertical friendship*, so to speak. Can we find, or at least imagine, any such thing?

Parent and child. A potentially promising candidate—and one often appealed to by the theorists of authority—is the relation between parents and children. Historically, arguments for political or legal authority have often attempted to assimilate the government to a parent—on the assumption that parental authority itself is secure and obvious.

Thus, in Plato's *Crito*, the condemned Socrates argues that he is obligated to obey even the unjust decree mandating his execution by imagining the laws of Athens appearing in personified form and invoking parental authority. "[Y]ou are our offspring," the laws say; "[w]e have given you birth, nurtured you, educated you." Consequently, if "[i]t is impious to bring violence to bear against your mother or father," then "it is much more so to use it against your country."[14]

Similarly, Robert Filmer, the seventeenth-century apologist for monarchy who is today remembered mostly as the sparring partner for John Locke's more consent-based theorizing, insisted that "fatherly authority" was the basis of all authority. Filmer's book *Patriarcha* was an extended argument, based on both scripture and Aristotelian philosophy, that monarchs stand in relation to their subjects as fathers stand to their children. The "subjection [of children] to their parents . . . is the only fountain of all regal authority, by the ordination of God himself."[15]

On a more popular level, similar appeals are implicit in common descriptions of one's country as "the Fatherland" or "the Motherland."

The assimilation of government to a parent—a government that is typically distant, impersonal, bureaucratic—may seem flatly untenable today. Donald Trump, or the federal government, as your father? The very suggestion may provoke revulsion. But whether or not the parent-child relationship can be used to support legal or governmental authority, do we at least still understand the relation between parent and child as one in which genuine authority resides? So that in response to Hannah Arendt's claim that authority has vanished from the modern world and that we no longer understand what it is, we can respond: "No, you are mistaken. Authority has not disappeared, and we do still understand it; we understand it in the context of parents and children."

Perhaps. The philosopher Michael White, while arguing (much as Arendt did) that what he calls "natural authority" has largely disappeared from the contemporary world, suggests that the parent-child relationship may be "the last bastion" of such authority. "The idea of parental authority as natural authority seems to me to represent a sort of vestigial idea that is not comfortably at home with the wider modern *Zeitgeist*."[16]

So we need to ask: does the parent-child relationship satisfy our three conditions? Between a father or mother and a son or daughter, there is a relationship that is personal and also, typically, hierarchical, at least when the children are young. So two of the three conditions seem to be met. It is also commonly supposed that a child has at least some prima facie obligation to do as the parent instructs. "Because I'm your mother" or "Because I'm your father and I told you to": these are familiar responses to the child's "Why should I?"

These are also reasons, of course, that children themselves often find to be wholly and woefully lacking in cogency. "Okay, you're my mother: *so what*?" And the indignant son or daughter may add, "It's not my fault that you're my mother" or "When you got made my father, nobody ever consulted *me*" (thus implicitly invoking the modern notion that there is no authority and hence no obligation without choice or consent). And so these responses call for closer examination. *Why* exactly should the child follow the orders or instructions of the parent?

White offers what will strike some as a commonsensical answer, but one which even if correct may fail to satisfy our conditions for "just because" authority. "The idea of parental authority," White suggests, "presupposes a degree of wisdom that [the parent] is prepared to exercise on behalf of the child. It implies that, whatever the child's subjective preferences may be, the parent possesses knowledge about the child's objective good and what the most effective means are for procuring that good."[17]

Let us suppose that White is correct, at least as a rough generalization. In that case, the parent's presumptively superior wisdom together with his or her devotion to the child's welfare might be enough to support "natural authority," as White puts it. But would this wisdom and devotion satisfy the conditions for genuine "just because" authority?

It seems not. In this analysis, to be sure, the child presumptively *should* follow the parent's instructions—but not because something like "obey your parents" is an intrinsic reason in its own right. The child should obey, rather, because doing so is likely to conduce to his or her own interests and welfare—interests and welfare that are themselves quite independent of the parent-child relation. People (including children) will be better off and will have more successful and satisfying lives if they get a good education, develop their talents and abilities, learn to be responsible, avoid getting into trouble, and so forth. And young children will be more likely to do these prudent things by following their parents' instructions than by acting just on their own impulses or immature judgments, or on the suggestions of similarly immature friends. The parent thus stands to the child much in the position of an expert in Joseph Raz's "service conception of authority," which we considered in the previous chapter. The responsible parent is like an all-purpose life coach, counselor, and investment adviser.

As we saw in the preceding chapter, we may have very good reasons to follow the advice of such experts. But these reasons do not add up to "just because" authority. It may be prudent to do as our doctor or our stockbroker advises; but we are not "obligated" to follow their advice, nor do they have "authority" to direct our lives. In the same way, if I am a child, it may be prudent to follow the instructions of my parents, but it similarly does not follow that they therefore have "just because" authority over me.

For the parent-child relationship to count as an instance of genuine authority, we would need to understand that relationship in deeper, less instrumentalist terms. However, we need not merely imagine such a possibility in the abstract: seemingly clear instances are on record and observable. Thus, in many traditionalist cultures, particularly in the Confucian and Buddhist cultures of Asia, filial piety has been widely regarded as a central virtue and component of personhood.[18] A child should honor and respect a parent not just because this may be the best strategy for doing well in life but because even aside from its practical results, treating parents with respect is in itself an essential quality of a good and respectable person. So teaches the Confucian *Classic of Filial Piety*: "The Master replied, 'Of all creatures with their different natures produced by Heaven and Earth, man is the noblest. Of all the actions of man there is none greater than filial piety. In filial piety there is nothing greater than the reverential awe of one's father. In the reverential awe shown to one's father there is nothing greater than the making him the correlate of Heaven.'"[19] And Confucius explains in more detail what filial piety entails: "The Master said, 'The service which a filial son does to his parents is as follows:— In his general conduct to them, he manifests the utmost reverence; in his nourishing of them, his endeavour is to give them the utmost pleasure; when they are ill, he feels the greatest anxiety; in mourning for them dead, he exhibits every demonstration of grief; in sacrificing to them, he displays the utmost solemnity. When a son is complete in these five things he may be pronounced able to serve his parents.'"[20]

To be clear: Filial piety does not entail a servile and delusional pretense that parents are infallible. "Therefore when a case of unrighteous conduct is concerned," Confucius instructs, "a son must by no means keep from remonstrating with his father."[21] Even so, recognition of and even remonstrance against parental failings must be performed within the bounds of the respect due to parents.

Moreover, the duties of filial piety do not extend only to one's natural or biological father and mother. Rather, they reach farther back to ancestors, and more broadly to elders and societal leaders generally.[22]

This sort of filial piety surely might be described as the kind of vertical friendship we are investigating. So we might understand this traditional virtue in the terms of "relational personhood" noted earlier with respect to friends. You are a person, we might say, not just in yourself, but in relation to others. And because humans are not flat or two-dimensional entities, those person-constituting relations will not be merely horizontal (with friends) but vertical as well (upward, with parents and elders and ancestors, and also downward, with children or descendants). The individual who disrespects or defies such relationships is not merely committing a moral error; he is failing to realize or fulfill his own personhood. As Mencius, a Confucian thinker, put it, "To be without sovereign or parent is to be a beast."[23] Conversely, honoring such relationships is essential to one's fulfillment or completion as a person. It is, to use our earlier term, a constitutive good. "The substance of humanity," Mencius taught, "is to serve one's parents."[24]

But can this sort of filial piety be translated so that it is comprehensible and plausible in contemporary Western cultures? Can we get beyond the more instrumentalist conception of the parent-child relationship noted earlier?

We might think of the matter in this way: In Western cultures, particular traits are thought to be valuable or admirable for their own sake. It is good for a person to be intelligent, perhaps, or well informed or open-minded and tolerant or compassionate or musically or athletically gifted—and not just because these qualities will likely produce other goods like wealth or popularity or fame, but because these qualities are deemed to be good in themselves. A person who has these traits is a more complete and admirable human being than someone who lacks them. Occasionally someone will comment disparagingly, "Sure, Susan is smart and artistic, and kind, but how much good has it done her? She is still as poor as an ordinary schoolteacher."

But the comment, we understand, reflects a lamentably shallow view of life and humanity. Being smart and artistic and kind are good things in themselves; they are constitutive ingredients of a more complete person.

So, could we add to this list of intrinsically valuable qualities the feature of, say, filial piety? Of deference to parents? So that we could say: It is not just that the child who follows his or her parents' instructions is likely to "do better in life." It is that a person who fails to respect and support his parents is ipso facto a less complete, less admirable human being.

On this conception, if we can regard it as plausible, honoring the wishes or needs of a parent would be an intrinsic reason for acting. Just as "because my friend asked me to" is an intelligible and prima facie sufficient reason for acting, so also "because my mother (or father) asked me to" would be a perfectly apt and intelligible explanation, and not just a shorthand reference to some other good.

But is this a conception that is accessible *to us*? Is it one that we can take seriously? Filial piety is a cherished virtue in some cultures, but it is not a prominent theme in modern Western cultures. Might this be the source of the condition observed by Hannah Arendt—the loss of a conception of authority?

And yet perhaps this conception is still accessible in our time and place. To be sure, contemporary Western cultures may not celebrate "filial piety" among the principal character traits that society seeks to instill in people. Unlike children in Confucian cultures, young people in Western countries are not typically brought up on books like *The Classic of Filial Piety* or *Twenty-Four Stories of Filial Piety*. And yet would it be accurate to say that this quality is wholly missing from Western cultures? After all, there are still thousands or millions of people who care for aging parents and who treat those parents' wishes as prima facie reasons for action. The phenomenon can be observed even in incongruous settings. In the television series *The Sopranos*, for example, it is evident from the very first episodes that although mob boss Tony Soprano is not averse to killing rivals or blowing up buildings in furtherance of the family business, he earnestly tries to respect the wishes of his delusional and cantankerous mother.

So perhaps in the instance of parents and children we have found a case of genuine authority that can be appreciated even in contemporary Western cultures. And yet doubts remain. Take the familiar instances of people caring for aging parents, sometimes at considerable sacrifice to themselves. Upon reflection, does this example satisfy the requirement of a vertical or hierarchical relationship?

It is true, as we have noticed already, that young children are typically treated as subordinate to their parents. The parents are older, more experienced, larger and stronger. But when adult children care for aging parents, these relationships are typically leveled out, or even reversed. Now it is the adult sons or daughters who are healthier, stronger, more capable, and the parents who are frail and needy. There is as much condescension as deference, perhaps, in such care. So perhaps the example does not satisfy our conditions after all. When children are young, we might say, they should follow their parents' instructions for instrumental reasons—because their lives will go better if they do. By contrast, when children become adults, they are no longer in a vertical relationship; or, if they are, it is now *they*, and not the aged parents, who are vertically superior.

Or perhaps the most accurate description is that adult children should support their parents for reasons of gratitude, or maybe for the same kinds of reasons that they ought to support those in need generally. At no point would genuine authority necessarily enter the picture.

In sum, the example of parental authority is a complex and debatable one. In the parent-child relationship, or at least in the filial piety that we can observe more clearly in traditional and non-Western cultures, we find instances of "just because" authority that we may (or may not) regard as admirable. These instances would seem to count against Arendt's claim that authority has "vanished" and that we can no longer understand what it is. Yes, we *can* understand, we might reply, and point to instances of filial piety. And yet these instances, at least as they are realized in modern Western culture, have a marginal and contestable character. As Michael White observes, "[P]arental authority fits uncomfortably within the intellectual milieu" of the modern West.[25]

God's authority, revisited. In the previous chapter, we saw that the dissolution of authority reflected in H. L. A. Hart's criticism of John Austin's "command" account might be applied—and has been applied—even to God. It might seem that if anyone has authority, God would have it (if there is a God in the classic sense). And yet a criticism going back to Plato and developed in detail by modern philosophers suggests the contrary.[26] Why should we do what God commands? If the answer is that God will reward us for obedience and punish us for disobedience, then it seems that God is in much the same position as Hart's gunman, who threatens to kill us unless we do as he orders. Or if the answer is that an omniscient and omnibenevolent God will infallibly command us to do what would be right and to avoid what would be wrong anyway—it would be wrong to kill or rape or rob whether or not God prohibited these things—then it seems that God is at best a kind of consummate moral adviser. Either way, God would lack "just because" authority.

Although sometimes viewed as compelling, however, this criticism overlooks a central aspect of the way religious believers have typically regarded their relationship with God.[27] The devout have regarded God not just as a bestower of rewards and sanctions, but as an intrinsic good—indeed as our highest good. In the Christian tradition, for example, the beatific vision or the loving contemplation of God is sometimes thought to be the greatest joy and the ultimate good that humans can attain. As Augustine famously put the point: "Thou hast made us for thyself, and restless is our heart until it comes to rest in thee."[28]

The notion of "vertical friendship" provides one way of understanding the point. God is often viewed, at least by analogy, as a supreme and supremely loving friend.[29] "What a Friend We Have in Jesus," declares a much-loved Christian hymn. And just as on a relational conception of personhood, friendship among persons is not just something enjoyable or satisfying but rather a constitutive good—an essential part of what constitutes us as the people we are— so friendship with God is thought to be essential to our being the persons we are. Without God, we are not fully ourselves.

The seventeenth-century pastor-poet George Herbert offered a provocative meditation on the point:

> Lord, thou art mine, and I am thine,
> If mine I am: and thine much more,
> Then I or ought, or can be mine.
> Yet to be thine, doth me restore;
> .... *If I without thee would be mine,*
> *I neither should be mine nor thine.*³⁰

So just as "because my friend asked me to" is an apt explanation for something you did (because friendship is intrinsically and not merely instrumentally valuable), so also "because God commanded me to" would be a perfectly apt explanation—and for basically the same reason. A fortiori, actually. In religious devotion, in short, we see another possible answer to Arendt's claim that authority has vanished and that we no longer know what it is.

To be sure, many today will regard this ostensible relationship with God as just another fiction. Even so, in this example, fictional or not, we may at least discern a conception of vertical friendship, and hence a conception of genuine authority.

Other examples? Setting out to see whether we could find examples of "vertical friendship"—namely, valuable or even constitutive but also hierarchical relationships in which "because he or she asked me to" provides an intrinsic and not merely instrumental reason for acting—we have encountered one exotic possibility (in the ideal of chivalry) and two more serious candidates. One is the relationship between parents and children. The other is the relationship between religious believers and (what they take to be) a supremely loving God. Both examples are contestable, to be sure, and complex. Even so, we see in these examples possible instances of relationships that at least seem to satisfy the conditions of genuine authority.

Are there other such instances? With a bit of reflection, it may seem that there are numerous examples. Teachers and students— sometimes, not necessarily always. Coaches and players—sometimes. More generally, mentors and mentees. Conceivably, even supervisors or bosses in an employment setting and the employees who work under them—sometimes (perhaps rarely).

These examples are all contestable in the same way that the examples of parental and divine authority are. It is possible, that is, to characterize all of these relationships in instrumentalist terms. The student follows the teacher's instructions because this is the best way to learn what the student wants to learn and to earn a degree. The player follows the coach's counsel because this is the best way to become a better athlete and to get playing time, and thus to move to the next level of competition (and maybe even earn a scholarship or a lucrative contract). And so forth.

Often the purely instrumentalist characterization *will* seem the most accurate—especially in employment contexts. You follow the boss's orders because you want to get paid and promoted. Period. And yet it seems that many people experience and describe at least some of these relationships in loftier terms—in terms of a kind of vertical friendship. It is not just that the teacher or the coach or the mentor imparted useful instruction or guidance. Rather, the relationship itself contributed to making the student or athlete or mentee the person he or she is. Perhaps the person could have acquired equivalent information from books or online programs or podcasts; but mere information obtained in that way would not have allowed for realization of the student's full personhood in the way that a personal relationship with a caring superior could. And that relationship depends, among other things, on a sort of sincere deference in which the subordinate partner—the student, the player, the mentee—genuinely respects the superior partner and responds to his or her instructions or orders. "Because the teacher told me to" or "because the coach asked me to" is a reason for action—and a reason that is not reducible into purely instrumentalist terms referring to other independent goods or goals.

"I would willingly do anything he asked me to do": we sometimes hear this said of a beloved teacher or coach. If sincere (and is there any reason to doubt their sincerity?), such reports seem indicative of a relationship that satisfies all of our conditions for genuine authority.

Autonomy and the Corrosion of Authority

We set off on this chapter's inquiry wondering whether it would be possible to find instances of genuine authority—instances that would satisfy the three conditions for "just because" authority, and also that would seem normatively attractive rather than contemptible in the way that the servility conspicuous in mass movements like fascism does. By now it may seem that our search has been more successful than we could have anticipated. Even setting aside marginal and debatable instances like romantic love and chivalry, we have encountered any number of plausible candidates for genuine authority. Parental authority (at least in traditional cultures, and possibly in our own). Divine authority. The authority of outstanding and dedicated teachers and coaches and mentors.

All of these examples are contestable, to be sure. And yet the examples are numerous enough, and familiar and commonsensical enough, that it seems unlikely that all of them could persuasively be explained away.

Indeed, the examples are common enough that an opposite question may arise. Why would anyone think that authority has somehow vanished from the modern world? Why would astute observers like Hannah Arendt and various others characterize our period in this way? It may be true that, as previous chapters sought to show, much of what passes for authority in our world is grounded in fictions, and is not even genuine authority: it is more a kind of *faux* authority. This may be especially true for legal or political authority. Even so, the instances of genuine authority are sufficiently familiar, arguably, that it may seem surprising that anyone would think that authority has disappeared. So, how to account for this surprising and (if our discussion thus far in this chapter is sound) mistaken assessment?

In our earlier chapters, though, we have already observed the likely answer to that question. More specifically, we have seen that modern life in the West, in contrast to life in many other times and places, has been powerfully influenced by the development of an ethic of egalitarian autonomy. The development has been the subject of voluminous scholarship and analysis; for our purposes here, we can hardly pretend even to summarize this work. It will be enough, hopefully, to indicate the basic nature of the change that has left authority as a beleaguered and obfuscated reality.

Until relatively recently, most societies even in the West were hierarchical: there were nobles and commoners, in a whole array of degrees. And people were mostly identified by their relations to other people and institutions—by family and class. Asked to identify yourself, you would probably say something like "I'm Robert, William's son" or "I'm Mary, Arthur's daughter." How else could you explain who you are? And depending on the status of William or Arthur, you would have been entitled to receive—or obligated to give—indications of recognition and respect. "With the possession of a certain social rank came a certain 'dignity,'" Kenneth Abraham and G. Edward White observe, "meaning that the status itself was expected to trigger some public acknowledgment, in the form of one or another ritual of obeisance, of the superiority of the individual holding it."[31]

Perhaps most importantly, this stratified and relational order of things was thought to be fitting and right. "God bless the squire and his relations, and keep us in our proper stations."

A critic might object that our contemporary society is still hierarchical—wealth and influence and opportunity are still distributed in grossly uneven proportions—and that people are still identified in part by their relations to other people and institutions. "Trevor is the nephew of Senator Muckamuck." "Maria is a Harvard alum." "Aaron is a partner at Slick and Shuffle." And yet there is a huge difference—namely, that these hierarchies today, however pervasive, are viewed with skepticism or even indignation.[32] You and I are entitled to be taken and accepted for *who we are*—not for who our father or mother is. And each one of us possesses, and is entitled to be taken as possessing, "equal dignity," or "equal moral worth."[33]

Or so we say. There is consequently, in many quarters at least, a discernible horror (or at least a professed horror) of hierarchy and "privilege," and the reigning ethic is of "autonomy" and "equal concern and respect."

These commitments—to autonomy and to equality—are intimate partners, or perhaps merely different aspects of the same normative vision. Thus, J. B. Schneewind explains how for Kant, the seminal theorist of what we might call "strong autonomy"[34] (because the term "autonomy" is used in different and sometimes more compromised senses),[35] the autonomous agent is one who in the exercise of his reason gives the moral law to himself rather than receiving it from anyone else. And insofar as each of us is his or her own legislator and sovereign, hierarchy is (or would be) done away with. True, there is no denying that some of us are wealthier, more attractive, more intelligent, than others of us. And yet we are all equal, in the sense that we are all equally sovereign over ourselves. Indeed, although God has an important role in Kant's moral philosophy, not even God can exercise authority over us. "[Kant's] astonishing claim," Schneewind explains, "is that God and we can share membership in a single moral community only if we all equally legislate the law we are to obey."[36]

Consequently, Kant exhibited a characteristically modern aversion to hierarchy. Schneewind notes in Kant's writings a "hatred of servility and of the class hierarchy that requires it from inferiors. He resents the nobility whose members always despise the 'rabble.'"[37] These commitments—to autonomy and equality—are pervasively evident in modern thought and culture. Gerald Dworkin notes that a commitment to "the conception of moral persons as free and equal" (as John Rawls put it) runs through modern political philosophizing.[38] And in a book aptly called *The Twilight of Authority*, Robert Nisbet observes that "it would be hard to exaggerate the potential spiritual dynamic that lies in the idea of equality at the present time. One would have to go back to certain other ages, such as imperial Rome, in which Christianity was generated as a major historical force, or Western Europe of the Reformation, to find a theme endowed with as much unifying, mobilizing power, especially among intellectuals, as the idea of equality carries now."[39]

But this ethic of egalitarian autonomy seems antithetical to the idea of authority. The commitment to equality negates the hierarchical or vertical relationship that is one of the conditions of authority. The commitment to autonomy in the Kantian sense is an explicit rejection of the possibility of receiving normative law from anyone except oneself.

So although we continue to be surrounded by de facto hierarchies of various kinds and by assertions of ostensible authority, insofar as the ethic of egalitarian autonomy prevails, we would seem to have two possible responses to such hierarchy and ostensible authority.

These responses might be described as "reductive rationalization" and "rejection."

The first kind of response seeks to uphold an apparent relationship of authority, and the reasons for action or compliance that flow from it, by analyzing the relationship into terms of self-interest and/or independent moral duties. The apparent subject should do as the apparent authority instructs *not* "just because" the apparent authority so instructed, but rather because it is in the subject's own interest to comply (Raz's service conception of authority), or because the apparent subject has an independent obligation to comply based on his or her own consensual promise or duty of gratitude or obligations to fellow citizens, or something of that sort. As we saw in the previous chapter, this is exactly how the leading accounts of authority today function. They attempt to supply reasons for obedience to law and government; but these reasons sound either in the self-interest of the citizens or in independent moral obligations (such as, in the official "consent" account, the obligations of promise-keeping). Far from explaining or justifying genuine authority, the accounts work to dissolve it into something else—and also to render it unnecessary. What might have looked like authority isn't. Not *real* authority. But it doesn't matter, because there are other ways of achieving the orderliness that it was authority's purpose to provide.

The other possible response to situations of seeming authority—the other response consistent with a commitment to egalitarian autonomy, that is—is to reject as illegitimate the claims of authority as well as the hierarchy from which those claims issue. Again, this response is perfectly familiar. In recent decades, all of the traditional hierarchies and their accompanying claims of authority—familial, cultural, religious, political—have provoked intense criticism and opposition.[40]

Insofar as we retain the commitment to egalitarian strong autonomy, it is hard to see what other responses to seeming authority could be available to us.[41] Reduction and rejection seem to exhaust our alternatives. As Kant and more truculent descendants like Robert Paul Wolff have accurately perceived, the idea of autonomy in a strong sense is simply incompatible with authority. You cannot say that the mature person must give law to himself, accepting law from no other source, and at the same time say that the person may or should respect the genuine authority of anyone or anything else. Joseph Raz suggests that modern theorizing about authority has had as its central purpose to find an answer to this challenge.[42] But if so, then the project has been doomed from the start. It has been a project seeking to support a logical contradiction.

To Be or Not to Be?

So then, has it turned out that Arendt was right after all? Authority has disappeared, and we can no longer conceive of what it is? Yes and no. Or, rather, no and yes.

Arendt was wrong because, as we have seen, there are instances of seeming authority all around us; and if we are in a commonsensical rather than critical mode, we will easily and naturally understand these instances as genuine authority. Authority is as real and as ordinary as toast for breakfast or dew on the morning grass. What is so hard to understand? What could Arendt (and Professor White and Kierkegaard) have been thinking? Was theirs the kind of brilliance that renders one blind to the obvious?

And then our commitment to autonomy rises up and asserts itself, and our understanding of authority sullenly slinks away. What had *seemed* to be authority must either be something else—something like consent or promise or gratitude—or else it is simply illegitimate authoritarianism. Inherited, oppressive, socially constructed hierarchy. And so authority—genuine authority, which a moment earlier had seemed comfortably avuncular—vanishes. And we are left befuddled as to what real authority might be. How could even God (assuming there is a God) have authority over us? And so it seems that Arendt was right after all.

In sum, it seems that authority—genuine authority, as opposed to *faux* authority—both has and hasn't vanished from the modern world. It has vanished quite unambiguously from the realm of law and government; the prevalence of theories like "consent of the governed" and the leading alternatives on offer are already a testament to that disappearance. Such theories, insofar as they succeed, supply us not with genuine authority but rather with a sort of authority substitute. They give us reasons to obey the law, but not real authority.[43]

Is that a loss to regret? Maybe not. So long as we have reasons to obey the law, who cares whether those reasons proceed from genuine authority or rather from some kind of authority substitute? If we can have the benefits of authority without being burdened down by actual authority, why complain?

In the nongovernmental realm, conversely, the situation is more ambiguous. Authority, it seems, has not actually vanished: it is all around us, arguably, in the relations (some of them, anyway) between parents and children, teachers and students, coaches and players. And yet insofar as we are in the thrall of commitments to egalitarian strong autonomy, we are pushed to interpret away the authority that is manifest in these relationships—to interpret those relationships and their associated obligations as based on something other than authority or, failing that, as illegitimate. So authority has not vanished, exactly; but it has vanished *for us*, so to speak, or vanished from our field of comprehension. Authority is still there, but we cannot see it, cannot understand it. It is hidden in plain sight.

Liberation or Loss?

Let us consider our situation under this aspect or, in other words, on the supposition that authority *has* disappeared from our world. Is this a development that we should celebrate, as liberating? Or does it reflect a "loss of the groundwork of the world," as Arendt suggested?

Our discussions earlier in this chapter on personhood have already anticipated the response: the question comes down, it seems, to one of anthropology. Not the descriptive or cultural anthropology that studies the ethnography of the Trobriand Islanders and other exotic cultures, but rather what is sometimes called normative or philosophical anthropology.[44] *What are we*—we human beings? What constitutes us as a distinctive species—and, arguably, a species with a distinctive value or dignity?[45] We have not thus far posed this question directly—and in fact only rarely does anyone pose the question directly. But we have tacitly been considering possible answers to the question, and those answers reflect two basic (and fundamentally different) conceptions of human personhood.

One answer—the one that was perhaps most deliberately articulated by Kant and that pervades modern culture—identifies our distinctive essence and dignity with our autonomy. We are distinctively creatures who can reason, think for ourselves, give law to ourselves. We do this as individuals. I am my own legislator—the master of my fate, the captain of my soul.[46] You are your own legislator, master, and captain. That is our peculiar dignity.

To be sure, many individuals, perhaps most, fall short of this ideal. They rely on other people to think for them, choose for them. "I have a book that has understanding for me," Kant says mockingly, "a pastor who has a conscience for me, a doctor who judges my diet for me." But this sort of behavior, however pervasive, is a manifestation of "laziness," "cowardice," and "immaturity." When we become fully ourselves, we will leave such dependence behind. It is, ultimately, "the vocation of every man to think for himself," and to choose for himself.[47]

The other answer to the anthropological question that we have encountered lies in what we have called the "relational conception of the person." Far from being independent and autonomous, every person realizes himself or herself only in relation to others. Just as a point has an identity only in relation to other points on a grid or in a figure ($x5$, $y7$), so that outside the figure it becomes unidentifiable, indistinguishable, and (as we might say) pointless, so individuals have an identity only within a network of relationships. Some of those relationships are horizontal—with friends (and, for that matter, neighbors and co-workers and even enemies). But because we are not flat, two-dimensional beings, some of the relationships are vertical: relationships with parents (and children) and teachers (and students) and coaches (and players). Even (or rather especially), in a Christian perspective, with God. It is these relationships—even (or perhaps especially) the vertical relationships—that allow us to realize our personhood. Recall George Herbert's conclusion:

> If I without thee would be mine,
> I neither should be mine nor thine.

These two conceptions appear to be antithetical. To be sure, the commitment to autonomy can no doubt accommodate relationships such as friendship—so long, that is, as they are freely chosen and do not impinge on our ability to think and choose for ourselves. But the claim that we are *dependent* on others, and indeed dependent on our relationships with others for our very personhood: this claim must be offensive to the view that locates our dignity in our autonomy.[48] And dependency on persons who by stipulation are our superiors—parents, teachers, . . . God—seems a special affront to our autonomy, and hence to our dignity. Such dependency may be unavoidable in children or in beginning students. But as we mature, and so become more fully ourselves, we pass beyond such dependency. So a sentiment like that expressed by George Herbert must inevitably be dismissed as a sign of abject "immaturity," as Kant put it.

To Herbert, by contrast, or to proponents of the relational conception, such charges of immaturity will seem deeply ironic. The fact is, they might say, that we *are* dependent on others, in all sorts of ways—emotional, psychological, financial, spiritual, prudential. We just are. Not merely children, but college grads and parents and stockbrokers and even professors of law or philosophy are dependent on their relations with others. Look around yourself: isn't that fact painfully obvious? And, contra Kant, it is actually a mark of maturity to acknowledge such dependency—just as it is a mark of maturity to acknowledge any other kind of truth.

From this perspective, the individual who goes around insisting on his autonomy and his ability to think and choose for himself is like the adolescent who refuses much-needed guidance with the protestation "I'm the boss of myself, and nobody is going to tell *me* what to do." Far from being "the boss of himself," the adolescent is not really a complete person at all; he is more a sort of a proto-person. And it is only when he learns to abandon his pretensions to autonomy and acknowledge his inescapable dependence that he will be on the path to becoming fully himself. That acknowledgment would not entail a sacrifice of his identity but rather its more complete realization. In this respect, moreover, we are all like the adolescent: we are incomplete persons who will realize our personhood over time, in part through the horizontal and vertical relationships that we develop.[49]

So it seems that the autonomy-oriented and the relational conceptions are directly opposed to each other,[50] at least in their implications for authority. If the Kantian, autonomy-oriented conception is correct, then the loss of authority from the modern world would be nothing to lament. On the contrary, this disappearance would reflect a necessary stage in the process by which humanity matures and becomes what it is capable of being. The achievement of full maturity would be attended by, to borrow a phrase, the "withering away" of authority.

Conversely, if the relational conception is correct, then the loss of authority would indeed be a tragic deprivation. In effect, the disappearance of authority and of the conditions and conceptions under which authority is intelligible would amount to the loss of the vertical relationships that are essential for us to be fully ourselves.[51]

The situation would become even more threatening if our law were to deploy its majesty and force to seize jurisdiction over the residual structures and institutions in which authority is still embodied—the family, the local community, the schools, the church—and subject those institutions to its ideal of egalitarian autonomy. If this campaign were to succeed, the possibilities for genuine authority would dwindle, and we would thus be condemned to a sort of enduring incompleteness, a perpetual adolescence. To a condition of being always protopersons, never really and fully ourselves.

Would it be too strong too strong to describe this condition as the loss of "the groundwork of the world"?

Epilogue

Authority outside the Cave?

We are living deep underground, in a subterranean cave. Our heads are fastened facing forward, toward a large cave wall. Behind us, although we cannot see them, fires burn, and someone walks back and forth, between the fires and us, carrying moving figures of people, animals, and other objects: in the firelight, these figures cast shadows on the wall. The shadows are the only things we can observe. And so we naturally take them as realities. We speak with each other about men, women, children, about horses and dogs and trees. But for us, these words refer not to real people and animals and objects, but only to the shadows that flicker on the wall and that we take to be real.

It is an eerie and far-fetched scenario, probably, but also a celebrated and influential one. The allegory of the cave[1] conveyed Plato's conviction that most of the ephemeral things we observe and talk about are only shadows of the true realities—or, we might say, fictional representations of the true realities. They are shadows or fictions of more enduring and substantial realities, or "forms," that we do not perceive directly but that we might infer, through a sort of Socratic examination and reflection, from the more transitory and insubstantial things we do perceive.

Plato's shadow/forms view of reality is not widely embraced today. On the contrary, in our empirically inclined, science-doting society, we are more likely to adopt the opposite stance: the empirical, observable items we see and touch are the most completely and obviously real things (transitory and contingent though they may be), whereas the "forms" or "ideas" under which we conceive of those empirical things are constructed artifices, necessary for our own thought and discourse, but not as real or substantial as the observable things themselves.

Whatever we might think of Plato's metaphysics generally, though, his allegory might seem to capture the condition of political authority today—or at least the condition of authority as perceived by thinkers like Hannah Arendt, whose claim that "authority has vanished from the modern world" launched our inquiry in this book. Contrary to Arendt, it *seems* that authority is all around us. Governments claiming to possess authority accost us on every side; they are constantly insisting on their credentials as they press and pester us with their incessant demands for money and service and obeisance. Arendt was perfectly aware of these claims and demands, of course; but she implied that this sort of observable authority is not the real thing, but only a shadow of authority. Like the denizens of Plato's cave, we take the appearance for the real thing because we lack the actual experience of genuine authority.

Does the analysis of this book, and in particular of the last two chapters, help to confirm this understanding of our situation, or instead to refute it? The previous chapter suggested that, contrary to Arendt's assessment, we do have instances of genuine authority. But these are all contestable cases, as we have seen, and easy to dismiss or misunderstand in our current intellectual environment. Moreover, our discussion has suggested that even if genuine authority does continue to exist—in, for example, parent-child relationships—Arendt's criticism is still largely correct (and hence Plato's allegory might still be applicable) with respect to *political and legal* authority. If we ask about government, that is, or law, it seems that what presents itself as authority is not the real thing. It is a shadow of the real thing. *Faux* authority, as we put it in chapter 5.

So, at least with respect to law and government, is the shadow of authority the most we could ever have or hope for?

Maybe. And yet ... can a shadow even *be* a "shadow" unless there is something more substantial that it is the shadow *of*?

In Plato's story, one of the captives within the cave manages to escape and to ascend upward into the light, where he sees reality itself, not just the shadows of reality. Might something similar be possible with respect to political authority? Does real political authority exist somewhere, somehow? And is there any possibility, for us, of coming to encounter or perceive that authority?

At this point, the guidance of Plato's allegory runs out. Even if we are persuaded of Plato's metaphysics, it does not seem that we end up with real authority. That is because, for Plato, the ultimate reality seems to be something that sounds quite impersonal—an "idea" or a "form." "The idea of the good," or something of that sort. Whereas authority, if it exists, would need to be something personal, as we have discussed.

One later set of interpreters, however, did push Plato's notions in a more personalistic direction. I refer to Christians like Augustine, bishop of Hippo, who were led by Plato's writings to embrace a faith in which the ultimate reality was not merely some inanimate "form," but rather a supreme Person. (Or even, as Augustine and his fellow Christians enigmatically conceived, three Persons who were also in some inscrutable sense one Person.) On this Christian view, the shadows of authority that we see around us might indeed be shadows of something real—something that is ultimate, and an intrinsic good (indeed our highest good)—and also Personal. So in this view, the elements of true authority would thus seem to be present. If, that is, the view is true, which is of course a fiercely contested matter.

And in fact throughout the centuries Christians have taught that there is—or at least there *will be*—a true political authority, with respect to which the earthly governments we see around us are pale imitations or temporary stand-ins. Indeed, in the West the idea is pervasive in our inherited traditions and cultures: to appreciate this, all you need to do is actually pay attention to the lyrics at any Christmastime performance of Handel's *Messiah*? You will hear exultant praises of the "King of Kings" who will come to "reign for ever and ever." The theme runs through familiar Christmas carols ("Joy to the world! / the Lord is come: / Let earth receive her King.") and through Christian scripture and later Christian teaching. You will see it even on the names of some church buildings: "Christ the King." To be sure, it is hard to know how many people today, including Christians, actually pay attention to these words or, even if they do pay attention, actually take them seriously. But the idea is surely there—hidden in plain sight, so to speak.

In this view, secular governments enjoy a kind of simulated authority. That is not an unimportant fact, in either its positive or its negative implications. Even though (or because) simulated authority may be the best we can have at present, it serves an indispensable function in preserving a kind of peace, in punishing the violent and disorderly, in providing a framework within which we can coordinate our various activities. Earthly government is presumptively entitled to our respect and support.

Even so, we are mistaken if we suppose that it is the real thing. It is, once again, a shadow of the real authority that is to come. A fictional representation of the reality.

This distinction is clearly presented in Augustine's major opus dealing with government (and much else). Early in the *City of God*, Augustine discusses Cicero's claim that not just any organized group of people qualifies as a republic; rather, a republic must be characterized by "true justice." Cicero had argued that on this understanding, the Rome of his time—he was writing during a period in which Roman society and institutions were in the process of collapsing into chaos and civil war—was not merely a defective republic; it was not a republic at all. Augustine provisionally accepts the point, and then extends it: on the Ciceronian conception, "Rome *never was* a republic, because true justice had never a place in it."[3]

And indeed, "true justice has no existence save in that republic whose founder and ruler is Christ."[4] On this demanding conception, "what are kingdoms but great robberies? . . . [W]hat are robberies themselves, but little kingdoms?"[5] Augustine illustrates the point with an anecdote about a pirate who had been captured by Alexander the Great. The ruler for his criminality, the pirate replied: "Because I do it with a petty ship, I am called robber, whilst thou who dost it with a great fleet art styled emperor."[6]

This is an inconvenient and even nihilistic conclusion, though, and so Augustine backs away from it. The Ciceronian conception that any government falling short of "true justice" is not a republic at all is not "feasible," he says. On a more practically realistic understanding, Augustine agrees with Cicero that "there was [at an earlier period of Roman history] a republic of a certain kind, and certainly much better administered by the more ancient Romans than by their modern representatives."[7] Much later in the book, Augustine returns to clarify the point. If instead of requiring "true justice" we define a republic more modestly—basically as an assembly of people bound together by common agreement on their shared interests—then we can consider Rome and other kingdoms to be republics after all, and not equivalent to large-scale criminal enterprises.[8]

And indeed, throughout the book Augustine insists on the value of this sort of government in promoting earthly peace. Even so, such government is in a sense a shadow and anticipation of the government that will exist when "all unrighteousness [will] pass away, and all principality and every human power be brought to nothing, and God be all in all."[9]

This will seem like an eccentric view today, no doubt. Not many people now—probably not many people who list themselves as Christians—think about government in this way. So then, what are the viable choices *for us*?

We might insist that the authority of governments—or at least of those governments that are relatively just and humane—*is* true authority. (This view would seem idolatrous on Augustinian premises.) Or we might say, less ambitiously, that true authority of the kind that people like Augustine and others (maybe even including, in a murky and modest way, H. L. A. Hart) have sought after is an illusion. Shadows of authority—authority grounded in fictions, faux authority, as we have called it: that is all we have or will ever have.

Which is all right, we might hasten to add, because faux authority is all we really need. So long as the fictions hold, faux authority can punish criminals, enforce contracts, and formulate and implement domestic and foreign policy. What more would we even want from our authorities? Indeed, if faux authority is all we will ever have or need, then we might as well drop the "faux" and just call it "authority"—granting that it is not authority in the lofty sense that some have envisioned.

This seems a more modest and commonsensical view, even if not a deeply satisfying one. (Because, once again, it is just a bit unsettling to accept that the majesty of our governments and our laws is grounded in fictions.) And yet if we do take this view, then do we behave incongruously when we then proceed to talk and act as if real rather than shadow or fiction-based authority *does* exist? As we implicitly do when we insist on finding, or at least arguing about, the true or "correct" meaning of a statute or constitutional provision or presidential edict? On the contrary, if shadowy, fiction-grounded authority is all we have, then we might expect it to be elusive, hard to pin down, always the subject and provocation for endless, irresolvable debates about what is "constitutional" or "legal." Because, as we saw in earlier chapters, there will be no fact of the matter that might bring such debates to a definite or correct conclusion. Authority, and hence law, are just not that kind of solid thing. They are more like the pleasant or terrifying projections of an illusionist.

Or, if these alternatives seem unsatisfying, it is perhaps still open to us to hope that the shadows of authority that flicker about us are cast by something, or by Someone, that for the most part we can perhaps only intuit or infer or learn of through rumor, but that is somehow real and substantial. Something or Someone that might be, to borrow a phrase from Hannah Arendt, "the groundwork of the world" with which we ostensibly autonomous selves in the modern world have largely lost touch.

NOTES

PROLOGUE

1. Hannah Arendt, "What Was Authority?," in *Authority: NOMOS I*, ed. Carl J. Friedrich (Cambridge, MA: Harvard University Press, 1958), 1:81–82.
2. Ibid., 105.
3. Ibid., 112.
4. Murphy v. Steeplechase Amusement Co., 250 N.Y. 479, 166 N.E. 173 (1929).
5. R. B. Friedman, "On the Concept of Authority in Political Philosophy," in *Authority*, ed. Joseph Raz (New York: New York University Press, 1990), 56. See also Joseph Vining, *The Authoritative and the Authoritarian* (Chicago: University of Chicago Press, 1988), 157, remarking on the "widespread observation that a sense of the authoritative in society is collapsing."
6. Michael White, "The Disappearance of Natural Authority and the Elusiveness of Non Natural Authority," in *Civilizing Authority: Society, State, and Church*, ed. Patrick McKinley Brennan (Lanham, MD: Lexington Books, 2007), 57.
7. Quoted in Friedman, "On the Concept of Authority," 57.
8. Hannah Arendt, *The Origins of Totalitarianism* (San Diego: Harcourt Brace Jovanovich, 1973).
9. See, e.g., Laurence Claus, *Law's Evolution and Human Understanding* (London: Oxford University Press, 2012); Heidi Hurd, "Why You Should Be a Law-Abiding Anarchist (Except When You Shouldn't)," *University of San Diego Law Review* 42, no. 1 (2005): 75.

10. See, e.g., Maurizio Passerin d'Entreves, "Hannah Arendt," in *Stanford Encyclopedia of Philosophy*, Fall 2019 ed., ed. Edward N. Zalta, https://plato.stanford.edu/entries/arendt/.

CHAPTER ONE The Fictional Foundations of (Modern) Political Authority

1. Cf. Joseph Vining, *From Newton's Sleep* (Princeton: Princeton University Press, 1995), 5, 110–18, 242, 248.
2. See Michael J. White, *Political Philosophy: An Historical Introduction* (Oxford: Oneworld, 2003), 204.
3. Don Herzog, *Happy Slaves: A Critique of Consent Theory* (Chicago: University of Chicago Press, 1989), 215.
4. See Amanda R. Greene, "Is Political Legitimacy Worth Promoting?," in *NOMOS LXI: Political Legitimacy*, ed. Jack Knight and Melissa Schwartzberg (New York: New York University Press, 2019), 76.
5. Thus, Amanda Greene maintains that "legitimacy rests on the assent of all and only the subjects," and she explains that "[a]ssent to being ruled involves a voluntary element of endorsement, i.e., 'I willingly accept my subjection.'" Greene, "Is Political Legitimacy Worth Promoting?," 71–72.
6. Although there is no single or uniform usage, "authority" and "legitimacy" are closely related concepts; "legitimacy" is typically taken to denote something like "morally justified authority," as opposed to mere power or unjustified, "de facto authority." See, e.g., Jeffrey A. Lenowitz, "On the Empirical Measurement of Legitimacy," in Knight and Schwartzberg, *NOMOS LXI*, 296.
7. Marbury v. Madison, 5 U.S. 137, 179 (1803).
8. Alexander Meiklejohn, *Political Freedom: The Constitutional Powers of the People* (New York: Harper, 1960), 9.
9. Rogers Smith, *Liberalism and American Constitutional Law* (Cambridge: Cambridge University Press 1990), 4 (italics added).
10. See John F. Crosby, *The Selfhood of the Human Person* (Washington, DC: Catholic University of America Press, 1996), 1.
11. Gerald Dworkin, *The Theory and Practice of Autonomy* (Cambridge: Cambridge University Press, 1988), 34.
12. See generally J. B. Schneewind, *The Invention of Autonomy: A History of Modern Moral Philosophy* (Cambridge: Cambridge University Press, 1998); Lawrence M. Friedman, *The Republic of Choice: Law, Authority, and Culture* (Cambridge, MA: Harvard University Press, 1990): 18–19, 23.
13. Ekow N. Yankah, "The Sovereign and the Republic: A Republican View of Political Obligation," in Knight and Schwartzberg, *NOMOS LXI*,

102–3; see also Horacio Spector, *Autonomy and Rights: The Moral Foundations of Liberalism* (Oxford: Clarendon, 1992), 90–100, 179–81.

14. Cf. Glenn Tinder, "Authority and Liberty," in *Civilizing Authority: Society, State, and Church*, ed. Patrick McKinley Brennan (Lanham, MD: Lexington Books, 2007), 59–60: "Autonomy ... is living in accordance with self-created and self-given laws and values. At its core, it is simply self-will. It is therefore in no need of authority and is by its nature intolerant of authority."

15. Robert Paul Wolff, *In Defense of Anarchism* (Berkeley: University of California Press, 1998).

16. Ibid., 71–72: "It is out of the question to give up the commitment to autonomy. . . . When I place myself in the hands of another, and permit him to determine the principles by which I shall guide my behavior, I repudiate the freedom and reason which give me dignity. I am then guilty of what Kant might have called the sin of willful heteronomy."

17. Ibid., 14.

18. Ibid., 18. See also ibid., 19 (arguing that "the concept of a *de jure* legitimate state would appear to be vacuous").

19. Ibid., 19.

20. Hurd, "Why You Should Be a Law-Abiding Anarchist." Hurd discusses a variety of considerations that make it "generally appropriate, indeed, generally obligatory, to comport one's conduct in accordance with social and legal rules." But "[n]one of these considerations gives us a reason to follow the law because it's the law." Ibid., 80–81.

21. See Joseph Raz, *The Authority of Law* (New York: Oxford University Press, 1979), 3.

22. Greene, "Is Political Legitimacy Worth Promoting?," 66.

23. See A. John Simmons, "The Duty to Obey and Our Natural Moral Duties," in *Is There a Duty to Obey the Law?*, by Christopher Heath Wellman and A. John Simmons (New York: Cambridge University Press, 2005), 118. "Real citizens in real political communities seldom do anything that can be plausibly described as either a promise to obey or any other kind of freely made commitment to comply with domestic laws."

24. Leslie Green, *The Authority of the State* (Oxford: Oxford University Press, 1990), 166.

25. Cf. White, *Political Philosophy*, 150: "Locke needs the state of nature to be pretty bad but not as bad as Hobbes had thought. It must be bad enough that human beings have adequate motivation to enter into a social contract by means of which a civil state is formed. However, it must not be so bad that the only alternative to it is for human beings to relinquish their political and moral wills to an absolute sovereign."

26. See ibid., 118–80.

27. Kent Greenawalt, "Promissory Obligation: The Theme of Social Contract," in Raz, *Authority*, 268; R. George Wright, *Reason and Obligation: A Contemporary Approach to Law and Political Morality* (Lanham, MD: University Press of America, 1994), 19–36.

28. Ronald Dworkin, *Law's Empire* (Cambridge, MA: Belknap Press, 1986), 194.

29. Edmund S. Morgan, *Inventing the People: The Rise of Popular Sovereignty in England and America* (New York: W.W. Norton, 1988), 87.

30. Ibid., 73.

31. Cf. Herzog, *Happy Slaves*, 193: "One sometimes encounters the suggestion that people consent to the government by paying taxes. In our own society, that invites a short and impatient answer. We have no real choice in the matter, no way of withholding consent. . . . True, one could choose not to pay taxes and risk going to jail. One could also choose to meet the proverbial gunman's challenge, 'your money or your life,' by refusing to hand over one's wallet and risking death. Yet that hardly makes the gunman's offer a proposed voluntary transaction. It's coercive, and so is the IRS's offer."

32. For persuasive criticism of this claim, see Randy Barnett, *Restoring the Lost Constitution* (Princeton: Princeton University Press, 2004), 14–29.

33. Cf. Abner Greene, *Against Obligation* (Cambridge, MA: Harvard University Press, 2012), 38: "For tacit (or implied) consent to work as a type of consent—and not as a ruse to pull us into a nonknowing, nonvolitional cession of authority—there must exist a clear set of social norms indicating that the action in question constitutes consent."

34. Cf. Dworkin, *Law's Empire*, 192–93: "Consent cannot be binding on people . . . unless it is given more freely, and with more genuine alternative choice, than just by declining to build a life from nothing under a foreign flag."

35. Cf. Herzog, *Happy Slaves*, 184: "I'm born under a government that already exists. No one ever asks me if I like it, if I'd prefer some very different government, or no government at all. From a dishearteningly wee age, I am indoctrinated with the merits of my government, an exercise often involving ugly streaks of xenophobia."

36. See Barnett, *Restoring the Lost Constitution*, 29–30.

37. For a helpful critical discussion, see M. Beth Valentine, "'Constructive' Consent: A Problematic Fiction," *Law and Philosophy* 37 (2018): 499–521, https://doi.org/10.1007/s10982-017-9320-6; Cf. Herzog, *Happy Slaves*, 4, arguing that "sometimes hypothetical consent arguments aren't genuinely consent arguments at all: sometimes we might as well argue directly from the substantive merits of what we're defending instead of going through the circumlocutions of hypothetical consent."

38. Cf. Michael J. White, "The Disappearance of Natural Authority and the Elusiveness of Nonnatural Authority," in Brennan, *Civilizing Authority*, 32, observing that "idealized consent is not really consent."

39. See, e.g., Michael Huemer, *The Problem of Political Authority* (New York: Palgrave Macmillan, 2013); Greene, *Against Obligation*, 35–113.

40. See John Finnis, *Natural Law and Natural Rights* (New York: Oxford University Press, 1980), 231. A similar point is argued for at length in Yves Simon, *A General Theory of Authority* (Notre Dame, IN: University of Notre Dame Press, 1962); see also Jean Porter, *Ministers of the Law: A Natural Law Theory of Legal Authority* (Grand Rapids, MI: Eerdmans, 2010), observing that "authority emerges out of the exigencies of joint activity and relational actions" (131) and linking authority to "the need for coordination by some agency directly responsible for social existence" (229).

41. Finnis, *Natural Law and Natural Rights*, 246–47.

42. Ibid., 249.

43. Ibid., 251.

44. Ibid., 250.

45. See Frederick Schauer, *The Force of Law* (Cambridge, MA: Harvard University Press, 2015).

46. Robert Cover, "Violence and the Word," *Yale Law Journal* 95 (1986): 1607, https://doi.org/10.2307/796468.

47. See Barnett, *Restoring the Lost Constitution*, 12: "[M]ost citizens think that when a command is called a 'law,' it carries with it a moral duty of obedience, even if that duty is not absolute."

48. Empirically minded scholars have in recent years tried to determine the extent to which perceptions of legitimacy as opposed to fear of governmental force influence obedience to law. Tom Tyler argues that legitimacy is at least as important a factor as fear of force. See Tom R. Tyler, "Evaluating Consensual Models of Governance: Legitimacy-Based Law," in Knight and Schwartzberg, *NOMOS LXI*, 257–292. Critics question whether the evidence supports Tyler's assessment. See, e.g., Lenowitz, "On the Empirical Measurement of Legitimacy"; Schauer, *Force of Law*. But probably most observers would agree that both factors—perceived legitimacy and fear—play some role.

49. See Blaise Pascal, *Pensées*, trans. A. J. Krailsheimer (Harmondsworth: Penguin, 1966), 11 (#44): "Our magistrates have shown themselves well aware of this mystery. Their red robes, the ermine in which they swaddle themselves like furry cats, the law courts where they sit in judgement, the fleurs de lys, all this august panoply was very necessary. If physicians did not have long gowns and mules, if learned doctors did not wear square caps and robes four times too large, they would never have deceived the world, which finds such an authentic display irresistible."

50. Huemer, *Problem of Political Authority*, 116.

51. Ibid., 116–23.

52. See, e.g., James J. O'Donnell, *Pagans: The End of Traditional Religion and the Rise of Christianity* (New York: Ecco, 2015), 28–44. See also Peter Heather, *The Fall of the Roman Empire: A New History of Rome and the Barbarians* (Oxford: Oxford University Press, 2006), 123: "Roman imperialism had claimed, since the time of Augustus, that the presiding divinities had destined Rome to conquer and civilize the world. The gods had supported the Empire in a mission to bring the whole of humankind to the best achievable state, and had intervened directly to choose and inspire Roman emperors. After Constantine's public adoption of Christianity, the long-standing claims about the relation of the state to the deity were quickly, and surprisingly easily, reworked. . . . The claim that the Empire was God's vehicle, enacting His will in the world, changed little: only the nomenclature was different. Likewise, while emperors could no longer be deified, their divine status was retained in Christian Roman propaganda's portrayal of God as hand-picking individual emperors to rule with Him, and partly in His place, over the human sphere of His cosmos."

53. See, e.g., Elk Grove Unified School Dist. v. Newdow, 542 U.S. 1 (2004), upholding use of the words "under God" in the Pledge of Allegiance; see also Lynch v. Donnelly, 465 U.S. 668 (1984), at 693 (O'Connor, J., concurring) and at 717 (Brennan, J., dissenting) (arguing that use of religious imagery and language is sometimes appropriate for the purpose of solemnizing public occasions and functions).

54. For a classic analysis, see Edward Shils and Michael Young, "The Meaning of the Coronation," *Sociological Review* 1 (1953): 63–81.

55. Cf. Horacio Spector, "Legal Fictionalism and the Economics of Normativity," in *Theoretical Foundations of Law and Economics*, ed. Mark D. White (New York: Cambridge University Press, 2009), 73, discussing "legal normativity as a form of ideological advertising developed by state power in order to increase law-abiding."

56. For an account of this mode of legitimation in early modern England, see Morgan, *Inventing the People*, 17–37. For an account of this thinking in the Middle Ages, see Walter Ullmann, *Principles of Government and Politics in the Middle Ages*, 2nd ed. (London: Methuen, 1966), 117–37.

57. Yuval Noah Harari, *Sapiens: A Brief History of Humankind* (New York: Harper, 2015), 24–25.

58. Ibid., 27.

59. Ibid., 28.

60. Susan Haack observes that "novels, and the fictional characters, places, etc., that figure in them, are real; but at the same time, . . . the places

and people they describe, and the events they narrate, are not real, but imaginary." Susan Haack, "The Real, the Fictional, and the Fake," in *Spazio Filosofico* (2013): 216. Haack acknowledges that "this sounds disturbingly like a contradiction," but she thinks closer analysis shows that the apparent contradiction is resolvable: the fictional characters are real imaginary people but not "real people."

61. Cf. Harari, *Sapiens*, 31–32: "An imagined reality is not a lie. . . . Unlike lying an imagined reality is something that everyone believes in, and as long as this communal belief persists, the imagined reality exerts force in the world."

62. See A. Brad Schwartz, "The Infamous 'War of the Worlds' Broadcast Was a Magnificent Fluke," *Smithsonian Magazine*, May 6, 2015, https://www.smithsonianmag.com/history/infamous-war-worlds-radio-broadcast-was-magnificent-fluke-180955180/.

63. Jerome Frank, *Law and the Modern Mind* (New York: Tudor, 1930), 317.

64. Cf. Terry Eagleton, *Literary Theory* (Minneapolis: University of Minnesota Press, 1983), 1–2, suggesting that the distinction between fact and fiction is "questionable."

65. Helen Dale, "Author's Note" from *Kingdom of the Wicked*, Libertarianism.org, October 1, 2017, https://www.libertarianism.org/publications/essays/authors-note-kingdom-wicked.

66. Morgan, *Inventing the People*, 13, 93.

CHAPTER TWO Fictional Authority and the Problem of Constitutional Interpretation

1. Cf. Antonin Scalia, "Assorted Canards of Contemporary Legal Analysis," *Case Western Reserve Law Review* 40 (1989–90): 589: "That is why, by the way, I never thought Oliver Wendell Holmes and the legal realists did us a favor by pointing out that all these legal fictions were fictions: Those judges wise enough to be trusted with the secret already knew it."

2. Patrick McKinley Brennan, "Locating Authority in Law," in Brennan, *Civilizing Authority*, 174: "Although there is some serious (if generally shallow) discussion of it in the Anglo-American jurisprudential literature, authority remains an outlier in scholarly legal discourse."

3. This is not *all* that lawyers and judges do, of course. They do other things, including other things *with* laws: a judge, for example, not only interprets a statute but also has to figure out how to *use* the statute in deciding a case. Interpreting a law is part of using it to decide a case. But a judge may

also need to decide whether to follow the law, to ignore it, to "update it" (or allow an agency to do so), and so forth. See Jody Freeman and David Spence, "Old Statutes, New Problems," *University of Pennsylvania Law Review* 163 [2014–15]: 1–94. See generally Steven D. Smith, "Why Should Courts Obey the Law?," *Georgetown Law Journal* 77 (1988): 113–64, discussing different reasons why and ways in which courts use statutes.

4. Cf. Vining, *From Newton's Sleep*, 115: "Close reading, reading in every detail and in every way, is at the very center of what lawyers *qua* lawyers do."

5. Occasionally, to be sure, a historian will read legal texts for purposes of a purely historical inquiry, but that is an unusual and specialized use.

6. Quoted in Richard A. Posner, *The Problems of Jurisprudence* (Cambridge, MA: Harvard University Press, 1990), 264–65. Posner agreed with Holmes's idea and castigated the justice for not consistently adhering to that idea.

7. Cf. William Baude and Stephen E. Sachs, "The Law of Interpretation," *Harvard Law Review* 130 (2017): 1082, describing the view that "there are many ways to read a legal text, each with its own claim to authority." See also Posner, *The Problems of Jurisprudence*, 265, describing "the *variety* of interpretive methods that compete for the law's attention" (emphasis original).

8. A major qualification might be noted here. Suppose that the king has issued an edict: as it happens, I hold the king in contempt and feel not the slightest respect for his decrees, but I know that *you* are a loyal subject who reveres the king and would never willfully neglect to follow his orders. And I see the chance of using the edict to persuade you to do something that would benefit me (or that would benefit *you*, if I happen to care about your welfare). In this situation, I might read the king's edict not to ascertain what the king was *actually* commanding, but rather to figure out what *you might be persuaded to believe* the king was commanding. Even in this case, though, the king's intended meaning will still in a sense be what we might call the primary or assumed or pretended object of interpretation, much in the way that conveying the truth is the assumed or pretended object of a calculated lie. My strategic use of the edict presupposes that the king has commanded something and that his command is the assumed object of our interpretation: without that presupposition, my strategy would collapse.

This qualification may have widespread application in a legal system. Most obviously, lawyers are trying to win cases for their clients, and their purpose, often, will not be to ascertain what legal authorities *really* meant by a law, but rather what some other decision maker (often a judge) can be persuaded to believe the legal authorities meant.

Nor does the possibility of strategic or manipulative use end with lawyers; it extends, potentially, to agencies and judges and other officials. And, in a sense, to all of us. When dealing with laws, we often do *not* primarily care about what the lawmaker intended or, for that matter, about what the law "really" means. What we care about, rather, for practical purposes, is what *someone else*—a judge, a police officer, a building inspector—will *say* the law means. So there is what the original lawmaker—the one to whom legal authority was assigned—meant to communicate; and then there is what the Supreme Court will *think* or at least say that legal authority meant, . . . and what a lower court will think or say the Supreme Court thinks or says the legal authority meant, and what a police officer or building inspector will think. . . . And so forth. We might describe the situation by saying that laws have primary meanings, and also secondary meanings, and tertiary meanings, and so on, indefinitely. And often, or usually, we will for our practical purposes be more concerned with some derivative meaning than with the primary meaning—the one the legal authority that made the law intended.

Even so, these derivative meanings are still parasitic on the primary meaning. They all necessarily make reference to, and get their sense and significance from, that primary meaning. Eliminate the primary meaning and the derivative meanings would all lose their sense, and their authority. Our interpretations will consequently be oriented to that primary meaning, albeit at one or more removes. And so we can still say, perhaps paradoxically, that what the legal authority meant to communicate by a legal text is our primary criterion of interpretation, even if it sometimes almost disappears from view under the layers of qualifications and derivative interpretations.

9. Larry Alexander, "Originalism, the Why and the What," *Fordham Law Review* 82 (2013): 540.

10. Larry Alexander, "Telepathic Law," *Constitutional Commentary* 27 (2010): 140–41.

11. A corollary point is that when lawyers and judges disagree about "what the law is," as they routinely do, they are commonly disagreeing about what the legal authorities were seeking to communicate through their texts. Cf. Steven Knapp and Walter B. Michaels, "Not a Matter of Interpretation," *University of San Diego Law Review* 42 (2005): 664, arguing that "we can only make sense of what people are doing when they disagree with each other about the meaning of a text if we suppose that they regard the text as meaning what its author actually (and not just apparently) intended."

12. We could of course say that the command was *really* authored by some conniving priest, who only pretended to be delivering the message of Apollo. And we might try to figure out what this priest meant. We *could* do that; but why should we? Who cares what some conniving priest has advised us to do?

13. See, e.g., Mitchell N. Berman, "Our Principled Constitution," *University of Pennsylvania Law Review* 166 (2018): 1325–1413.

14. Robin West, *Progressive Constitutionalism: Reconstructing the Fourteenth Amendment* (Durham, NC: Duke University Press, 1994), 196.

15. U. S. Const., Art. VI, para. 2.

16. Listing for *The Constitution of the United States*, 2nd ed. (Malta, ID: National Center for Constitutional Studies), Amazon.com, https://www.amazon.com/Constitution-United-Delegates-Constitutional-Convention/dp/0880801441/ref=sr_1_2?keywords=the+constitution+in+full&qid=1558021229&s=gateway&sr=8-2.

17. See Ilan Wurman, *A Debt against the Living: An Introduction to Originalism* (Cambridge: Cambridge University Press, 2017), 59: "The idea is familiar, if not intuitive, to most Americans: 'We the People' enacted the Constitution in a public act of ratification, and because the Constitution is thus clothed with the consent of the governed, we must continue to adhere to it today."

18. Barnett, *Restoring the Lost Constitution*, 14; Cf. Gary Lawson and Guy Seidman, "Originalism as a Legal Enterprise," *Constitutional Commentary* 23 (2006): 49, observing that "the Constitution itself identifies its author as 'We the People of the United States,' which is clearly a legal fiction rather than a historical fact."

19. James Boyd White, *Acts of Hope: Creating Authority in Literature, Law, and Politics* (Chicago: University of Chicago Press, 1994), 84. White adds that "the idea that the framers of the Constitution, and the Constitution itself, are fictive is no argument against them. All thought about collective life requires simplification; all such thought is constitutive; and this 'fiction' . . . has been at times a source of enormous good." Ibid., 84n2.

20. See Morgan, *Inventing the People*.

21. Cf. Lawson and Seidman, "Originalism as a Legal Enterprise," 58, asserting that "[t]he Constitution declares itself to be authored by, and to speak on behalf of, 'We the People of the United States.' As a matter of political theory, of course, this declaration is a preposterous pretension with no grounding in reality."

22. Morgan, *Inventing the People*. Morgan traces seminal developments back to the English civil wars of the mid-seventeenth century.

23. Edward J. Larson and Michael P. Winship, *The Constitutional Convention: A Narrative History from the Notes of James Madison* (New York: Modern Library, 2005), 187.

24. See Joseph J. Ellis, *The Quartet: Orchestrating the Second American Revolution, 1783–1789* (New York: Knopf, 2015), 150–51.

25. While arguing that "We the People" is a fiction, Randy Barnett acknowledges that "[t]he founders' claim of legitimacy was based not on the divine right of kings, but on the right of 'We the People' to govern them-

selves.... They made the declaration because they believed that the consent of 'We the People' was necessary to establish a legitimate government." *Restoring the Lost Constitution*, 11.

26. See, e.g., ibid., 136–37.

27. See Pauline Maier, *Ratification: The People Debate the Constitution, 1787–1788* (New York: Simon & Schuster, 2010), 107, 260. It was hardly the last time that Americans appealed to We the People to circumvent the legal requirements for constitutional change. See, generally, Bruce Ackerman, *We the People: Foundations* (Cambridge, MA: Harvard University Press, 1991).

28. See Maier, *Ratification*, 260.

29. Cf. David Erskine, *The Great Lester: Ventriloquism's Renaissance Man* (Fort Worth, TX: David Erskine, 2013).

30. Cf. Barnett, *Restoring the Lost Constitution*, 11: "Though 'the People' can surely be bound by their consent, this consent must be real, not fictional—unanimous, not majoritarian. Anything less than unanimous consent simply cannot bind nonconsenting persons."

31. See John O. McGinnis and Michael B. Rappaport, *Originalism and the Good Constitution* (Cambridge, MA: Harvard University Press, 2013), 9–10. See also Barnett, *Restoring the Lost Constitution*, 20: "Though voting requirements varied with local jurisdictions, in no place could women, children, indentured servants, or slaves vote. Moreover, it was not uncommon to have a property requirement that limited the voting rights of white males and free black males. How can a small minority of inhabitants presuming to call themselves "We the People" consensually bind anyone but themselves? And assuming they could somehow bind everyone then alive, how could they bind, by their consent, their posterity?"

32. For discussion of this criticism, see Allen C. Guelzo, "How Slavery Is and Isn't in the Constitution," *Public Discourse: The Journal of the Witherspoon Institute*, Nov. 8, 2018, https://www.thepublicdiscourse.com/2018/11/42658/.

33. Wurman, *Debt against the Living*, 62–64.

34. In this spirit, Thomas Jefferson, who took very seriously the requirement of "consent of the governed," famously argued that a constitution would expire at the end of every nineteen-year period, which he took to be the approximate length of a generation. See Richard K. Matthews, *The Radical Politics of Thomas Jefferson: A Revisionist View* (Lawrence: University Press of Kansas, 1984), 19–29. He wrote to Madison: "Every constitution then, and every law, naturally expires at the end of 19 years. If it be enforced longer, it is an act of force, and not of right." Ibid., 23.

35. Lawson and Seidman, "Originalism as a Legal Enterprise," 59.

36. Cf. Sanford Levinson, "Divided Loyalties: The Problem of 'Dual Sovereignty' and Constitutional Faith," *Touro Law Review* 29, no. 2 (2013): 247: "The notion of a single sovereign is scarcely unproblematic, and doubling that number only makes things ever more complicated."

37. James Madison, *Federalist* no. 39, in *The Federalist Papers*, ed. Clinton Rossiter (New York: New American Library, 1961), 242.

38. See, e.g., James Madison, *Notes of Debates in the Federal Convention of 1787 Reported by James Madison*, with an introduction by Adrienne Koch (Athens: Ohio University Press, 1966), 203–30, 293–96.

39. Thomas Jefferson, "Draft of the Kentucky Resolutions," para. 1, reprinted in *The Constitution of the United States*, ed. Michael Stokes Paulsen, Steven G. Calabresi, Michael W. McConnell, Samuel L. Bray, and William Baude, 3rd ed. (St. Paul: Foundation Press, 2017), 52.

40. Quoted in Paulsen, *Constitution of the United States*, 59 (emphasis added).

41. Martin v. Hunter's Lessee, 14 U.S. 304 (1816).

42. See Paul M. Bator, Herbert Wechsler, and Henry M. Hart Jr., *Hart and Wechsler's The Federal Courts and the Federal System*, 2nd ed. (Mineola, NY: Foundation Press, 1973), 445.

43. *Martin*, 14 U.S. at 324.

44. McCulloch v. Maryland, 17 U.S. 316, 404–5 (1819).

45. John C. Calhoun, speech in the Senate, January 22, 1833, reprinted in *The Essential Calhoun*, ed. Clyde N. Wilson (New Brunswick, NJ: Transaction Publishers, 1992), 287 (emphasis added).

46. Ibid., 288.

47. Ibid., 287.

48. *McCulloch*, 17 U.S. at 403.

49. On this interpretation, any nonratifying states would presumably be deemed to have separated themselves from "the People" to which they formerly had belonged.

50. See McGinnis and Rappaport, *Originalism and the Good Constitution*.

51. See, e.g., Madison, *Notes of Debates in the Federal Convention of 1787*, 215 (Alexander Hamilton: states are "artificial beings"), 221 (James Wilson: "the imaginary beings called *States*" [emphasis in original]).

52. Ilan Wurman makes a similar move, arguing that although "the consent of the governed" would ideally entail actual consent by all of the governed, because that sort of consent is impossible we are compelled to treat the closest practical approximation of consent as the decision of the people. *Debt against the Living*, 61–62.

53. See Benedict Anderson, *Imagined Communities: Reflections on the Origin and Spread of Nationalism*, 2nd ed. (London: Verso, 1991).

54. Agitation for nullification arose again in the wake of Brown v. Board of Education, 347 U.S. 483 (1954), but was put down in Cooper v. Aaron, 358 U.S. 1 (1958).

55. U. S. Term Limits, Inc. v. Thornton, 514 U.S. 779, 801–3, 821n31 (1995).

56. Ibid., 838 (Kennedy, J., concurring).

57. Ibid., 846 (Thomas, J., dissenting) (emphasis added).

58. Ibid., 846–47.

59. See Steven D. Smith, "That Old-Time Originalism," in *The Challenge of Originalism: Essays in Constitutional Theory*, ed. Grant Huscroft and Bradley W. Miller (Cambridge: Cambridge University Press, 2011).

60. Cf. Thomas Colby and Peter J. Smith, "Living Originalism," *Duke Law Journal* 59 (2009): 244, asserting that "originalism" refers to "a smorgasbord of distinct constitutional theories that share little in common except a misleading reliance on a single label." See also Lawrence B. Solum, "Simple-Minded Originalism? Simply Wrong!," in *Moral Puzzles and Legal Perplexities: Essays on the Influence of Larry Alexander*, ed. Heidi M. Hurd (Cambridge: Cambridge University Press, 2019), 189–91, listing a range of originalist positions; Mitchell N. Berman, "Originalism Is Bunk," *NYU Law Review* 84 (2009): 1, classifying a variety of different versions of originalism.

61. For helpful histories of originalism by proponents, see Lawrence B. Solum, "What Is Originalism? The Evolution of Contemporary Originalist Theory," in Huscroft and Miller, *Challenge of Originalism*, 13–29; Vasan Kesavan and Michael Stokes Paulsen, "The Interpretive Force of the Constitution's Secret Drafting History," *Georgetown Law Journal* 91 (2003): 1134–48. For a recent history by an originalist critic, see Eric J. Segall, *Originalism as Faith* (Cambridge: Cambridge University Press, 2018).

62. "Originalism" is sometimes said to be a movement that began in the 1970s as a reaction to the more adventurous and textually untethered constitutional decisions of the Warren and Burger courts—decisions like *Miranda v. Arizona* and *Roe v. Wade*. But this description is tendentious: the originalists themselves have contended that they are merely articulating an approach to interpretation that had always been—and had been understood to be—the correct one, and that a self-conscious "originalist" movement became necessary. See Wurman, *Debt against the Living*, 13–14. More recently, scholarly proponents of what is sometimes called "New New Originalism" have argued that originalism has from the outset been the officially recognized mode of constitutional interpretation. See, e.g., William Baude and Stephen E. Sachs, "Grounding Originalism," *Northwestern University Law Review* 113 (2019): 1455–91.

63. See, e.g., Raoul Berger, *Government by Judiciary: The Transformation of the Fourteenth Amendment*, new ed. (Indianapolis: Liberty Fund,

1997), 4, 9, 402. See Lawrence B. Solum, "Originalism versus Living Constitutionalism: The Conceptual Structure of the Great Debate," *Northwestern University Law Review* 113 (2019): 1263: "Old-fashioned intentionalists argued that the original meaning was the original intent of the Framers."

64. An influential early critique was Paul Brest, "The Misconceived Quest for the Original Understanding," *Boston University Law Review* 60 (1980): 204–238.

65. See, e.g., ibid., 218–22.

66. Ibid., 225: "Even if the adopters freely consented to the Constitution, . . . this is not an adequate basis for continuing fidelity to the founding document, for their consent cannot bind succeeding generations. We did not adopt the Constitution, and those who did are dead and gone."

67. See ibid., 214–15. See also McGinnis and Rappaport, *Originalism and the Good Constitution*, 121–22, arguing that "whatever the advantages of original intent in the case of a single author, it is much more problematic in situations where multiple authors are involved"; Keith E. Whittington, "On Pluralism within Originalism," in Huscroft and Miller, *Challenge of Originalism*, 72, noting that "it is hard as a practical matter to identify the coherent intentions of a collective author (potentially across multiple ratification conventions on many aspects of the text)."

68. See Michael Stokes Paulsen and Luke Paulsen, *The Constitution: An Introduction* (New York: Basic Books, 2015), 123–26.

69. See Kesavan and Paulsen, "Interpretive Force," 1137–39, describing this shift in emphasis from the Philadelphia delegates' understandings to the ratifiers' understandings. See also Larry Alexander, "Appreciation and Responses," in Hurd, *Moral Puzzles and Legal Perplexities*, 407, 424: "First, let me make it clear that I view the Constitution's ratifiers, not its authors, as those who had authority to create constitutional norms."

70. See Solum, "What Is Originalism?," 19–20.

71. Cf. Solum, "Originalism versus Living Constitutionalism," 1250: "Original intent fell out of favor among originalists more than thirty years ago."

72. See Solum, "Simple-Minded Originalism?," 199: "The public meaning of a constitutional provision is the meaning that the provision had for the public at the time the provision was framed and ratified." Cf. Wurman, *Debt against the Living*, 16: "The original public understanding version maintains that the meaning of a constitutional provision is the meaning the public that ratified the Constitution would have understood it to mean."

73. Segall, *Originalism as Faith*, 85–87; Kesavan and Paulsen, "Interpretive Force," 1132.

74. See, e.g., Stanley Fish, "The Intentionalist Thesis Once More," in Huscroft and Miller, *Challenge of Originalism*, 99. Fish argues that academic

efforts to separate textual meaning from authors' intentions have become "scholastic, a dizzying structure of cycles and epicycles built on a mistake."

75. John O. McGinnis and Michael B. Rappaport, "Unifying Original Intent and Original Public Meaning," *Northwestern University Law Review* 113 (2019): 1378, arguing that interpretation depends on linguistic "rules and conventions."

76. See Solum, "Simple-Minded Originalism?," 196: "Intentional action by individual speakers (or authors) is necessary to get conventional semantic meanings going, but once such a meaning is established, it is not reducible to the communicative intentions of individual speakers (or authors)."

77. See Connie S. Rosati, "Alexander's 'Simple-Minded Originalism,'" in Hurd, *Moral Puzzles and Legal Perplexities*, 153–54. For elaboration, see Solum, "Simple-Minded Originalism?," 193–98. Solum asserts that "[t]he sentence meaning of a written text is the conventional semantic meaning of the words and the phrases as structured by the conventions of syntax and punctuation." Ibid., 196.

78. Wurman, *Debt against the Living*, 17, describing the leading view that "original public understanding should aim at what *a hypothetical reasonable observer*, someone fully informed about the history and context of various constitutional provisions and skilled in linguistic conventions, would have understood" (emphasis in original); Kesavan and Paulsen, "Interpretive Force," 1132, asserting that the question is what a "hypothetical, objective, reasonably well-informed reader of those words and phrases, in context, at the time they were adopted, and within the political and linguistic community in which they were adopted," would understand the words to mean. Gary Lawson and Guy Seidman argue that the controlling understanding should be that of "the reasonable American person as of 1788" or "the hypothetical understandings of a reasonable person who is artificially constructed by lawyers." "Originalism as a Legal Enterprise," 48.

79. The linguistic conventions appropriate for interpreting the Constitution might in particular emphasize the prevailing modes of legal interpretation. See McGinnis and Rappaport, *Originalism and the Good Constitution*, 116–38.

80. See Lawson and Seidman, "Originalism as a Legal Enterprise," 57.

81. Richard Kay, "Original Intention and Public Meaning in Constitutional Interpretation," *Northwestern University Law Review* 103 (2009): 714–16.

82. They argue that it makes no difference whether we ask about an author or a reader. Lawson and Seidman, "Originalism as a Legal Enterprise," 56. The point seems plausible only on the assumption that since either the author or the reader is hypothetical anyway, we can construct these hypothetical personages to have convergent understandings.

83. See ibid., 54, 58, 66n57, 68.

84. Cf. Marbury v. Madison, 5 U.S. 137 (1803).

85. See, e.g., Antonin Scalia, *A Matter of Interpretation* (Princeton: Princeton University Press, 1997), 17.

86. Jeffrey Goldsworthy, "The Case for Originalism," in Huscroft and Miller, *Challenge of Originalism*, 42, 44 (emphasis added).

87. Cf. Vining, *From Newton's Sleep*, 166: "In legal thought the meaning of the word or words is not separate from the meaning of the speaker." See also ibid., 58: "[W]ords divorced from person—what is sometimes called the literal—is nothing more than sounds of leaves rustling and branches clicking."

88. See Goldsworthy, "Case for Originalism," 44, arguing that treating law as text with meaning to be supplied "entails that the legislatures cannot really make law or have genuine authority to make law: They can only provide raw material to be turned into law by the legal profession." See also Steven D. Smith, "Law without Mind," *Michigan Law Review* 88 (1989): 104.

89. Cf. Lawrence B. Solum, "Originalism and Constitution Construction," *Fordham Law Review* 82 (2013): 464, observing that "as competent speakers and writers of . . . English, the Framers are likely to have understood that the best way to convey their intentions would be to state them clearly in language that would be grasped by the officials and citizens to whom the constitutional text was addressed."

90. See Mitchell N. Berman, "Reflective Equilibrium and Constitutional Method," in Huscroft and Miller, *Challenge of Originalism*, 246: "Non-originalists do not deny that the original meaning constitutes a reason, possibly even a weighty reason, in favor of a given contemporary constitutional interpretation; they only deny the originalist contention that original meaning (or the like) is a conclusive or exclusive reason."

91. Justice William J. Brennan, "The Constitution of the United States: Contemporary Ratification," speech delivered at Georgetown University, Oct. 12, 1985, reprinted in *American Constitutional Law*, by Alpheus T. Mason and Donald Grier Stephenson (Englewood Cliffs, NJ: Prentice-Hall, 1987), 607–15.

92. See Grant Huscroft, "Vagueness, Finiteness, and the Limits of Interpretation and Construction," in Huscroft and Miller, *Challenge of Originalism*, 205–8.

93. Cf. Larry Alexander, "Goldsworthy on Interpretation of Statutes and Constitutions: Public Meaning, Intended Meaning and the Bogey of Aggregation," in *Law under a Democratic Constitution: Essays in Honour of Jeffrey Goldsworthy*, ed. Lisa Burton Crawford, Patrick Emerton, and Dale Smith (Oxford: Hart, 2019), 7: "[Goldsworthy] thinks that if the planners

trust others with a delegation of planning authority, that undermines originalism. But that is a confusion. If the plan is to delegate, that *is* its original meaning."

94. Obergefell v. Hodges, 576 U.S. 644 (2015).

95. See Jon Butler, *Awash in a Sea of Faith: Christianizing the American People* (Cambridge: Cambridge University Press, 1990), 257–88.

96. Holy Trinity Church v. United States, 143 U.S. 457, 470 (1892).

97. See, e.g., Segall, *Originalism as Faith*, 12, 156–57.

98. See, e.g., Michael J. Perry, *The Constitution, the Courts, and Human Rights* (New Haven: Yale University Press, 1982), 37; John Hart Ely, "Constitutional Interpretivism: Its Allure and Impossibility," *Indiana Law Journal* 53 (1978): 399. But they quickly repented of that audacity. See Thomas Grey, "The Constitution as Scripture," *Stanford Law Review* 37 (1984): 1: "It is common to call the opposing schools of thought on the question 'interpretivist' and 'noninterpretivist,' but this distorts the debate. If the current interest in interpretive theory, or hermeneutics, does nothing else, at least it shows that the concept of interpretation is broad enough to encompass any plausible mode of constitutional adjudication. We are all interpretivists."

99. Alexander M. Bickel, *The Least Dangerous Branch: The Supreme Court at the Bar of Politics* (Indianapolis: Bobbs-Merrill, 1962), 25–26.

100. See Dworkin, *Law's Empire*.

101. Edward Foley, while praising Ronald Dworkin for advocating the use of political philosophy in constitutional law, sharply criticizes Dworkin for his continuing insistence on adherence to the constitutional text: on Dworkin's own premises, Foley persuasively argues, this continuing textualism makes little sense. Edward P. Foley, "Interpretation and Philosophy: Dworkin's Constitution," *Constitutional Commentary* 14 (1997): 151.

102. Ronald Dworkin, *Freedom's Law: The Moral Reading of the Constitution* (Oxford: Oxford University Press, 1996), 7.

103. Ibid., 78.

104. Ibid., 10.

105. Herbert Wechsler, "Toward Neutral Principles of Constitutional Law," *Harvard Law Review* 73 (1959): 18–19. See also Laurence Tribe, "Comment," in Scalia, *Matter of Interpretation*, 89, admiring the "inspiring generality" of many of the Constitution's provisions; Ackerman, *We the People*, 94, describing the "rich lode of principle" contained in the Constitution.

106. Jack M. Balkin, *Living Originalism* (Cambridge, MA: Harvard University Press, 2011), 14, 25, 23.

107. Ibid., 59.

108. Jack M. Balkin, *Constitutional Redemption: Political Faith in an Unjust World* (Cambridge, MA: Harvard University Press, 2011), 11; see also Berman, *Our Principled Constitution*.

109. Robert H. Bork, *The Tempting of America* (New York: Free Press, 1990), 81–83.

110. William N. Eskridge Jr., "Original Meaning and Marriage Equality," *Houston Law Review* 52 (2015): 1092. In a similar vein, see Steven G. Calabresi and Hannah M. Begley, "Originalism and Same-Sex Marriage," *University of Miami Law Review* 70 (2016): 648.

111. But see Mike Rappaport, "Abandoning Originalism Wouldn't Be Very Conservative," Law & Liberty, July 16, 2019, https://www.lawliberty.org/liberty-forum/abandoning-originalism-wouldnt-be-very-conservative/, arguing that originalism can be used in a way that avoids the problems of "living constitutionalism."

112. Bator, Wechsler, and Hart, *Hart and Wechsler's The Federal Courts*, 18–19.

113. See, e.g., Earl M. Maltz, "Brown v. Board of Education," in *Constitutional Stupidities, Constitutional Tragedies*, ed. William N. Eskridge Jr. and Sanford Levinson (New York: New York University Press, 1998), 207: "On its face, Section 1 [of the Fourteenth Amendment] might appear to be a general, open-ended statement of principles of justice and equality, leaving the judiciary free to fill in the details as it sees fit. However, in the Reconstruction period, privileges and immunities, due process, and equal protection of the laws were all principles with well-established legal pedigrees, whose meanings were uncertain only at the margins."

114. Ackerman, *We the People*, 96–99.

115. See Steven D. Smith, *The Constitution and the Pride of Reason* (New York: Oxford University Press, 1998), 39–44.

116. 410 U.S. 113 (1973) and 558 U.S. 310 (2010), respectively.

117. Lawson and Seidman, "Originalism as a Legal Enterprise," 53.

CHAPTER THREE   Our Quasi-Fictional Government

1. For a discussion of an imaginative variety of hypothetical situations in which the question whether it was "Congress" that acted might arise, see Matthew D. Adler and Michael C. Dorf, "Constitutional Existence Conditions and Judicial Review," *Virginia Law Review* 89 (2003): 1127–45.

2. See U.S. Constitution, Art. I.5.1.

3. Related questions arise with respect to *time*: must the different branches of Congress pass a law at (approximately) the same time? Saikrishna

Prakash explains the current working assumption that "[a]ll bills must be passed within a single two-year Congress." Saikrishna Bangalore Prakash, "Of Synchronicity and Supreme Law," *Harvard Law Review* 132 (2019): 1234. Once that time period has expired, a bill passed in one house is treated as having failed, and the measure must begin all over again. This understanding has developed even though "the Constitution says nothing about" the question. Ibid., 1256.

4. In fact, the question whether a statute was actually enacted *has* occasionally been contested, and the question has usually been addressed under the so-called enrolled bill doctrine, under which a statute is deemed by a court to have been properly enacted if the statute has been certified by the speaker of the House and the president of the Senate, sent to the president, and filed in the statutory archives kept by the secretary of state. Field v. Clark, 143 U.S. 649 (1892). However, the doctrine does not actually answer the questions of whether a statute has been validly enacted and, if so, how, but rather defers those questions to other actors and indulges for judicial purposes a presumption that the requirements (whatever they might be) have been met. Moreover, as Adler and Dorf have explained, the constitutional and theoretical bases for the enrolled bill doctrine are eminently contestable. Adler and Dorf, "Constitutional Existence Conditions," 1172–81.

5. The Court eventually answered the question in the affirmative. Brief additional discussion of the decision will be given later in the chapter.

6. Cf. Edwards v. Aguillard, 482 U.S. 578, 637 (1987) (Scalia, J., dissenting): "In the present case, for example, a particular legislator need not have voted for the Act either because he wanted to foster religion or because he wanted to improve education. He may have thought the bill would provide jobs for his district, or may have wanted to make amends with a faction of his party he had alienated on another vote, or he may have been a close friend of the bill's sponsor, or he may have been repaying a favor he owed the majority leader, or he may have hoped the Governor would appreciate his vote and make a fund-raising appearance for him, or he may have been pressured to vote for a bill he disliked by a wealthy contributor or by a flood of constituent mail, or he may have been seeking favorable publicity, or he may have been reluctant to hurt the feelings of a loyal staff member who worked on the bill, or he may have been settling an old score with a legislator who opposed the bill, or he may have been mad at his wife, who opposed the bill, or he may have been intoxicated and utterly unmotivated when the vote was called, or he may have accidentally voted 'yes' instead of 'no,' or, of course, he may have had (and very likely did have) a combination of some of the above and many other motivations. To look for the sole purpose of even a single legislator is probably to look for something that does not exist."

7. Richard Ekins collects statements by thinkers from Aquinas and Hobbes to Blackstone affirming that the goal of statutory interpretation is to ascertain and give effect to, as one writer put it, "the legal meaning taken to be intended by the legislator." Richard Ekins, *The Nature of Legislative Intent* (Oxford: Oxford University Press, 2012), 1–2.

8. Matthew Bacon, *A New Abridgement of the Laws of England* (1768), 4:647–48, quoted in McGinnis and Rappaport, *Originalism and the Good Constitution*, 136.

9. William Blackstone, *Commentaries on the Laws of England*, 1:*59–*61.

10. See William N. Eskridge Jr. and Philip P. Frickey, *Cases and Materials on Legislation: Statutes and the Creation of Public Policy*, 2nd ed. (St. Paul: West Publishing Company, 1995), 514: "For most of this country's history, both the theory and the practice of statutory interpretation have been 'eclectic' rather than systematic." Cf. Antonin Scalia and Bryan A. Garner, *Reading Law: The Interpretation of Legal Texts* (St. Paul: West Publishing Company, 2012), 9, asserting that "the field of interpretation is rife with confusion." A recent empirical study of federal appellate judges found that their approaches to statutory interpretation continue to be characterized by "intentional eclecticism." Abbe R. Gluck and Richard A. Posner, "Statutory Interpretation on the Bench: A Survey of Forty-Two Judges on the Federal Courts of Appeals," *Harvard Law Review* 131 (2018): 1302.

11. Kosak v. United States, 465 U.S. 848 (1984).

12. Ibid., 863 (Stevens, J., dissenting).

13. Ibid., 856.

14. See Eskridge and Frickey, *Cases and Materials on Legislation*, 514: "Three different theoretical approaches have dominated the history of American judicial practice: *intentionalism*, in which the interpreter identifies and then follows the original intent of the statute's drafters; *purposivism*, in which the interpreter chooses the interpretation that best carries out the statute's purpose; and *textualism*, in which the interpreter follows the 'plain meaning' of the statute's text."

15. See McGinnis and Rappaport, "Unifying Original Intent and Original Public Meaning," 1376–77, noting that original public meaning is often associated with textualism and original intent with intentionalism.

16. Quoted in Gluck and Posner, "Statutory Interpretation on the Bench," 1301.

17. See generally William N. Eskridge Jr., "Dynamic Statutory Interpretation," *University of Pennsylvania Law Review* 135 (1987): 1479. See also T. Alexander Aleinikoff, "Updating Statutory Interpretation," *University of Michigan Law Review* 87 (1988): 20.

18. See, e.g., Richard A. Posner, *The Problems of Jurisprudence* (Cambridge, MA: Harvard University Press, 1990), 299–309. See ibid., 300: "Maybe the best thing to do when a statute is invoked is to examine the consequences of giving the invoker what he wants and then estimate whether those consequences will on the whole be good ones."

19. See, e.g., Jody Freeman and David B. Spence, "Old Statutes, New Problems," *University of Pennsylvania Law Review* 163 (2014): 1–94. For an early, innovative proposal along these lines, see Guido Calabresi, *A Common Law for the Age of Statutes* (Cambridge, MA: Harvard University Press, 1984).

20. See, e.g., Scalia, *Matter of Interpretation*, 17; see also Alexander, "Appreciation and Responses," 424.

21. Roscoe Pound, "Spurious Interpretation," *Columbia Law Review* 7 (1907): 381.

22. But see Ekins, *Nature of Legislative Intent*, 52, arguing that even a convergent majority intention would be insufficient because "[t]he legislators who form a majority do not have authority to make law. Only the legislature has that authority."

23. Describing the idea of a legislative intent as a "transparent and absurd fiction," the legal realist Max Radin observed that "[t]he chances that of several hundred men" a majority would share an understanding of a statute were "infinitesimally small." Max Radin, "Statutory Interpretation," *Harvard Law Review* 43 (1930): 870–71. See also Ryan D. Doerfler, "Who Cares How Congress Really Works?," *Duke Law Journal* 66 (2017): 981: "[A]s an empirical matter, members of Congress do not *share* intentions"; Kenneth A. Shepsle, "Congress Is a 'They' Not an 'It': Legislative Intent as Oxymoron," *International Review of Law and Economics* 12 (1992): 239–256.

24. Larry Alexander, "Originalism, the Why and the What," *Fordham Law Review* 82 (2013): 542. For a similar example, see Larry Alexander, "Legal Positivism and Originalist Interpretation," San Diego Legal Studies Paper No. 15-200, Elsevier, November 18, 2015, 20–21, http://ssrn.com/abstract=2691740.

25. Alexander, "Legal Positivism and Originalist Interpretation," 20–21.

26. See Tommy Christopher, "The Context behind Nancy Pelosi's Famous 'We Have to Pass the Bill' Quote," Mediaite, November 17, 2013, http://www.mediaite.com/tv/the-context-behind-nancy-pelosi-famous-we-have-to-pass-the-bill-quote/.

27. The bills may, to be sure, be read by congressional staffers, but an empirical study suggests that staffers often by their own admission cannot understand the bills they are assigned to review and assess. See Lisa Schulz

Bressman and Abbe R. Gluck, "Statutory Interpretation from the Inside—an Empirical Study of Congressional Drafting, Delegation, and the Canons: Part II," *Stanford Law Review* 66 (2014): 743. Whether the staffers are different in this respect from the actual legislators is perhaps an open question.

28. In this vein, Larry Solum hypothesizes that "a member of Congress could have a second-order communicative intention to enact the meaning created by the first-order communicative intentions of the individuals who drafted a statute." In this case, Solum reasons, "we would have a kind of delegation of the authority to create communicative content." Solum, "Simple-Minded Originalism?," 203. Larry Alexander appears to adopt this response to the aggregation problem, albeit tentatively. See Alexander, "Appreciation and Responses," 429.

29. See n. 11 in this chapter and the accompanying text discussing *Kosak v. United States*.

30. Cf. Eskridge and Frickey, *Cases and Materials on Legislation*, 530, suggesting that "statements by sponsors and committees might reasonably be thought to represent congressional consensus unless denied by other Members." See also Lawrence M. Solan, "Private Language, Public Laws: The Central Role of Legislative Intent in Statutory Interpretation," *Georgetown Law Journal* 93 (2005): 427–486.

31. See, e.g., Ekins, *Nature of Legislative Intent*, 52–76.

32. See Alexander, "Appreciation and Responses," 429: "Is it an improper delegation of my legislative authority as a voting faculty member for me to declare, with respect to a faculty committee's proposed modification of the faculty rules, one that I have been too busy or too lazy to read, 'I vote to approve whatever it is they recommended'?"

33. On the complex questions raised by congressional delegations, see Larry Alexander and Saikrishna Prakash, "Delegation Really Running Riot," *University of Virginia Law Review* 93 (2007): 1035–1079. I leave aside here the enormous question of legislators delegating their lawmaking authority to particular kinds of *nonlegislators*—e.g., administrative agencies. The question would lead us into realms of legal fictions exceeding anything contemplated in this book. See, e.g., Gary Lawson, "The Rise and Rise of the Administrative State," *Harvard Law Review* 107 (1994): 1231–1254.

34. The point is vividly made in Scalia and Garner, *Reading Law*, 392–93.

35. Scalia, *Matter of Interpretation*, 17. For the same point, see John F. Manning, "What Divides Textualists from Purposivists?," *Columbia Law Review* 106 (2006): 79. See also Oliver Wendell Holmes Jr., "The Theory of Legislation," *Harvard Law Review* 12 (1899): 417–19: "[W]e ask, not what this man meant, but what those words would mean to a normal speaker of

English, using them in the circumstances in which they were used.... We do not inquire what the legislature meant; we ask only what the statute means."

36. See, e.g., Frederick Schauer, "Intentions in Tension," in Hurd, *Moral Puzzles and Legal Perplexities*, 216, asserting that "existing rules and conventions of language can generate meaning"; Anita S. Krishnakumar, "Backdoor Purposivism," *Duke Law Journal* 69 (2020): 1286: "linguistic rules or conventions."

37. John F. Manning, "Textualism and Legislative Intent," *Virginia Law Review* 91 (2005): 424.

38. Scalia, *Matter of Interpretation*, 17. See Abbe R. Gluck, "Justice Scalia's Unfinished Business in Statutory Interpretation: Where Textualism's Formalism Gave Up," *Notre Dame Law Review* 92 (2017): 2060, explaining how Scalia's textualism "seeks to realize 'rule of law' values." Cf. Jeffrey Goldsworthy, "Subjective versus Objective Intentionalism in Legal Interpretation," in Hurd, *Moral Puzzles and Legal Perplexities*, 180: "Lawmakers have authority to make laws, but it is the laws they make that inherit their authority, not—when there is a difference—the laws they intended to make. If the will of the lawmaker were binding, then it would be the true law, and what we currently call laws—which are promulgated by the lawmaker—would merely be evidence of the true law."

39. For classic expositions, see Lon Fuller, *The Morality of Law*, rev. ed. (New Haven: Yale University Press, 1964); Friedrich Hayek, *The Constitution of Liberty* (Chicago: University of Chicago Press, 1960).

40. Jeffrey Goldsworthy, "The Case for Originalism," in Huscroft and Miller, *Challenge of Originalism*, 44.

41. This concern is pressed in Goldsworthy, "Subjective versus Objective Intentionalism," 180–83.

42. Cf. Alexander, "Goldsworthy on Interpretation," 10: "So if the author intends her audience to think 'cat,' then 'cat' is her intended meaning, even if she claims in her secret diary to mean 'dog.' Secret intended meanings are incoherent." On this point, Goldsworthy appears to agree. See Goldsworthy, "Subjective versus Objective Intentionalism," 182.

43. See, e.g., McNally v. United States, 483 U.S. 350 (1987).

44. Cf. Alexander, "Goldsworthy on Interpretation of Statutes and Constitutions," 11: "No one should suffer because of reasonable reliance on an interpretation later shown to have been mistaken."

45. Bostock v. Clayton County, 140 S. Ct. 1731 (2020).

46. Fish, "Intentionalist Thesis Once More," 99.

47. See Ekins, *Nature of Legislative Intent*, 23, arguing that "what is significant is the action of the legislature itself ... rather than the intentions of each member of the legislature considered for his or her part only." Cf.

Vining, *Authoritative and the Authoritarian*, 120: "If one looks at what lawyers say while they are going about their work, it will be found that their questions are in the form 'What did Congress mean by this?' or 'What was the purpose of Congress in enacting this?' and legal conclusion arrived at from the reading of statutes . . . are couched in the form 'Congress intended this' or 'The purpose of Congress was thus and so.'"

48. Cf. Vining, *Authoritative and the Authoritarian*, 121, describing "the personification of Congress." Cf. Lawson and Seidman, "Originalism as a Legal Enterprise," 65: "The metaphor works by positing the collective as a fictitious individual. We anthropomorphize the collective and attribute to it a single mind. We act *as though* it were a concrete person able to act in an intentional way."

49. In this vein, Antonin Scalia and Bryan Garner approvingly quote Tony Honore: "The point of speaking of the intention of the legislature . . . is not that any particular person's views should govern the interpretation of the text. It is rather that the interpreter should treat the text *as if* it represented the view of a single individual, and make it as coherent as possible." Scalia and Garner, *Reading Law*, 393–94 (emphasis added).

50. Morgan, *Inventing the People*, 93.

51. A recent empirical study by Professor Abbe Gluck and Judge Richard Posner found that although textualists such as Justice Scalia inveigh against the use of legislative history, nearly all appellate judges continue to draw on such materials. Gluck and Posner, "Statutory Interpretation on the Bench," 1310.

52. Cf. Scalia and Garner, *Reading Law*, 56: "Of course, words are given meaning by their context, and context includes the purpose of the text. The difference between textualist interpretation and so-called purposive interpretation is not that the former never considers purpose. It almost always does."

53. Henry M. Hart Jr. and Albert M. Sacks, *The Legal Process: Basic Problems in the Making and Application of Law* (New York: Foundation Press, 1994), relevant sections reprinted in Eskridge and Frickey, *Cases and Materials on Legislation*, 539–40.

54. Cf. Scalia and Garner, *Reading Law*, 18: "Where purpose is king, text is not—so the purposivist goes around or behind the words of the controlling text to achieve what he believes to be the provision's purpose."

55. See Freeman and Spence, "Old Statutes, New Problems," 163; Calabresi, *Common Law*.

56. See Amul R. Thapar and Benjamin Beaton, "The Pragmatism of Interpretation: A Review of Richard A. Posner: *The Federal Judiciary*," *Michigan Law Review* 116 (2018): 823: "Judges should not worry so much about doctrine, precedent, or text, [Posner] contends, and should instead

work to improve society by determining the most sensible resolution of a dispute, so long as it's not unavoidably blocked by an authoritative precedent."

57. Cf. Gluck, "Justice Scalia's Unfinished Business," 2067: "No one needs to be reminded that most federal judges generally do not believe they have free-floating federal-lawmaking power."

58. See, e.g., the remarks of Professor Michael Seidman in "The Sotomayor Nomination, Part I," Federalist Society, July 9, 2009, https://fedsoc.org/commentary/publications/the-sotomayor-nomination-part-i.

59. Marbury v. Madison, 5 U.S. 137, 177 (1803).

60. See Gluck and Posner, "Statutory Interpretation on the Bench," 1311, reporting the view of many judges who "were forthright about the quasi-legislative activity that statutory interpretation by judges entails." See also ibid.: "In such situations, the judge's function is, realistically, more legislative than interpretive."

61. See Southern Pac. Co. v. Jensen, 244 U.S. 205, 221 (1917) (Holmes, J., dissenting): "I recognize without hesitation that judges do and must legislate, but they can do so only interstitially; they are confined from molar to molecular motions."

62. See n. 102 and accompanying text.

63. Consider, for example, this summary from the syllabus to the recent decision in American Legion v. American Humanist Association, 139 S. Ct. 2067 (2019): "ALITO, J., announced the judgment of the Court and delivered the opinion of the Court with respect to Parts I, II–B, II–C, III, and IV, in which ROBERTS, C. J., and BREYER, KAGAN, and KAVANAUGH, JJ., joined, and an opinion with respect to Parts II–A and II–D, in which ROBERTS, C. J., and BREYER and KAVANAUGH, JJ., joined. BREYER, J., filed a concurring opinion, in which KAGAN, J., joined. KAVANAUGH, J., filed a concurring opinion. KAGAN, J., filed an opinion concurring in part. THOMAS, J., filed an opinion concurring in the judgment. GORSUCH, J., filed an opinion concurring in the judgment, in which THOMAS, J., joined. GINSBURG, J., filed a dissenting opinion, in which SOTOMAYOR, J., joined."

64. Cf. Vining, *From Newton's Sleep*, 9: "The forms of speech adopted in the Supreme Court opinions themselves . . . imply the existence of a single mind, that of 'this Court.'"

65. Bakke v. Regents, 438 U.S. 265 (1978).

66. See chapter 4, text accompanying note 95.

67. Some time after writing this section, I discovered a recent article thoroughly and thoughtfully developing a similar theme along quite similar lines. See Daphne Renan, "The President's Two Bodies," *Columbia Law Review* 120 (2020): 1119–1214.

68. See, e.g., Frank H. Buckley, *The Once and Future King* (New York: Encounter Books, 2014).

69. Ernst H. Kantorowicz, *The King's Two Bodies* (Princeton: Princeton University Press, 1957; repr., 1997).

70. Ibid., 7. In a similar vein, medieval and early modern theorists would frequently distinguish between "the king" (who was a mortal human being) and "the crown" (which transcended the human king). Ibid., 336–83.

71. Ibid., 9.

72. Ibid., 8, 16–20.

73. Ibid., 23.

74. Ibid., 7, 14.

75. Ibid., 317.

76. Ibid., 314–450.

77. Ibid., 21.

78. Ibid., 23.

79. Ibid., 3.

80. Morgan, *Inventing the People*, 17.

81. More examples are contained in Renan, "President's Two Bodies."

82. See ACLU v. Allegheny County, 492 U.S. 573 (1989); Lynch v. Donnelly, 465 U.S. 668 (1984).

83. See *ACLU v. Allegheny County*; McCreary County, Kentucky v. American Civil Liberties Union of Kentucky, et al., 545 U.S. 844 (2005); Wallace v. Jaffree, 472 U.S. 38 (1985).

84. See David M. Smolin, "Consecrating the President," *First Things*, Jan. 1997, https://www.firstthings.com/article/1997/01/consecrating-the-president.

85. David Smolin explains: "Indeed, it is far more problematic, in terms of a theory of a secular or religiously neutral government, to allow religious adornment of inaugurations than it is to permit prayers at graduation. A graduation ceremony is predominately a personal and communal rite of transition. An inauguration, by contrast, is indelibly a political event for securing the orderly transfer of power and the political allegiance of a people. Inaugural religious oaths administered upon holy scripture and accompanying prayers signal something not profoundly different from the famous coronation of the emperor Charlemagne by the Pope in Rome in *a.d.* 800 — namely, that God and His voice in organized religion are authoritatively blessing the endowment of an individual with political office and power. Of course, Billy Graham, unlike some medieval popes, has never claimed the jurisdiction to select the civil ruler. But the role of legitimating the office, transferring power, and endowing individuals with political authority remains the same." Ibid.

86. See, e.g., Newdow v. Roberts, 603 F.3d 1002 (D.C. Cir. 2010).

87. Critics often find such explanations wildly implausible. See, e.g., Douglas Laycock, "Theology Scholarships, the Pledge of Allegiance, and Religious Liberty: Avoiding the Extremes but Missing the Liberty," *Harvard Law Review* 118 (2004): 235, observing that "[t]his rationale is unconvincing both to serious nonbelievers and to serious believers."

88. Kent Greenawalt, "Secularism, Religion, and Liberal Democracy in the United States," *Cardozo Law Review* 30 (2009): 2387.

89. Kent Greenawalt, *Religion and the Constitution: Establishment and Fairness* (Princeton: Princeton University Press, 2008), 2:61–62 (emphasis added). Cf. Larry Alexander, "What's inside and outside the Law?," *Law and Philosophy* 31 (2012): 229: "Most state officials are state officials only part of the time; the rest of the time they are spouses, parents, taxpayers, automobile drivers, Presbyterians, club and union members—in short, most of the time they are indistinguishable from 'private citizens.'"

90. Cf. Alexander, "What's inside and outside the Law?," 227: "If the mayor goes home at night and tells his wife to 'shut up,' he is not unconstitutionally enjoining her free speech, for he is not, on that occasion, acting as 'the state.' He is just an obnoxious private person."

91. Hawaii v. Trump, 138 S. Ct. 2392 (2018).

92. 138 S. Ct. at 2418: "But the issue before us is not whether to denounce the statements. It is instead the significance of those statements in reviewing a Presidential directive." One can imagine other approaches the Court might have taken. For example, the Court might have contended that if someone uses religion as a proxy for some other factor, such as propensity to violence, one is not acting on antireligious animus. But this explanation would raise troubling questions not only for the Establishment Clause but for equal protection law generally, and the Court did not adopt this approach.

93. Ibid. at 2418.

94. The majority began by suggesting that it would be enough for the exclusion order to be supported by a "facially legitimate and bona fide reason," but then proceeded to employ a still-deferential "rational basis" standard. Ibid. at 2418–20.

95. Ibid. at 2423. Cf. Renan, "President's Two Bodies," 1198: "The majority opinion, authored by Chief Justice Roberts, embraces an impersonal, thoroughly institutional presidency. Any anti-Muslim animus of the sitting president is nearly irrelevant to the doctrinal question whether the presidential proclamation violated the First Amendment."

96. Ibid. at 2435–36 (Sotomayor, J., dissenting).

97. Ibid. at 2436.

98. Ibid. at 2439.

99. In Washington's case, the perceived magnificence of the man arguably elevated the new office, not the other way around. See Edward J. Larson, *The Return of George Washington* (New York: William Marrow, 2015).

100. Psalm 39:5 (KJV).

101. Jim Beam Distilling Co. v. Georgia, 501 U.S. 529, 549 (1991) (Scalia, J.).

102. See also Scalia and Garner, *Reading Law*, 5: "In the 20th century, the legal realists convinced everyone that judges do indeed make the law. To the extent that this was true, it was knowledge that the wise already possessed and the foolish could not be trusted with." For an argument that Scalia's jurisprudential claims generally may have been based on a self-conscious commitment to maintaining "noble myths" about law that he himself did not actually believe, see Daniel A. Farber and Suzanna Sherry, *Desperately Seeking Certainty: The Misguided Quest for Constitutional Foundations* (Chicago: University of Chicago Press, 2002), 38–44.

103. For example, the bulk of Scalia and Garner, *Reading Law*, consists of a discussion of a large variety of canons.

104. For discussion and evidence, see Gluck and Posner, "Statutory Interpretation on the Bench," 1327–34.

105. On the gaping gap between canons of interpretation and actual congressional practice, see generally Bressman and Gluck, "Statutory Interpretation from the Inside."

106. See Scalia and Garner, *Reading Law*, 174–79; Eskridge and Frickey, *Cases and Materials on Legislation*, 644–45.

107. Cf. Eskridge and Frickey, *Cases and Materials on Legislation*, 638 ("A more important problem is that this canon, like many of the others, assumes that the legislature thinks through statutory language carefully, assessing every possible variation. This is clearly not true."); ibid., 709, describing the critical view that "canons of construction . . . are part of the linguistic and logical pretense that the legislature goes about its work in a methodical, rational way." For sharp criticism of the canons, see Richard Posner, "Statutory Interpretation—in the Classroom and in the Courtroom," *University of Chicago Law Review* 50 (1983): 800–822.

108. Gluck, "Justice Scalia's Unfinished Business," 2059.

CHAPTER FOUR   From Political Fictions to "Living with Lies"

1. Morgan, *Inventing the People*, 14.

2. See "The 1619 Project," *New York Times*, August 2019, https://www.nytimes.com/interactive/2019/08/14/magazine/1619-america-slavery.html.

3. See, e.g., Gerard Baker, "How the 1619 Project Slandered America," *New York Post*, May 8, 2020, https://nypost.com/2020/05/08/how-the-1619-project-slandered-america/.

4. Vaclav Havel, "The Power of the Powerless," in Havel, *Living in Truth*, ed. Jan Vladislav (London: Faber, 1986), 36; Havel, "Letter to Dr. Gustav Husak, General Secretary of the Czechoslovak Community Party," in Havel, *Living in Truth*, 3.

5. Aleksandr Solzhenitsyn, *The Gulag Archipelago* (1958–68), vols. 1–3.

6. Hannah Arendt, *The Origins of Totalitarianism* (New York: Harcourt, 1979).

7. Havel, "Letter to Gustav Husak," 6.

8. Ibid., 6–7.

9. Havel, "Power of the Powerless," 41.

10. Ibid.

11. Ibid., 42.

12. Ibid.

13. Ibid., 55.

14. Havel, "Letter to Gustav Husak," 31.

15. Ibid., 8.

16. Ibid., 5.

17. Ibid., 4–5.

18. Havel, "Power of the Powerless," 45.

19. Ibid., 44.

20. Ibid., 59.

21. Havel, "Letter to Gustav Husak," 7.

22. Havel, "Power of the Powerless," 62.

23. Ibid., 45.

24. Havel, "Letter to Gustav Husak," 15.

25. Ibid., 12.

26. Ibid., 24.

27. Havel, "Power of the Powerless," 42.

28. See George Orwell, *1984* (San Diego: Harcourt Brace Jovanovich, 1977), 214: "Doublethink means the power of holding two contradictory beliefs in one's mind simultaneously, and accepting both of them. . . . The process has to be conscious, or it would not be carried out with sufficient precision, but it also has to be unconscious, or it would bring with it a feeling of falsity and hence of guilt. . . . To tell deliberate lies while genuinely believing in them, to forget any fact that has become inconvenient, and then, when it becomes necessary again, to draw it back from oblivion for just as long as it is needed, to deny the existence of objective reality and all the time to take account of the reality which one denies—all this is indispensably necessary."

29. Leszek Kolakowski, *Main Currents of Marxism*, trans. P. S. Falla (New York: W. W. Norton, 2008), 859 (emphasis added): "Ideology is not simply an aid or adjunct to the system but an absolute condition of its existence, irrespective of *whether people actually believe in it or not*. . . . The Soviet system could not do without this ideology, which is the sole *raison d'etre* for the existing apparatus of power."

30. Havel, "Power of the Powerless," 78.

31. Arendt, *Origins of Totalitarianism*, 474.

32. Ibid., 382; see also ibid., 334, explaining that "the audience . . . did not particularly object to being deceived because it held every statement to be a lie anyhow."

33. Ibid., 333.

34. Ibid., 382.

35. Havel, "Letter to Gustav Husak," 13.

36. Havel, "Power of the Powerless," 57.

37. For development of this idea, see Steven D. Smith, "Believing Persons, Personal Believings: The Neglected Center of the First Amendment," *University of Illinois Law Review* 1233 (2002): 1233–1320.

38. In a chapter on what he calls "the Vital Lie tradition," Mike Martin discusses a number of noted thinkers who have argued in one form or another that certain kinds of self-deception are unavoidable, necessary to human life, and indeed admirable. Mike W. Martin, *Self-Deception and Morality* (Kansas: University of Kansas Press, 1986), 109–37.

39. John 8:32 (KJV).

40. Thomas Aquinas, *Summa Contra Gentiles* I, ch. 1, trans. Anton C. Pegis (Notre Dame, IN: University of Notre Dame Press, 1975), 60.

41. Thomas Aquinas, *Summa Theologica* I, Q. 16, art. 5.

42. Kolakowski, *Main Currents of Marxism*, 857.

43. Ibid., 857.

44. Ibid., 857–58.

45. Orwell, *1984*, 81.

46. Ibid., 249–58, 277.

47. Havel, "Letter to Gustav Husak," 31.

48. Havel, "Power of the Powerless," 52.

49. Kolakowski, *Main Currents of Marxism*, 849.

50. C. S. Lewis, *The Abolition of Man* (Oxford: Oxford University Press, 1943).

51. Havel, "Letter to Gustav Husak," 24.

52. Havel, "Power of the Powerless," 60.

53. Ibid., 65, 73.

54. Ibid., 102.

55. Ibid., 100.
56. Cf. Finnis, *Natural Law and Natural Rights*.
57. See, e.g., Vaclav Havel, "Address Given to Trinity College, June 28, 1996," in *The Art of the Impossible: Politics as Morality in Practice* (New York: Fromm International, 1998) 246–47: "[A] legal relationship or legal order must be preceded by a connection to an order from the realm of morality, because only a moral commitment imbues the legal arrangements with meaning and makes them truly valid. Nor can the moral order be narrowed to a mere 'moral contract': in the end, its roots are always found to be metaphysical.... And what is conscience or responsibility, if not a certain attitude of man toward that which reaches beyond him—that is, toward infinity and eternity, the transcendental, the mystery of the world, the order of Being or the Omniscient?"
58. Havel, "Power of the Powerless," 65.
59. Kolakowski, *Main Currents of Marxism*, 858.
60. *The Gulag Archipelago* was published in three volumes over a ten-year period. I will cite Aleksandr Solzhenitsyn, *The Gulag Archipelago: An Experiment in Literary Investigation*, authorized abridgment by Edward E. Ericson Jr. of the translation by Thomas P. Whitney (parts 1–4) and Harry T. Willetts (parts 5–7) (New York: HarperPerennial, 2007). The quotation here is from p. 325.
61. Ibid.
62. Ibid., 326.
63. Ibid., 325, 326.
64. Ibid., 326.
65. Aleksandr Solzhenitsyn, "Live Not by Lies!," in *The Solzhenitsyn Reader*, ed. Edward E. Ericson and Daniel J. Mahoney (Wilmington, DE: ISI Books, 2006), 556, 557–58.
66. Ibid., 559.
67. Ibid.
68. Czeslaw Milosz, *The Captive Mind*, trans. Jane Zielonko (London: Secker & Warburg, 1953), 54.
69. Ibid., 56.
70. Ibid., 197.
71. Ibid., 55.
72. Ibid., 6.
73. Ibid., 110.
74. Ibid., 66.
75. Arendt, *Origins of Totalitarianism*, 333.
76. Ibid., 413.
77. Morgan, *Inventing the People*, 21.

78. Ibid., 23.

79. Ibid., 24.

80. See John Hart Ely, *Democracy and Distrust* (Cambridge, MA: Harvard University Press, 1980).

81. Whether Jefferson actually made this statement is uncertain, although it was attributed to him by Thoreau. See Eugene Volokh, "Who First Said, 'The Best Government Is That Which Governs Least'? Not Thoreau," *Washington Post*, Sept. 6, 2017, https://www.washingtonpost.com/news/volokh-conspiracy/wp/2017/09/06/who-first-said-the-best-government-is-that-which-governs-least-not-thoreau/.

82. Orwell, *1984*, 69, 82.

83. Milton Mayer, *They Thought They Were Free: The Germans, 1933–45* (Chicago: University of Chicago Press, 1955; repr., 2017), 48.

84. Ibid., 47.

85. The classic text is Isaiah Berlin, "Two Concepts of Liberty," in *Four Essays on Liberty* (London: Oxford University Press, 1969). See also Michael J. Klarman, "Rethinking the History of American Freedom," *William and Mary Law Review* 42 (2000): 270.

86. See, e.g., Ronald Dworkin, *Justice for Hedgehogs* (Cambridge, MA: Belknap Press, 2011), 330. See also Martha Minow and Joseph William Singer, "In Praise of Foxes: Pluralism as Fact and Aid to the Pursuit of Justice," *Boston University Law Review* 90 (2010): 905, explaining that equality is "a foundational value. . . . It is a fundamental principle in our society that all people are . . . entitled to be treated with equal concern and respect."

87. Robert Nisbet observed that "it would be hard to exaggerate the potential spiritual dynamic that lies in the idea of equality at the present time. One would have to go back to certain other ages, such as imperial Rome, in which Christianity was generated as a major historical force, or Western Europe of the Reformation, to find a theme endowed with as much unifying, mobilizing power, especially among intellectuals, as the idea of equality carries now." Robert Nisbet, *Twilight of Authority* (Oxford: Oxford University Press, 1975), 184.

88. See Maimon Schwarzschild, "Point of Crisis, or Is It All Over?," *San Diego Law Review* 56 (2019): 1083, describing "scenes of groveling apologies, reminiscent of confessions at show trials, by accused faculty and staff, some of them subjected to 're-education' by their far from educated accusers."

89. Milosz, *Captive Mind*, 197.

90. Douglas Murray, *The Madness of Crowds: Gender, Race and Identity* (London: Bloomsbury Continuum, 2019), 8–9.

91. Ibid., 7.
92. Ibid., 9.
93. Anthony T. Kronman, *The Assault on American Excellence* (New York: Free Press, 2019), 119.
94. Ibid., 120–21.
95. Ibid., 137.
96. Ibid., 135, 134.
97. Havel, "Letter to Gustav Husak," 13.

CHAPTER FIVE   Authority and Faux Authority

1. Arendt, "What Was Authority?," 81–82, 112.
2. Hart "was never convinced that he had satisfactorily resolved this dilemma about the restricted, but genuinely normative, notion of obligation in law." Nicola Lacey, *A Life of H. L. A. Hart: The Nightmare and the Noble Dream* (Oxford: Oxford University Press, 2004), 228. Late in life, in personal ruminations, Hart described the problem of obligation as "[q]uite panic-generating!" and worried about whether he could be "honest about errors [in *The Concept of Law*] without *wrecking* the book." Ibid., 336.
3. Much of the content of this chapter is distilled (and revised) from Steven D. Smith, "Hart's Onion: The Peeling Away of Legal Authority," *Southern California Interdisciplinary Law Journal* 16 (2006): 97–135.
4. See John Austin, *The Province of Jurisprudence Determined*, ed. Wilfred E. Rumble (1832; Cambridge: Cambridge University Press, 1995), 18–25. Citations are to the 1995 edition.
5. Ibid., 21–22.
6. Ibid., 166.
7. These criticisms occupy chapters 2 through 4 of Hart's book *The Concept of Law*, 2nd ed. (Oxford: Oxford University Press, 1997), and are summarized at ibid., 79.
8. Ibid., 82–83.
9. Joseph Raz, *The Morality of Freedom* (Oxford: Clarendon, 1986), 23. See also R. B. Friedman, "On the Concept of Authority in Political Philosophy," in *Authority*, ed. Joseph Raz (Oxford: Clarendon, 1990), 65: "[T]he point of claiming that an imperative comes from authority is to put a person under an obligation to obey it"; White, "Disappearance of Natural Authority," 29, asserting that "obligation and authority are correlative notions"; Austin, *Province of Jurisprudence Determined*, 22. Leslie Green quotes Hannah Pitkin's assertion that "[i]t is part of the concept, the meaning of 'authority' that those subject to it are required to obey, that it has a

right to command. It is part of the concept, the meaning of 'law,' that those to whom it is applicable are obligated to obey it." Leslie Green, *The Authority of the State* (Oxford: Clarendon, 1990), 193–94.

10. Describing the view that sees authority and obligation as correlative as "the inseparability thesis," William Edmundson notes that some philosophers now reject this thesis. But Edmundson acknowledges that "the inseparability thesis expresses a deeply held view of the nature of political and legal authority." William A. Edmundson, "State of the Art: The Duty to Obey the Law," *Legal Theory* 10 (2004): 220. Even those who separate "authority" from "obligation" may admit that they thereby depart from the more conventional understanding. See, e.g., Philip Soper, "Law's Normative Claims," in *The Autonomy of Law: Essays on Legal Positivism*, ed. Robert P. George (Oxford: Oxford University Press, 1996), 231.

11. Thus, Hart argued that we would find it unnatural even to describe the gunman's order as a "command": that is because "a command is primarily an appeal not to fear but to respect for authority." Hart, *Concept of Law*, 20. See also H. L. A. Hart, "Commands and Authoritative Legal Reasons," in Raz, *Authority*, 103–7.

12. Oliver Wendell Holmes, "The Path of the Law," *Harvard Law Review* 10 (1887): 459: "If you want to know the law and nothing else, you must look at it as a bad man, who cares only for the material consequences which such knowledge enables him to predict, not as a good one, who finds his reasons for conduct, whether inside the law or outside of it, in the vaguer sanctions of conscience."

13. See A. J. Ayer, *Philosophy in the Twentieth Century* (London: Orion, 1992), 234–39.

14. Exactly how Hart understood the relation between linguistic analysis and jurisprudence has generated extensive discussion among theorists. See, e.g., Timothy A. O. Endicott, "Herbert Hart and the Semantic Sting," in *Hart's Postscript: Essays on the Postscript to "The Concept of Law,"* ed. Jules Coleman (Oxford: Oxford University Press, 2001), 39–58; Nicos Stavropoulos, "Hart's Semantics," in Coleman, *Hart's Postscript*, 59–98. It seems clear, though, that Hart was not concerned with linguistic usage just for its own sake: he used it to achieve insights into the subjects that language users discuss. In this vein, Nicos Stavropoulos observes that "Hart claims . . . [that] the quest for definitions is not exclusively about language, but is meant to provide metaphysical knowledge. . . . A definition, Hart argues, achieves this by revealing the 'latent principle' that 'guides our use' of a word." Ibid., 64.

15. Thus, at the outset of his project Hart asserted that "the suggestion that inquiries into the meanings of words merely throw light on words is false. Many important distinctions, which are not immediately obvious, be-

tween types of social situation or relationships may best be brought to light by an examination of the standard uses of the relevant expressions." Hart, *Concept of Law*, vi.

16. Just what this term ("moral") means is itself an elusive question. Michael Smith has remarked that "if one thing becomes clear by reading what philosophers writing in meta-ethics today have to say, it is surely that enormous gulfs exist between them, gulfs so wide that we must wonder whether they are talking about a common subject matter." Michael Smith, *The Moral Problem* (Malden, MA: Blackwell, 1994), 3. Fortunately, we need not pursue that question here: it will be more than sufficient to occupy ourselves with "authority."

17. Cf. Brian Bix, *Jurisprudence: Theory and Context*, 2nd ed. (London: Sweet & Maxwell, 1999), 156: "The question is whether the legal status of a command, authorization or prohibition, by itself, without more, adds any *moral* reason for doing or not doing the action indicated."

18. Jules Coleman, *The Practice of Principle* (Oxford: Oxford University Press, 2001), 121 (emphasis added).

19. Friedman, "On the Concept of Authority," 63 (quoting R. S. Peters). Cf. the quotation from Bix, *Jurisprudence*, 156, in n. 17 above.

20. Cf. Tinder, "Authority and Liberty," 59: "Authority only exists where it is freely accepted, and for this reason liberty is a primary condition of authority."

21. Cf. Vining, *Authoritative and the Authoritarian*, 120.

22. It may well be, as lawyer and psychologist Benjamin Sells has argued, that we often do think of law itself as a person. A common image, Sells found, is of the law as "an older man, gray-haired and distinguished looking," who wears a leather or camel coat, carries a briefcase, and drinks his coffee black without sugar. Benjamin Sells, *The Soul of the Law* (Rockport, MA: Element, 1994), 24.

23. It is true that the storm does not actually issue any order to you ("Stay inside or I'll strike you with lightning"), whereas the gunman does give an order. But this difference also seems incidental. We can imagine a situation in which the gunman points his gun at your head but forgets to say anything, or nervously loses his voice; but you still understand what the threat is and how you can avert it—by handing over your money. Or maybe the gunman is hiding in the bushes with the obvious intent of shooting you and taking your wallet; but you see that you can prevent this by tossing your wallet at him and leaving. It seems that nothing in the analysis changes with these variations.

24. Vining, *Authoritative and the Authoritarian*, 248.

25. The point is intended as a practical one about ordinary human psychology and motivation, not a metaphysical or metaethical one. Aristotle

argued that we seek most things because they are instrumental to achieving the one thing that is intrinsically good—happiness. Aristotle, *Nicomachean Ethics* 1.1, 1.4. He may have been right, but that is not the way we are using "intrinsic" and "instrumental" here. A good might be merely "instrumental" from a certain ethical perspective but "intrinsic" as a matter of common and understandable human motivations. Take money. Money is perhaps the classic instance of a good that from one standpoint is merely instrumental. You can't eat it; you can't wear it; just in itself it is pretty much worthless. And yet if someone says "I took the job because it paid well," we will typically take this as an adequate explanation of what someone did; we will not react with "I don't understand. So it paid well? So what? What difference did that make?" Although in a deep sense money may be a purely instrumental good—it is good only for what it can buy—it is so closely connected to so many possibilities and goods that most people will treat it as a presumptively good thing. They will take the money and decide later what to spend it on. And we understand this.

26. Cf. Finnis, *Natural Law and Natural Rights*, 142, observing that "if A treats his relationship with B as being for his (A's) own sake, then the relationship will not be one of friendship and the benefits (if any) that A derives from it will not include the benefit of real friendship."

27. Cf. Aristotle, *Nicomachean Ethics* 8.5.1158a: "Now friendship is said to be among equals."

28. See chapter 1, under "Consent as a Fiction."

29. Cf. Abner Greene, *Against Obligation* (Cambridge, MA: Harvard University Press, 2012), 40: "We owe such obligations to our neighbors, not to the state itself."

30. See Finnis, *Natural Law and Natural Rights*, 359–61.

31. Among other reasons, just laws may command what we have an independent moral obligation to do anyway. Consider, for example, laws prohibiting murder, rape, or theft.

32. In fact Finnis acknowledges that "the ruler has, very strictly speaking, no right to be obeyed . . . ; but he has the authority to give directions and make laws that are morally obligatory and that he has the responsibility of enforcing." Finnis, *Natural Law and Natural Rights*, 359.

33. Jules Coleman, though critical of Raz in significant respects, describes Raz's account of authority as "brilliant both in the depth of its problematic and in the perspicuity of its solution, and . . . it is certainly the most fully developed, sophisticated, and influential doctrine of legal authority to date." Coleman, *Practice of Principle*, 124. And though rejecting much in Raz's positivistic jurisprudence, John Finnis endorses his conception of authority. Finnis, *Natural Law and Natural Rights*, 234.

34. Joseph Raz, "Authority, Law, and Morality," *Monist* 68 (1985): 297.

35. More precisely, the authority's directive preempts further consideration of *the kinds of reasons that are reflected in the authority's directive*. Ibid., 297–98. But if the authority has not taken some class of reasons into account, then her directive would not preempt consideration of *those* reasons. For example, you might defer to your doctor's instructions with respect to health-related considerations. But if you have a faith-based objection to, say, receiving a blood transfusion, you might not regard the doctor's medical judgment as preempting consideration of *that* sort of reason: that is because the doctor has no competence with respect to that sort of reason and his directives presumably have not taken it into account.

36. Ibid., 299.

37. For a thorough critique of Raz's account, see Kenneth Einar Himma, "Just 'Cause You're Smarter than Me Doesn't Give You a Right to Tell Me What to Do: Legitimate Authority and the Normal Justification Thesis," *Oxford Journal of Legal Studies* 27 (2006): 121–50. See also Larry Alexander and Emily Sherwin, *The Rule of Rules* (Durham, NC: Duke University Press, 2001), 73–77, discussing deficiencies in Raz's account. See also Ronald Dworkin, *Justice in Robes* (Cambridge, MA: Belknap Press, 2006), 201, 206, describing Raz's account of authority as "eccentric" and as "presuppos[ing] a degree of deference toward legal authority that almost no one shows in modern democracies."

38. Himma, "Just 'Cause You're Smarter than Me," 140.

39. For a helpful overview, see R. George Wright, *Reason and Obligation: A Contemporary Approach to Law and Political Morality* (Lanham, MD: University Press of America, 1994), 1–18.

40. Cf. A. John Simmons, "The Duty to Obey and Our Natural Moral Duties," in *Is There a Duty to Obey the Law?* (Cambridge: Cambridge University Press, 2005), 119: "Suppose that we do in fact owe benefactors a fitting return of some sort. Whatever else may be true of these debts, it is clear . . . that our benefactors are not entitled to themselves specify what shall constitute a fitting return."

41. Cf. Edmundson, "State of the Art," 245: "If you, unbidden, squeegee my windshield, I may owe you a duty to say thanks, but I do not owe a duty to do whatever you demand, even if what you demand is very important to you."

42. H. L. A. Hart, "Are There Any Natural Rights?," *Philadelphia Law Review* 64 (1955): 185.

43. For detailed criticism, see A. John Simmons, *Justification and Legitimacy* (Cambridge: Cambridge University Press, 2001), 1–42. For more sympathetic treatments, see Christopher Heath Wellman, "Samaritanism and the

Duty to Obey the Law," in Simmons, *Is There a Duty to Obey the Law?*, 3–89; George Klosko, "Presumptive Benefit, Fairness, and Political Obligation," in *The Duty to Obey the Law*, ed. William A. Edmundson (Lanham, MD: Rowman & Littlefield, 1999), 193–212.

44. Hart, "Are There Any Natural Rights?," 185: "The rules may provide that officials should have authority to enforce obedience and make further rules, but the moral obligation to obey the rules in such circumstances is due to the co-operating members of the society, and they have the correlative moral right to obedience."

45. Simmons, "Duty to Obey," 91, 94–95.

46. Plato, *Euthyphro*. For modern versions of the argument, see, e.g., David O. Brink, "The Autonomy of Ethics," in *The Cambridge Companion to Atheism*, ed. Michael Martin (Cambridge: Cambridge University Press, 2007), 149; Michael S. Moore, "Good without God," in *Natural Law, Liberalism and Morality*, ed. Robert P. George (Oxford: Oxford University Press, 1996), 221.

47. Cf. Jean Porter, *Ministers of the Law: A Natural Law Theory of Legal Authority* (Grand Rapids, MI: Eerdmans, 2010): "Willing obedience to God is reasonable and appropriate, because God is assumed to direct the agent to act in such a way as to conform to the demands of reason, as seen from the perspective of one who is supremely and uniquely qualified to make such a judgment."

48. Cf. Alasdair MacIntyre, "Which God Ought We to Obey?," in *Philosophy of Religion*, ed. Michael Peterson et al. (Oxford: Oxford University Press, 2001), 579: "Power without justice may give us reasons to obey commands because we fear to do otherwise; beneficence without justice may give us reasons to obey commands either from gratitude or because we have been provided with expectations of future beneficence. So that if we know of some god, such as [William Blake's] Nobodaddy or Jupiter, that he is powerful, or if we know of God that he is beneficent, we may indeed have good reason to obey the relevant set of commands, but not at all the kind of reason that we need to treat obedience as obligatory."

49. See, e.g., Arthur Leff, "Unspeakable Ethics, Unnatural Law," *Duke Law Journal* (1979): 1231: "It is of the utmost importance to see why a God-grounded system has no analogues. Either God exists or He does not, but if He does not, nothing and no one else can take His place."

CHAPTER SIX   Is Genuine Authority Possible?

1. Eric Hoffer, *The True Believer: Thoughts on the Nature of Mass Movements* (New York: Harper & Row, 1951), 118–19 (emphasis added).

2. John Stuart Mill issued a general complaint against "the servility of mankind toward the supposed preferences or aversions of their temporal masters, or of their gods." John Stuart Mill, "On Liberty," in *On Liberty, and Other Writings*, ed. Stefan Collini (Cambridge: Cambridge University Press, 1989), 10.

3. See Lynne Henderson, "Authoritarianism and the Rule of Law," *Indiana Law Journal* 66 (1991): 379–456.

4. Vining, *Authoritative and the Authoritarian*.

5. Immanuel Kant, "An Answer to the Question: What Is Enlightenment?," reprinted in *What Is Enlightenment?*, ed. James Schmidt (Berkeley: University of California Press, 1996), 58–63.

6. Quoted in Colin E. Gunton, *The One, the Three and the Many* (Cambridge: Cambridge University Press, 1993), 45.

7. Cf. Charles Taylor, *Sources of the Self* (Cambridge, MA: Harvard University Press, 1989), 38–39, observing in modern culture "a common picture of the self, as ... drawing its purposes, goals, and life-plans out of itself, seeking 'relationships' only insofar as they are 'fulfilling.'"

8. Alistair I. MacFayden, *The Call to Personhood* (Cambridge: Cambridge University Press, 1990), 9.

9. John Macmurray, *Persons in Relation* (Amherst, MA: Humanity Books, 1999; first published 1961), 61. Macmurray elaborates (emphasis added): "We need one another to be ourselves. This complete and unlimited dependence of each of us upon the others is the central and crucial fact of personal existence. Individual independence is an illusion; and the independent individual, the isolated self, is a nonentity. In ourselves we are nothing; and when we turn our eyes inward in search of ourselves we find a vacuum. Being nothing in ourselves, we have no value in ourselves, and are of no importance whatever, wholly without meaning or significance. *It is only in relation to others that we exist as persons. . . . We live and move and have our being not in ourselves but in one another.*" Ibid., 211. See also Gunton, *One, the Three and the Many*, 169, asserting that "persons mutually constitute each other, make each other what they are."

10. William Shakespeare, Sonnet 141.

11. See William Chester Jordan, *Europe and the High Middle Ages* (London: Allen Lane, 2001), 133–37.

12. See Norman Cantor, *The Civilization of the Middle Ages*, rev. ed. (New York: HarperCollins, 1993), 348–50; Johan Huizinga, *The Autumn of the Middle Ages*, trans. Rodney J. Payton and Ulrich Mammitzsch (Chicago: University of Chicago Press, 1921; repr. 1996), 82–88.

13. Cf. Huizinga, *Autumn of the Middle Ages*, 86: "The entire presentation of noble love in literature and social life frequently strikes us as intolerably stale and ridiculous." However, Huizinga also suggested that "the

motif . . . always comes back again in new forms, as, for instance, in the romance of the cinematic cowboy." Ibid., 83.

14. Plato, *Crito* 50e–51e, in *Plato: Complete Works*, ed. John M. Cooper (Indianapolis: Hackett, 1997), 45.

15. Robert Filmer, *Patriarcha*, in *Patriarcha, and Other Writings*, ed. Johann P. Sommerville (Cambridge: Cambridge University Press, 1991), 8, 7.

16. White, "Disappearance of Natural Authority," 25.

17. Ibid.

18. For a detailed exposition of the meaning and requirements of filial piety, see Li Fu Chen, *The Confucian Way*, trans. Shih Shun Liu (London: Kegan Paul International, 1986), 376–411.

19. *The Hsiao King, or Classic of Filial Piety*, trans. and ed. James Legge (Whitefish, MT: Kessinger, 2004), 26 (punctuation reformed).

20. Ibid., 30 (punctuation reformed).

21. Ibid., 33.

22. Ibid., 24, 32.

23. Quoted in *Sources of Chinese Tradition*, ed. William Theodore de Bary et al. (New York: Columbia University Press, 1960), 1:98.

24. Ibid.

25. White, "Disappearance of Natural Authority," 27.

26. See, e.g., Plato, *Euthyphro*; see also David O. Brink, "The Autonomy of Ethics," in *The Cambridge Companion to Atheism*, ed. Michael Martin (Cambridge: Cambridge University Press, 2007); Michael S. Moore, "Good without God," in *Natural Law, Liberalism and Morality*, ed. Robert P. George (Oxford: Oxford University Press, 1996), 221.

27. This argument is developed more methodically in Steven D. Smith, "Is God Irrelevant?," *Boston University Law Review* 94 (2014): 1339.

28. Augustine, *Confessions* 1.1, trans. Albert Cook Outler (New York: Dover, 2002), 1. Cf. Joel Harrison, *Post-Liberal Religious Liberty: Forming Communities of Charity* (Cambridge: Cambridge University Press, 2020), 170: "Augustine more fundamentally means that personhood is grounded in understanding the person as a subject destined for God."

29. Cf. John 15:15 (KJV): "Henceforth I call you not servants; for the servant knoweth not what his lord doeth: but I have called you friends." Cf. Porter, *Ministers of the Law*, 56, describing "our relation to God as a personal force in human life—as redeemer, father, and friend."

30. George Herbert, "Clasping of Hands," in *George Herbert: The Country Parson, The Temple*, ed. John N. Wall Jr. (New York: Paulist Press, 1981), 282 (emphasis added).

31. Kenneth Abraham and G. Edward White, "The Puzzle of Dignitary Torts," *Cornell Law Review* 104 (2019): 324.

32. Cf. Lawrence M. Friedman, *The Republic of Choice: Law, Authority, and Culture* (Cambridge, MA: Harvard University Press, 1990), 48: "Hierarchy and stratification still exist, of course, but with diminished legitimacy and in revised forms. In some senses, they have gone underground. Political theory and popular sentiment have bored holes in all forms of privilege; established churches and aristocracies have all but vanished. Popular sovereignty is the crucial basis of governing structures; older forms of government have gone under, while the kings and queens that survive are figureheads."

33. See, e.g., Martha Minow and Joseph William Singer, "In Praise of Foxes: Pluralism as Fact and Aid to the Pursuit of Justice," *Boston University Law Review* 90 (2010): 905: "It is a fundamental principle in our society that all people are . . . entitled to be treated with equal concern and respect."

34. J. B. Schneewind, *The Invention of Autonomy: A History of Modern Moral Philosophy* (Cambridge: Cambridge University Press, 1998), 3: "Kant invented the conception of morality as autonomy."

35. See Dworkin, *Theory and Practice of Autonomy*, 21–33, esp. 25, arguing for "a weaker conception of autonomy." See ibid., 32: "There is an intellectual error that threatens to arise whenever autonomy has been defended as crucial or fundamental: This is that the notion is elevated to a higher status than it deserves. Autonomy *is* important, but so is the capacity for sympathetic identification with others, or the capacity to reason prudentially, or the virtue of integrity. Similarly, although it is important to respect the autonomy of others, it is also important to respect their welfare, or their liberty, or their rationality. Theories that base everything on any single aspect of human personality, on any one of a number of values always tend toward the intellectually imperialistic."

36. Schneewind, *Invention of Autonomy*, 512.

37. Ibid., 490.

38. Dworkin, *Theory and Practice of Autonomy*, 3–4.

39. Nisbet, *Twilight of Authority*, 184.

40. See generally White, "Disappearance of Natural Authority."

41. Once again, however, there are different or more moderate versions of "autonomy" that need not have these corrosive implications. See generally Dworkin, *Theory and Practice of Autonomy*.

42. See Raz, *Authority of Law*, 3.

43. We might take Locke's celebrated treatises on government as indicative of this change. His first treatise—the one hardly anyone reads today—was a no-holds-barred attack on and refutation of the older view, in which governmental authority was linked to patriarchal and divine right models that reflected genuine authority (or would have, if the models had not been thoroughly fictional). The leading articulation of this position at the time

was a treatise by Robert Filmer, entitled *Patriarcha*, mentioned earlier; and Locke's first treatise carried the unsubtle title *The False Principles and Foundations of Sir Robert Filmer, and His Followers, Are Detected and Overthrown*. Having thus "overthrown" the older position, Locke proceeded in his second treatise — the one that people do still read and that was entitled *An Essay concerning the True Original Extent and End of Civil Government* — to elaborate the fictions of the state of nature and the social contract that have served to legitimize governments in the West in more recent centuries. But even treating these newer ideas as persuasive and disregarding their fictional quality, we have seen that what they give us is a kind of *faux* authority. Reasons to obey the law, perhaps, but not genuine authority.

44. Cf. White, *Political Philosophy*, 225–26, arguing that "[a]t the beginning of the twenty-first century in the constitutional democracies of the West, the point of studying political theory and its history is not to play the role of the philosopher-king or of the philosopher-parliamentarian. Rather, it is to consider the political implications of various normative anthropologies — that is, the implications of various conceptions of what human existence is all about."

45. Cf. Karol Wojtyla, *Person and Community: Selected Essays*, trans. Theresa Sandok, OSM (New York: Lang, 1993), 210: "[W]e must consider the question of the irreducible in the human being — the question of that which is original and essentially human, that which accounts for the human being's complete uniqueness in the world."

46. The well-known lines are from William Ernest Henley's poem "Invictus."

47. Kant, "Answer to the Question: What Is Enlightenment?," 58; see 58–59.

48. Cf. Wolff, *In Defense of Anarchism*, 71–72: "It is out of the question to give up the commitment to autonomy.... When I place myself in the hands of another, and permit him to determine the principles by which I shall guide my behavior, I repudiate the freedom and reason which give me dignity."

49. Cf. Wojtyla, *Person and Community*, 179, observing that "the dignity of the human person is always more of a call and a demand than an already accomplished fact."

50. But see Crosby, *Selfhood of the Human Person*, 3, arguing that both the Kantian and the relational perspective are essential and proposing a position of "'transcendent autonomy' proper to the human person."

51. Joseph Vining observes that "the less authority there is, the more alone in the world we are as individuals, and the more alone, the closer to the madness we see in those who feel themselves utterly alone." Vining, *Authoritative and the Authoritarian*, 149.

EPILOGUE Authority outside the Cave?

1. Plato, *Republic* 7.514a–518b.
2. The title reminds that if instead of the Christian tradition we look to the Jewish tradition, a similar idea is discernible—in the enduring hope and expectation of the Messiah.
3. Augustine, *City of God* 2.21, trans. Marcus Dodds (New York: Modern Library, 1993), 63 (emphasis added).
4. Augustine, *City of God* 2.21 (Dodds, 63).
5. Augustine, *City of God* 4.4 (Dodds, 112).
6. Augustine, *City of God* 4.4 (Dodds, 113).
7. Augustine, *City of God* 2.21 (Dodds, 63).
8. Augustine, *City of God* 19.24 (Dodds, 706–7).
9. Augustine, *City of God* 19.15 (Dodds, 694). Augustine probably alludes to two passages in the New Testament (both here given in the KJV, with emphasis added): 1 Corinthians 15:28 ("And when all things shall be subdued unto him, then shall the Son also himself be subject unto him that put all things under him, that *God may be all in all*") and Ephesians 1:21 ("[God has set Christ] far above *all principality, and power*, and might, and dominion, and every name that is named, not only in this world, but also in that which is to come").

INDEX

1619 project, 124
1984 (Orwell), 124, 137, 149

Ackerman, Bruce, 69
Affordable Care Act, 87
aggregation problem, 54–59, 82, 84–88, 95, 106–8, 109
"aims of life," 139–42
Alexander, Larry, 34–35, 86–88
Alien and Sedition Acts, 47
allegory of the cave (Plato), 219–21
Amendment, First, 112
Amendment, Fourteenth, 61, 64, 67, 69
Amendment, Twenty-Seventh, 42–43
Aquinas. *See* Thomas Aquinas, Saint
Arendt, Hannah, ix–xv, 1, 125, 146
Articles of Confederation, 39
Augustine, 206, 221–23
  City of God, 222–23
Austin, John, 159, 162
authority
  as a concept, x–xii
  cultivating perception of, 16–17
  as a fiction, xii, 12, 35–37, 51
  limitations of, 25
  and purposivism, 103
  tension with autonomy, 3–5
  See also "coordination account" of authority; delegation of legislative authority
autonomy, 3–5, 10, 149
  egalitarian, 209–213

Bacon, Matthew, 83
Bakke v. Regents, 107, 154
Balkin, Jack, 67–69
Barnett, Randy, 38
Bill of Rights, 67
Blackstone, William, 83
Bork, Robert, 67
Bostock v. Clayton County, xv, 96–97, 101–2
Brown v. Board of Education, 67
Burke, Edmund, 198
Bush, George, 113–14

Calhoun, John C., 48–51
"cancel culture," xv, 153–54
"canons of construction," 120
Carolingian dynasty, 103–4
Christmas Carol, A (Dickens), 25–26

Citizens United v. Federal Election Commission, 71
City of God (Augustine), 222–23
Civil War, 52
Clinton, Bill, 116
Congress
  compared with Supreme Court, 106
  and legislative reassignment, 103
  as quasi-fiction, 77, 98, 117, 121
consent
  "consent of the governed," 2, 23, 30, 42, 72, 104, 147, 148–49, 174–76
  consent proposition, 2
  constructive, 10–11
  as a fiction, 5, 23–24
  implied, 8–10
Constitution
  authority of, 52
  as quasi-fiction, 38, 71–74
  as a social contract, 38, 47, 49
  See also originalism
"coordination account" of authority, 13, 176–78
Cover, Robert, 15
COVID-19, xv, 81
Crosby, John, 3

Dale, Helen, 22
Darkness at Noon (Koestler), 137
"death principle," 128
"declaratory" view of judicial function, 105
delegation of legislative authority, 88–92, 95
Dickens, Charles
  Christmas Carol, A, 25–26
divine right, 17
doublethink, 253n.28
due process clause, 69
Dworkin, Gerald, 3, 211
Dworkin, Ronald, 7, 67–68

Edmundson, William, 258n.10
Ekins, Richard, 244n.7, 245n.22, 247n.47
enrolled bill doctrine, 243n.4
equal protection clause. *See* Amendment, Fourteenth
Eskridge, William, 244n.14, 244n.17, 252n.107
ethos of chivalry, 197–98

"fair play," 182–83
fiction
  compared with falsehood, 18–20
  as cooperative conspiracy, 20–22, 118
  intentions of, 99
  limitations of, 25–27
  political fiction, dark and benign depictions compared, 124
  and statutory interpretation, 101
  and suspension of disbelief, 22, 101
filial piety, 202–4
Filmer, Robert, 199
Finnis, John, 13–17, 176
Fish, Stanley, 238n.74
Floyd, George, xv, 124
"framers' intent." *See* originalism
Frank, Jerome, 20
"Frank the Magnificent," 41, 45
Frickey, Philip P., 244n.14, 244n.17, 252n.107
Friedman, Richard B., xi, 165
friendship, 171–73, 192–97

Gluck, Abbe, 120
God's authority, 185, 206–7
Goldsworthy, Jeffrey, 61, 94
Green, Leslie, 6
Greenawalt, Kent, 7, 112–13
Greene, Abner, 228n.33, 260n.29
Greene, Amanda, 5
Gulag Archipelago, The (Solzhenitsyn), 143–44

Haack, Susan, 230n.60
Hamilton, Alexander, 39, 51, 54, 59
Hart, H. L. A., xiv
  comparing "obligation" to "being obliged," 161
  objection to John Austin's account of authority, 159–60, 161–63
Hart, Henry, 102
Havel, Vaclav, xii, 121, 123, 146
  on authentic living and "the real aims of life," 139–42
  on dishonesty vs. nonaffirming assent, 127–30
  on existential reasons for assent to a Marxist regime, 125–28
  on "human disposition to the truth," 135–39
  and political fictions generally, 123–47
Hawaii v. Trump, 114–16
Henry, Patrick, 40
Herbert, George, 206–7, 215–16
Herzog, Don, 2
Himma, Kenneth, 180
Hitler, Adolph, 146, 150
Hobbes, Thomas, 6, 7
Hoffer, Eric, 190
Holmes, Oliver Wendell, Jr., 33, 162
Hurd, Heidi, 4

"imagined community," 51
intentionalism, 84

Jefferson, Thomas
  and "consent of the governed" as a political fiction, 147, 149
  and Kentucky Resolutions, 47
  and originalism, 54
  and "self-evident truths" as a political fiction, 147
Johnson, Lyndon B., 76–77, 116
"just because" concept of authority defined, 164, 173

Jules Coleman account, 165
Richard Friedman account, 165
  and prima facie reasons, 165–66, 198
  requirement of intrinsic reason to act, 168–72, 192–93, 198
  requirement of person in authority rather than external facts, 166–68, 198
  requirement of vertical relationship, 172–74

Kagan, Justice Elena, 84
Kant, Immanuel, 192, 210, 211–17
Kantorowicz, Ernest, 110–11
King's Two Bodies, The, 114–16
Kay, Richard, 60
Kennedy, Justice Anthony, 52
Kierkegaard, Soren, xi
King's Two Bodies, The, 114–16
Koestler, Arthur
  Darkness at Noon, 137
Kolakowski, Leszek, 136–138, 141
Kosak v. United States, 83
Kronman, Anthony, 107, 154–55

Lawson, Gary, 43, 60, 73
Leff, Arthur, 262n.49
Levelers, 7
Locke, John, 6, 7, 187, 199

MacFayden, Alistair, 194
Macmurray, John, 195
Madison, James, 39, 47, 54, 59
Manning, John, 93
Marshall, Chief Justice John, 48
Martin v. Hunter's Lessee, 47
Marxism, 123–47, 148
McCulloch v. Maryland, 48
McGinnis, John, 235n.31, 238n.67, 239n.79, 244n.15
Meiklejohn, Alexander, 3
Merovingian dynasty, 103

Milosz, Czeslaw, 145
   on citizens acting or performing, 145
   on performative unity, 146
Morgan, Edmund, 100, 111
   on the Agreement of the People, 7
   on the invention of "We the People," 38–40
   on political fiction, 22
   on relying on fictions, 123
   on struggles between the king and the House of Commons, 148–49
Morris, Gouverneur, 39, 42, 49
Murray, Douglas, 153–54

Nisbet, Robert
   Twilight of Authority, 211
Nixon, Richard, 116
"no endorsement" doctrine, 112–13
nonoriginalism, 53, 62

Obama, Barack, 114, 116–17
Obamacare. *See* Affordable Care Act
Obergefell v. Hodges, 64–65
"obligation" and "being obliged," compared, 161, 163
"original public meaning," 56, 60
originalism, 53–62
Orwell, George
   1984, 124, 137, 149

parental authority, 199–205
Pascal, Blaise, 16
Paul, Saint, 12
Pelosi, Nancy, 87
person/office distinction, 113–17
personhood, 194–97
personification, 99–100, 108
Philadelphia Convention, 39–40, 46
philosophical anthropology, 135, 139, 214

Plato, 187, 206
   allegory of the cave, 219–21
   on parental authority, 199
plausibility. *See* "truishness"
"political aesthetics," 16
Porter, Jean, 262n.47
Posner, Judge Richard, 104
Pound, Roscoe, 85, 99
Powell, Justice Lewis, 107
Prakash, Saikrishna, 242n.3
presidency
   characterization of, 113
   and endorsement of religion, 112
   as quasi-fiction, 113, 116–17
purposivism, 84, 102

quorum requirement, 78

Radin, Max, 245n.23
Rambo situation, 163, 177
Randolph, Edmund, 54
Rappaport, Michael, 235n.31, 238n.67, 239n.79, 242n.111, 244n.15
Rawls, John, 7, 8, 211
Raz, Joseph, 4, 178–81
"reasonable person," 10, 93
"reductive rationalization," 212
Roberts, Chief Justice John, 114
Roe v. Wade, 71

Sacks, Albert, 102
Santa Claus, xiii
Scalia, Justice Antonin, 92–93, 98, 119
Schauer, Frederick, 229n.45, 247n.36
Schneewind, J. B., 210–11
Schwarzschild, Maimon, 256n.88
Seidman, Guy, 43, 60, 73
"separation error," 34, 55
"service conception of authority," 178–81
Simmons, John, 184

Smith, Rogers, 3
Smolin, David, 250n.85
social contract, 6–9, 18, 38
Solum, Larry, 237n.61, 239n.77, 240n.89, 246n.28
Solzhenitsyn, Aleksandr, 125, 143
   on culture of lying as dilemma for parents, 144
   Gulag Archipelago, The, 143–44
Sotomayor, Justice Sonia, 115
Stalin, Joseph, 138, 146
Star Wars, 118
state sovereignty
   and authority of the Supreme Court, 46–48
   compared with federalism, 45–47
Story, Joseph, 46
Supreme Court
   authority of, 46
   compared with Congress, 106

textualism, 84, 92
Third Reich, 146, 150
Thomas, Justice Clarence, 52
Thomas Aquinas, Saint, 136

totalitarianism, xi, 146
"truishness," 21–24, 72–73, 100–101, 123, 149
Trump, Donald, 114, 116–17, 200
Twilight of Authority (Nisbet), 211

universities, 152, 154–55, 191
U.S. Term Limits, Inc. v. Thornton, 52

verticality, 172–74, 199–205
Vining, Joseph, 168, 191–92
"Vital Lie tradition," 254n.38

War of the Worlds, 19
"We the People," 37–45, 53, 71–74, 104
Wechsler, Herbert, 67–69
White, James Boyd, 38
White, Michael, xi, 200–201
Wilson, James, 51
Wolff, Robert Paul, 4, 176, 192, 212
Wurman, Ilan, 236n.52, 237n.62

Yankah, Ekow, 3

STEVEN D. SMITH is the Warren Distinguished Professor of Law at the University of San Diego. He is the author of numerous books, including *The Rise and Decline of American Religious Freedom* and *Law's Quandary*.

CPSIA information can be obtained
at www.ICGtesting.com
Printed in the USA
LVHW091507280921
698928LV00001B/97